How to Fix Everything

How to Fix Everything

Prescription For a Dying America

John E. Jirgal

Northwest Publishing, Inc.
Salt Lake City, Utah

How to Fix Everything

All rights reserved.
Copyright © 1995 Northwest Publishing, Inc.

Reproduction in any manner, in whole or in part,
in English or in other languages, or otherwise
without written permission of the publisher is prohibited.

For information address: Northwest Publishing, Inc.,
6906 South 300 West, Salt Lake City, Utah 84047
BCC 1.27.95

PRINTING HISTORY
First Printing 1996

ISBN 1-56901-514-7

NPI books are published by Northwest Publishing, Incorporated,
6906 South 300 West, Salt Lake City, Utah 84047.
The name "NPI" and the "NPI" logo are trademarks belonging to
Northwest Publishing, Incorporated.

PRINTED IN TNE UNITED STATES OF AMERICA
10 9 8 7 6 5 4 3 2 1

To My Father,
Who Taught Me Values.

Publisher's Note

There is an unfortunate but necessary delay between the time a work is accepted for publication and its actual production date. Mr. Jirgal wanted us to bring this to the reader's attention because several of the ideas in this book are finally being considered by Congress even as our presses run. He states: "It is important that the American people recognize the recent conservative shift in Congress as being no more than it truly is: a small, but meaningful step in the right direction. This is not the war itself, merely the first battle in our attempt to get our nation back on proper course.

"The fact that many of the items and ideas I discuss (term limitations, a balanced budget, welfare reform, etc.) are now seeing the light of day in some form is not reason to rejoice, but rather to hope. Cautious optimism should be our position, and we must press on."

While waiting for this book to come out, Mr. Jirgal has spent the intervening time furiously mailing various individual chapters to members of Congress, media figures, and other influential people. Perhaps some of them have been paying attention.

At the author's request, this book has been produced entirely on virgin paper. It contains no recycled paper whatsoever.

Contents

Introduction by Dr. Herb London ix
Foreword xi
Preface xv
The Underlying Principle (Lies, Lies, Lies) xxi

Section I: That Which Steals Our Wealth
Welfare Reform 3
Unemployment 11
The High Cost of Medical Care 18
Taxes, Taxes, Taxes 32
The Economy 49
Immigration 55
Illegal Immigration 60
Foreign Aid 67
The Trade Balance 69
The National Debt 76
Our Failing Auto Industry 81

Section II: That Which Steals Our Health
Red Bag Medical Waste 91
Atomic Waste 94
Solid Waste Disposal 97
The Ozone Layer 107
The Environment and Pollution 110
Asbestos Removal 134
AIDS 137
Hazardous Waste Sites 151

Section III: That Which Steals Our Soul
The Government Itself 157
Government Mandates 162
The Electoral College 164
The Homeless 167
Racism 171
Race Relations 203
Prostitution 207
Drug Abuse 218
Abortion 228
The Criminal Justice System 241
Poverty 251

Section IV: And The Rest
- The Public Education Disaster 265
- Gun Control 273
- The Military and National Security 283
- Crime 295
- Prisons 303
- Capital Punishment 311
- Energy 317
- Social Security 327
- Congressional Reform 330
- Congressional Term Limitations 333
- The Non-Politician 337
- Citizen Empowerment 340

Postscript
- The Renaissance of America 351
- What You Can Do 353
- Suggested Reading 357

Introduction

With war clouds on the horizon in the 1930s, George Orwell surveying the European scene said "the first duty of intelligent men is the restatement of the obvious." That statement is no less true today than it was sixty years ago. Unfortunately the "restatement of the obvious" has been obfuscated by a variety of social and political concerns.

Edward Banfield, discussing the internal war in urban America, in his marvelous book *Unheavenly City* notes that the average person has a better grasp of what needs to be done in our cities than most analysts and professional politicians saddled with ideological baggage. This disparity of views accounts for the stasis in public policy. Those who know don't have a voice in what should be done and those who think they know are too politically "savvy" to make any changes.

Rarely does one read a book unfettered by the *zeitgeist*. Rarely is the "obvious" stated clearly and persuasively. Rarely is the man-on-the-street permitted to express his views without the apparent gravity of social science equations. Yet in the work of John Jirgal we have an unusual common sense guide to what ails us and what the antidote can be.

Jirgal doesn't pretend to be a Platonic philosopher king. He speaks as *Everyman,* aware of limitations and frustrated by the inexorable flow of events over which he exercises almost no control. Whether the issue is crime on the streets, the fiscal nightmare in government or schooling that doesn't translate into education, Jirgal has important ideas to convey.

In my judgment many academics will reject this book as insufficiently scholarly. But this reflexive response will be a disservice to potential readers and to policy analysts who would do well to read and imbibe the lessons of those unaffected by the Procrustean bed of numerical evidence.

Something is wrong in the body-politic and from my reading of Jirgal's book, the description of the problem and remedies suggested are worthy of consideration. After all, social science hasn't distinguished itself in finding answers to what ails us. Perhaps the answers are to be sought in the spiritual domain, in a return to first principles, to the moral core on which this nation was established. That is a point Jirgal understands quite well and for that understanding alone his book deserves the widest distribution and serious consideration.

Herb London

Foreword

The publication and distribution of this book will make me a great deal of enemies. So be it. This is not my intention but the natural outgrowth of attempting to say something substantive. When one endeavors to state the facts plainly as one sees them, neither glossing over the obvious nor making excuses for the conclusions that *must* be drawn, he cannot help but attract a lot of fire. This is an unfortunate fact of life.

So, for example, when I mention in my chapter on medical care that our nation could well do with twice as many doctors and half as many lawyers, I pen these words only to get a point across, not with any mean-spirited desire to insult those in the legal profession. But human nature being what it is, I am certain that a large number of people will choose to take what I have to say the wrong way rather than looking objectively at what I offer, examining my statements to see if they are valid. This is so much a part of the human condition as to be unavoidable, and indeed one of the reasons this book had to be written.

We have for too long been guided only by the most superficial of our emotions, and have commonly responded to corrective attempts not with proper introspection, but with an exceedingly thin-skinned intolerance for criticism. Sadly, much of this seems to take the form of a very childlike tossing of stones toward even the mildest suggestion of constructive criticism. It is as if when another tells us that we should be a little more careful with our finances, the only clever reply we can think of is "Yeah, well, you're ugly!"

I know that a good percentage of those who will be reading this book will fit into the various categories of people who I seem to "attack" (nearly everyone sooner or later), but again, this is unavoidable if I am to say anything more important than that you should have a nice day. I only ask of you that you put aside for the moment that sting of perceived insult and see if what I am telling you in this text is true, and if my solutions are workable. We are all to greater or lesser degrees responsible for America's sick condition. Were it not so wouldn't things be moving along rather swimmingly instead of having become the mess we find ourselves in today?

So, if you are able to look a bit beyond yourself, I believe you are going to find in this book the most workable solutions to our nations ills. They are those which may be most easily and inexpensively implemented, and many are unique to this work you are holding in your hands, never having been offered elsewhere.

On occasion, I do borrow the ideas of others, but always with the full credit due, and to those people who have been so generous as to allow me to include their ideas, I do wish to express my wholehearted appreciation.

And so reader, if you have not already shut this book and flipped on the television, please be open-minded enough to read on. I am sure that you will find much of what I have to say both interesting and provocative. It is my wish for you only that if you find something you agree with, you will take it as your own.

Is this nation worth saving? Yes. Can it still be saved? Again, yes, but only if *you* come on board.

Preface

The victim has managed to make it as far as the Emergency room. Bleeding profusely from multiple gunshot wounds, he has also been given a lethal dose of poison. The poison's indications have already become quite pronounced. For any chance of survival he requires immediate attention by experts of the highest qualifications, who must take a personal interest in his recovery. If there is to be any hope at all, the highly paid team of specialists, surgeons and other experts retained by the hospital for just such a time as this, must move quickly, with an economy of motion and exhibit a sense of urgency. Precious time goes by as vital blood, the fluid of life, continues to pour unabated onto the floor. No one has even attempted to staunch the flow making it's one-way trip from the victim's arteries. The poison continues to progress with it's ugly work, unchallenged by those who might properly interfere with "nature" taking its course. The hands of the clock move ceaselessly forward and still no one appears to address the problems of the obviously dying patient.

Far off in a distant room of the same hospital is a large, comfortable, and opulently furnished meeting room. It is crowded with doctors. A haze of smoke produced by some of the finest cigars that other people's money can buy fills the room. It is quite possible that the same smoke is being augmented with that from various controlled substances. Substances which would never be recommended to patients, but it seems are being consumed by the physicians nonetheless. One shudders to think of a doctor so impaired caring for any patient who truly needs his services. This apparently isn't a realistic concern, as the gathering of experts doesn't appear to being going anywhere right away. With drinks in hand and comfortably reclining, this enormous group of medical professionals discuss at great length possible courses of action to follow in the treatment of our unfortunate man in the emergency room. Some cool heads carefully outline each and every step that might be taken, even going to the extreme of recommending alternative methods in direct contradiction to their earlier statements. Neither logic, nor time constraints will be allowed to get in the way of a full examination of all the possible directions in which to go.

Other doctors possessing a more emotional nature also state their cases, their opinions. Their thoughts on the subject are given with rising voices and flailing arms. The majority of the crowd covers the spectrum between these two extremes. One common thread however does draw this team of experts together. It is the considered opinion of all involved that something must be done, and it really isn't important what that something is, as long as it doesn't actually involve going so far as treating the patient.

It probably wouldn't occur to you, but there is an enormous moral dilemma here. Should the victim prove terminal while all these necessary discussions are taking place then that certainly can't be considered their fault, now can it? God forbid that any action taken might prove to be the wrong one and the dying patient expire all the quicker. No, that would certainly allow for, perhaps even call for, the assignment of blame. The ability to hold, at least some of these great physicians, to some degree accountable for their actions. And thus it is that this esteemed gathering of doctors, these great medical experts and care providers continue their ever so well meaning discussions ad nauseam, while the clock runs out on our now doomed patient. He slips off to his death unaware that the exact people in which he had placed his trust to save him in his hour of need, really had no intention of doing anything to help him from the very beginning. And so he dies, as die he should with the entire staff of this great medical facility to be properly held blameless in his death, for after all they didn't do anything wrong, they simply didn't do anything at all.

The aforementioned patient in this not too unrealistic scenario is of course, The United States of America. The highly paid, some might say overpaid, Doctors, Surgeons and Specialists are none other than our President, Congressmen and other elected and appointed officials. The lengthy discussions they hold go on even now, while the patient will slowly, but without question, die. And die in fact with their blessings. For there are not just one, but two odd twists to this story. First the Physicians stand to inherit all the patient owns once he expires, so in actuality, it is in their best interest that the patient die. The second odd twist is that the gunshot wounds and the poisoning were inflicted by this same well-meaning group of health care providers while on the payroll of, and with the resources of the victim. The bullet wounds came in the form of unnecessary and burdensome taxes, restricted freedoms, ever-eroding Constitutional rights, and a diminishing quality of life. The victim's weakly pay check (poetic license intended) is not viewed as his own, but as belonging to the Government, the State if you will, with a small finder's fee to be turned over to the wage earner after withholding is taken out, for putting in his forty to eighty hours of labor. Why, such withholding even provided the hospital setting in which the country, the victim, the taxpayer is so callously allowed to die. And the poison comes in the form of racism, perpetrated by the same ones espousing the removal of racism. It comes in the form of a "Do as I say, Not as I do" Congress. It's ingredients are the Politically Correct Movement, removal of religious freedom in the name of Freedom of Religion or better termed freedom *from* religion, and the espousal of anything vain, anything perverse and anything base, under the guise of freedom of expression.

Ah, but there still remains one small irony. After his untimely death at the hands of these evil and slothful physicians, from wounds and poison actually inflicted by them, the final insult is yet to come. The hospital bill will be sent to the next of kin who will be held accountable for every last penny owed, and the doctors will party with his life insurance. At the party the doctors will speak of what a shame it was that nothing could be done to save the victim, while outside the ballroom, his descendants mourn their loss. Yes, a bleak picture I have painted. Is there any hope at all? No, none whatsoever. Not as long as we allow things to continue in their present direction. And neither will a slowing down of the process, nor a modest change in direction help us either. The changes necessary for the patient, that is to say *our* survival, are enormous and dramatic. What can be done? Read on.

I ask something bold of you. I ask nothing less than you adopt and fight for *all* the ideas in this book. Even the ones you might for a while disagree with. To do anything less would be to come to the battle (and make no mistake, it is the battle for your life) with a cafeteria mentality.

The man in the cafeteria doesn't take that except what he expressly likes, and that is fine as far as that goes. But without a cohesive and comprehensive plan, those who should be on the same side in this will find themselves disregarding different items, until there isn't enough fabric left of the original cloth for a handkerchief, much less enough to cover the entire body as required.

In the end the decision will be yours, as in fact it has been all along.

Firsthand I witnessed the death of a large union, one which I had been involved in for decades. There was much that could have been done, and still this patient likewise died while the doctors discussed what must be done, yet did nothing. And its thousands of members just could never agree on a course of action, and so quite naturally took none.

The good, the upright, the hard working all perished with the rest. And the real pity, the real crime is that it didn't have to end that way.

On a quiet night you can still hear their distant whimper. Don't let America follow suit.

The Underlying Principle
(Lies, Lies, Lies)

"There are no simple solutions!" The politicians' amplified voice bounces off the walls of the crowded auditorium as he slaps his hand down on the lectern for emphasis. There he stands, an American hero. One who is not afraid to tell it like it is, not afraid to take on the tough questions. The crowd cheers him. And as he continues his well-rehearsed speech, playing the audience he has carefully studied to know so well, you can almost hear the trumpets start up with the Star Spangled Banner as background music, feel an imaginary wind pick up the American flag craftly placed to his right rear. All would be well except for one thing. He is lying. Yes, he is lying. He has played to the emotion of the crowd, that he is one who stands ready to make these tough, but necessary choices. "Ah, such a man!" the audience almost thinks as one.

I tell you the truth, and hidden in his black, stony little heart, the aforementioned politician probably knows it too. There are almost nothing *but* simple solutions. That's right, as radical as it might sound, the answers to most of life's difficult problems usually lie in the most simple solutions. The wheel is round. The sky is blue. The shortest distance between two points is a straight line. You eat when you're hungry, rest when you're tired and yes, most certainly, the simplest solution is usually the best solution, as well as being the easiest to implement. This is not to say that simple solutions don't at times create their own small problems. But by their very nature, the simplest solutions create the smallest problems, and again by nature, ones that are not in themselves insurmountable. I possess these solutions and offer them up to you here in this book. Many people, particularly those of a political bent, will protest my ideas. The reason for this if you haven't guessed it, is precisely because they *will* work.

People of ill intent thrive on the failures of our society, for that is what empowers them. Therefore the last things they really want are solutions. But if you are one of those who does care about this country, this book was written for you. And now, without further delay, my version of "How To Fix Everything."

Section I:
THAT WHICH STEALS OUR WEALTH

Welfare Reform

The subject of Welfare Reform seems to be another one of those that our esteemed politicians want very much to talk about, ad infinitum, but the last thing they really want to do is work on its eventual solution.

Our officials don't want to admit that the system itself is rife with corruption and incompetence. They would also like to make certain that you remain unaware of the magnitude of welfare fraud.

Our beloved Liberals treat any reference to the growing problems as racism. They call anything reformers might say "code-words" for racism. These same Liberals are quick to remind us that the majority of people on public assistance are white. But wait, then isn't this a contradiction? Never having been bound by the constraints of logic, as normal people are, they insist on having it both ways.

Since it is true that the greatest number of people on the public dole are white, how then could any discussion on welfare reform and reduction be termed racist?

This leaves us with no alternative but to begin by doing the most important thing we can for these Liberals. Ignore them. For their opinion is as valueless as that of an individual who thinks that he is a lemon pie. Treating them with this well-deserved amount of respect, let's go on to do things my way.

The majority of the people on welfare haven't much alternative. Unwed and uneducated mothers with small children and no available day-care, retarded individuals, those with learning disabilities, the physically handicapped, few of us would attempt to deny them assistance despite the fact that help comes in the form of our tax dollars. Americans are not a stingy people.

But a large and seemingly growing minority of those who are quickly becoming an intolerable burden to us, fall into none of these categories.

Those who we need to get off our backs include perpetrators of fraud, either in the form of double booking or false claims, otherwise healthy people who simply choose not to work, unwed mothers who became that way by design (primarily an inner city problem), the chronically unemployable, and people misrepresenting a disability.

Although each recipient of welfare receives only about eight thousand dollars per year in direct benefits, not much to live on at all, thanks to the wonders of bureaucracy the actual cost to the taxpayer exceeds thirty thousand dollars per claim per year. Amazing how much you can add to a bill when you really work on it! Indirect benefits and bureaucratic accounting costs serve to balloon the cost to the taxpayer until we are no longer talking about small potatoes at all.

Figure out the total of the tens of thousands, or more likely, hundreds of thousands of people who really don't belong on welfare, and we're talking about saving billions of dollars per year. And as they say in Congress, A billion here, a billion there, and pretty soon you're talking about real money.

The first step in welfare reform is to identify and then remove the undeserving from the rolls. These people are not going to remove themselves. They are as spoiled adult children still living at home. Well past the age of maturity, they remain a large drain on their parents resources, and will continue to do so as long as "mom and dad" keep paying the bills.

It is time for the grown children to be kicked out of the nest, out into society and forced to fend for themselves.

We already have in place the way to accomplish this. A board of supervisors must be set up within the existing system of social workers. This board will be comprised of a group of citizens such as yourselves who have a vested interest in seeing to it that the plan works. The board would direct the case workers to research and provide them with a list of approximately twenty-five percent of their clients who they believe to be the least worthy to remain on the rolls. These might include, but not be limited to the following: The supposed disabled who have been witnessed otherwise, unwed mothers who have in fact moved in with some sugar daddy, yet continue to collect their checks, cases of abandonment, where the old man pretends to have fled, but in fact is still living with the woman, those who are known to be working a job off the books, and those who are working the racket of receiving multiple checks.

Along with the submission of these lists would come whatever documentation and evidence as can be provided to substantiate such claims.

When investigation of a particular case bears out abuse, the client will be removed from the eligibility rolls, and have ninety days to file an appeal. In this manner the truly needy are provided with proper recourse in the event of incorrect information or against the possibility of vindictive behavior from any particular social worker. Likewise even those thrown off the public dole with every good reason will be given three months from the time of notice in which to find a job. No one will simply be left high and dry.

This system should serve to reduce the number of people collecting public assistance by approximately twenty percent. It further serves to force a large amount of people back into society, now on the paying end. Once their participation in the welfare scam is over, the majority of these people will have no alternative than to go back to working for a living, even though in most cases that means starting at bottom of the ladder jobs. Employers would no longer find it as difficult to fill those bottom line positions, and so business benefits.

We also get to address a darker side of the welfare issue with this same program: Its tightly woven connection to street crime. It is no secret that many people on welfare are also small time criminals. The monthly check provides them with a base salary you might say, and a considerable amount of their true income is derived from theft, muggings, con games, prostitution, drug sales, etc., etc. This is especially a big city problem. Those young men on the street corner running a game of three card monte: do you really think they hold night jobs, and do this in their spare time? If you were to follow half the hookers home after a day of plying their trade they would lead you back to the projects where the majority of them live on public assistance, whoring to support their crack habits.

If you stroll down any street in cities like New York, you will see hundreds of cars with signs in the windows reading "No Radio." Now it's not that New Yorkers are too poor to afford a radio after having treated themselves to a new car, and wish to advertise that fact. Car radio theft in most cities has reached the proportion where if you haven't already had yours stolen, you've probably removed it yourself in order to avoid both the loss and the accompanying shattered window.

The proper equation is that excess time in the hands of less than well meaning people, breeds crime. Most people forced back to work would find little time or energy left for such activities.

The resulting additional benefit would be a much reduced crime rate and our ability to either refocus the efforts of our police or perhaps lay a few off, again saving tax dollars.

After we have managed to reduce the number of those on public assistance, there is still much work to be done. With a reduced need, there is a reduced need to fill. Thus we can begin laying off a proportional number of welfare workers whose services are no longer needed, and send them off to find work in the real world. Let us not lose sight of the fact that this accomplishes an important goal: to shrink government. It is hoped that the majority of those released from public service would find jobs in the private sector, jobs in which they actually produce something rather than only helping the taxpayer chase his tail.

A welfare system operating with a properly reduced staff leaves less room in which to hide internal scandal, corruption and fraud. It can be housed in smaller, more affordable offices. By definition a smaller more streamlined operation runs more efficiently.

Did you know that it takes three dollars worth of administrative effort to put each one dollar worth of food stamps into the hands of the recipient?

This would change rapidly once the bureaucracy has been reduced to the point that we could get an effective handle on it. That sort of nonsense has just got to be stopped. At present the government doesn't think so.

So far our plan is able, once implemented, to save us an enormous amount of money. But I don't wish to save all of it right away. Let us say that we take half the monetary savings and give that back immediately to the taxpayer. Let us then plow the other half back into the system to produce more dramatic savings down the line. This would be in the form of education and job training to work toward the goal of removing more people from welfare.

Next, actual monetary incentives would also be given to unwed mothers to go on a Norplant 17 program, and avoid becoming "Breeders" supplying us with our next generation of welfare recipients.

Norplant 17 is a birth control implant which may be removed at any time the individual is able to go back to work and pay her own way. Couple this with an actual reduction in benefits to those who continue to have children while on welfare and you'd soon see just how quickly people can become responsible.

Those of the Liberal persuasion would say "What right do you have to interfere with someone's reproductive freedom?"

To this I answer "*Every* right, so long as *I* am paying the bill, and *no* right, if I am not." While we are on the subject I must ask who gave them the right to coin the word "Entitlements," and where did they get the right to tax me against my wishes? I never gave it to them!

Please don't forget that Norplant 17 is being offered here as an option, and with a monetary reward. No one is to be forced into this program.

I can also feel the disapproval of my Catholic brothers and sisters. Please understand that I do love Catholics. Again I remind you that no one would be forced into this program. Which is the bigger of the sins in Catholicism anyway? Avoiding procreation, or sexual activity outside of the bounds of marriage? If the church opposes this plan (for people who are predominately not Catholic) let the church then pay their way, not the taxpayer supported public welfare system.

As for objections to the reduced payments for those who choose to continue to crank out children while on welfare, I simply ask: Where else in the natural world is a lack of responsibility rewarded? I mean outside of Congress that is?

The next idea will frighten those of you who will see it as "Big Brotherism." So be it.

A portion of this money which has been set aside for further welfare reform will be offered to welfare recipients and the public at large, for turning in cases of welfare fraud and corruption. This will reduce such fraud through actual exposure, and as a bonus stop fraud before it starts. One is less likely to engage in criminal activities when aware that someone may be looking over his shoulder.

These one time lump sum rewards would pay for themselves many times over and create a system of watchdogs who remain in place working behind the scenes, and free of charge until they uncover abuse.

Just one brief closing note. People often ask me if I agree with the concept of "workfare," and I tell them that I most certainly do not.

Workfare is where those on welfare who are able bodied, are required to perform some various tasks for the state such as street cleaning or whatever, in order to continue receiving their checks.

I counter that if they are able bodied I do not want them on the welfare rolls at all. Let them compete with the rest of us in the private sector for productive jobs. It is not my obligation to supply these people with government provided, and taxpayer funded opportunities. This was never the design nor intent of the welfare system. It was meant and should always be meant to act only as a life saving net for those individuals who for some reason *cannot* work, those who would otherwise starve.

The welfare system has only grown to today's disastrous proportions because of clouded thinking like "workfare." Let us not perpetuate the error.

Our choice is clear. We can implement the above ideas, straighten out a system gone wrong, and save our society countless billions while reducing crime.

Or we could just let things continue the way that they are.

Unemployment

The government does not create jobs, that is what the private sector does. Each time the government attempts to create jobs it does so at the expense of those in private business, paying taxes. If you think that government created jobs could possibly be a good thing, let us examine this situation from the viewpoint of logical extremes: so that we all have employment, we all go to work for the government. Since we all work for the government, we all draw our check from the government. But wait, where would the government get the money? Taxes, of course. Once we are all working for Uncle Sam, the tax rate would necessarily rise to one hundred percent, for each of us would be working in order to pay the salary of the worker next to us. And for the most part, what is produced? Nothing.

Productive, tax paying employment must by definition come from free enterprise. The equation is simple: for each job in government there is just that much more of a burden upon the private sector tax paying public. For each additional job created by non-government business on the other hand, there is just that much more of a sharing of the tax burden along with the accompanying production (goods, services, etc.).

So obviously the key to increased employment is to stimulate the economy by means of encouraging private sector jobs.,

Just how can this be accomplished?

Recently, our government has instituted a number of programs which were counterproductive to business growth. It would of course serve no ones interests to go back to the days of the sweat shop, child labor, and the sixty to eighty hour work week. No one is proposing that.

However, if jobs are to be created, the economy must be expanded and to do that, business must be encouraged. If business is to be encouraged, we must start by ending government's antagonistic approach toward business.

How can we look at big corporations as somehow being inherently evil, when they employ thousands and in some cases hundreds of thousands of American workers? The hostile climate business finds itself operating in today is exactly what has led to the shackling of enterprise which precluded taking on additional workers.

In reality, no company wishes to lay any of its workers off. The concept is that each worker is employed by a company on a cost plus profit basis. If you as a worker are so inefficient that your efforts earn for the company no more than your salary, or perhaps even a bit less, then of course that is another story. Similarly if the quantity of work needing to be done diminishes considerably, then layoffs are the natural progression.

But again, given healthy contracts and efficient workers any company would prefer to retain all of its employees so as to fulfill the production level required and meet market demands.

If government is to have a role in this at all, it should largely be to simply stay out of the way.

A good example of how government shackles enterprise is the recently imposed "Family Leave Bill." According to it's rules any company which employs fifty people or more must grant its employees up to thirteen weeks of unpaid leave per year. This leave would be for the purpose of allowing the employee to care for newborns and for other such good reasons and is meant to be applied to both men and women. Since we all love our children and this leave is of an unpaid nature thereby costing the company nothing, isn't this a good deal all the way around? Not exactly. Actually not even close.

If you understood what I said about each employee working in order to turn a profit for the company (no profit, no company), then you must realize that the loss of any employee costs the company more than just that workers salary.

A replacement worker must be brought in for the interim and with few exceptions must be trained at some expense, and will for quite a while operate with a lack of efficiency, perhaps even costing the company money for several weeks of training.

Just about the time that this workers productivity is showing profit potential, it is time to let him go again, as the person who he replaced for family leave is scheduled to return.

The higher the level of skill that the worker who takes such leave possesses, the more his absence impacts the company.

The legislators and news media have both downplayed another important aspect of this new law. It probably slipped your notice that although the employer doesn't have to pay a salary to the worker on leave, they are required by law to continue supplying medical coverage to same. With today's high cost of health insurance you can see where most companies will have to shell out several thousand dollars to cover each employee who will at the time be earning them nothing. Is that fair and proper? Does this encourage business? Help the employment outlook?

What impact will this have on certain sized companies and their employees?

As I have shown, the cost of compliance with this new law will be considerable. Any company having just a few more employees than the threshold, for example fifty-three people, would probably find it to their advantage to lay off a few, bringing the total to forty-nine, work those remaining a little harder and legally evade the new law. In this case four people are put out of work, and those who are left must work harder to make up for their shrinking ranks. Additionally each of these remaining employees will work under a bit more stress, wondering if their job will be the next to be cut.

Who will be the most likely to be let go? In an ideal world we'd all like to think that the most slothful and undependable would go first, or at least those who have the least seniority. The reality however is that the first to go more likely will be the "trouble maker" who has been trying to form a union, or someone who has been making disparaging remarks about the boss's nephew. Also likely to be on the "X" list are those that the company might consider to be future liabilities. Women of child bearing age would become prime candidates for the great good-bye, as would people of less than perfect health.

Similarly, companies on the borderline with, say, forty-five employees or so will abandon any ideas of expanding their staff. They will not be adding those few more workers to the payroll which they might have, that move now being too costly.

It doesn't take a great deal of imagination to visualize larger companies splitting themselves into smaller fractions (on paper only) in order to take advantage of the under fifty employees rule. Mr. and Mrs. Smith trucking and shipping would, with the stroke of their lawyers pen, become Mr. Smiths trucking and Mrs. Smiths shipping.

As is typical of the laws passed by a supposedly well meaning government, their effect is quite the opposite of the stated intent. Not only does this law and so many like it not help the people it was designed to, but it actually hurts them.

As I pointed out, business also suffers when the government sticks it's nose in where it doesn't belong. Odd, that government thinks that it can run business better than the managers and owners of the corporations can, this despite the fact that it can't even run itself properly.

Does there exist a better example of corruption, inefficiency and waste then you find within our own beloved government? Were businesses run in a like manner they would all fail, for business does not have the public jugular (taxpayer) to keep sucking on. And still they remain our self appointed moral voice?

Regardless of what should be obvious to anyone with half a brain, certain people like our favorite swimmer, Ted Kennedy, don't think that restrictive laws like the family leave bill do near enough damage to business and the problem of unemployment. He has vowed that the "Family Leave Bill" as it stands today is "only the beginning."

My plan for getting America back to work has eight basic components. The details of many of them are found in other chapters so I will only give you an overview here. Also as you read through the book you will see other things which were all meant to work together toward the goal of a healthier America, but which do not specifically come under the headings of these eight points.

1) We must stop trusting government to be capable of supplying any solutions to our employment problem. Not

capable of steering their own ship they have not a clue as to how to help us, except with the foolish idea of hiring more government workers. Each new layer of government, each new task force, every new fact finding mission serves only to make matters worse. As you would with a drunk or an insane man, it would be wise to avoid looking to them for proper direction.

2) Related to the first point, government must be pressured and in some cases forced to keep its big nose out of the way of business. Overly restrictive laws which shrink the economy, and the public sectors' desire to employ ever more people must be put to an end.

3) We must dramatically reduce and in fact nearly stop immigration as it is practiced today. What good would it do if my ideas (or anyone else's for that matter) were to put twenty thousand people to work immediately, if at the same time our government brought in an equal amount of people also looking for jobs? This madness has got to be stopped.

4) We must see to it that laws are repealed which make attractive for our companies to manufacture outside our borders, using foreign labor.

5) The measures which I proposed in the chapter "our failing auto industry" must be implemented. This would return a vast segment of our society to the workplace.

6) Tax incentives should be granted to companies of every description, but especially those willing to take on additional employees. Business should no longer be viewed by government as some huge cash cow, created for no other purpose than to be sucked dry by taxes, fees, penalties, surcharges, etc. Business must be encouraged, not punished, if we are to approach full employment.

7) Big government and its attending tax structure and schemes must be dismantled as I've called for in my chapter on taxes. Without the burden of a huge and wasteful

Unemployment

government to pay for, many people who currently must hold two jobs just to get by could afford to relax a little. Likewise in households where both husband and wife have found it necessary to work, many could go back to only one mate working.

Those additional jobs freed up would now be available for others.

8) The only place government does belong in this equation is to make America "user friendly" for business and hence, jobs. I detail this further in my chapter on the economy.

There you have it folks. You are down to only two choices. Go farther in the direction that those like Ted Kennedy would have us, and then wonder where all the jobs went, or get government off the back of free enterprise, relegating our "leaders" to their proper job, and watch things flourish.

Actually if you want to see America survive you have only one choice. Guess which one?

The High Cost of Medical Care

Of the many thousands of people I have talked to, few indeed do not count the skyrocketing cost of medical care among the top handful of problems facing us today.

The most common response to the question of what can be done is to move toward socialized medicine. The vast majority of those I have asked think that this is the best answer and perhaps the only one.

I find this response to be most unfortunate for I don't believe that socialized medicine is the only answer, nor do I believe that it is any answer at all. I'd like to see this nation stay as far away from that stretch of quicksand as possible. The common response saddens me for two reasons. First it shows a lack of willingness to exercise some imagination by the majority of respondents, and second it reveals how naive people are about a system which generally hasn't worked well elsewhere, and will with certainty fail miserably here.

"But" you say, "You've asked all those people who all agree that it's the direction to go in, surely they can't all be wrong and you right?"

It is hardly a matter which can be settled by consensus. I must remind you that in World War II the entire world stood by while a certain Mr. A. Hitler, no doubt an evil and deranged individual, took it upon himself (with help) to murder six million Jews and millions of others as well. While all this was going on the world basically did nothing until it was far too late.

So much for the majority having the right idea.

The problems of the medical system which have caused it to evolve into the monster we have with us today are many and varied. I will address the largest of them in this chapter. As usual there is much that can be done the only question being; are we willing to do what is necessary?

The first step we can take is totally within our control. We must stop worshipping doctors.

Physicians are people just like all of us. They have merely by choice of their own, studied to become experts in a field that is unfamiliar to most of us, very much in the same manner as has an architect or a plumber. What do I mean by worship? When was the last time you asked what the doctor charges prior to setting up an appointment? I am asking this whether or not insurance will be paying the bill. Though not a gambler at heart, I would put money on most of you answering "never."

Chances are you see the doctor and pay the office girl on the way out (or the insurance does), never having discussed the fee. Have you asked your doctor for references? How about his personal success ratio? That might really open a can of worms mightn't it? When was the last time you questioned his procedure or even asked for a full explanation of what he was doing? This is what I mean about worshipping doctors.

There isn't another tradesman or professional to whom you would grant such latitude, commit your trust to so wholeheartedly without restraint, question or comment.

A friend of mine once hired an exceedingly high priced specialist to perform a surgical procedure. After the operation he discovered that the specialist he had hired and paid quite a bit extra for did not execute the procedure himself. He stood by, providing advice and oversight while one of his trainees gained hands-on experience.

The strange thing is that my friend wasn't at all upset. Certainly he did not get his money's worth, nor that which he had bargained for. The case raises both contractual and ethical questions. My friend wasn't simply paying someone to see that a certain job gets done, (mowing the grass, etc.) but had hired a particular individual so as to insure the application of the skills of the precise individual in question. Furthermore it was not until later, after the operation, that he learned of the switch. This constitutes a breech of trust, does it not?

Yet the patient wasn't in the least bit perturbed. "How else would the trainees gain the needed experience?" He asked me. I only wonder where else in his life my friend has been so magnanimous. Nowhere, I am sure. This sort of behavior is again what I refer to as worshipping doctors.

The point is that medical costs cannot in any way be contained when we treat with such a cavalier attitude the physicians responsibility toward us, their bread and butter.

A major change in our attitude is the first step toward controlling medical costs. We must make it clear that we are interested in overseeing the entire process in the supervisory capacity which we have disdained in the past. Plainly, it is your body, your health, your money, and with the exception of certain details, it is you who should be calling the shots.

The next important move is to involve ourselves deeply in the area of insurance coverage. Much of the responsibility for the dramatic increase in the cost of medicine lies with us. For too long we have distanced ourselves from any interest in the costs so long as we are not directly paying them. This is entirely the wrong attitude. If we pay no attention to the cost of office visits etc., only because we are not directly paying

The High Cost of Medical Care

the bill, this cannot help but eventually come back and bite us on the posterior. In just a handful of years a doctor, a clinic, lab or hospital can easily double the fee and in fact will if no one objects. The insurance carrier will pay these higher costs and after a short delay, extract the increase from the policy holder (usually your boss) by upping the premium rate.

You may not be impacted by this right away but as the years roll by, each with a substantial increase in rates, sooner or later you will be. Your company will simply pay the higher rates for a while, but when it becomes burdensome will have no choice but to take action. They may choose to reduce your coverage. Dental and optical plans are usually the first to go when a company is feeling pinched. Your employer may instead opt to increase your deductible or your co-payment.

Finally, many employers have found it necessary to reduce the percentage of the work force which they are willing to provide coverage for, or eliminate it altogether. Those in the labor movement usually misinterpret such actions as an attempt by management to squeeze more profit out of operations at the workers expense. While on occasion this undoubtedly does happen, usually this is not the case at all. Most employers who have historically bought and paid for coverage for their men would prefer to continue if it is possible to do so. The last thing a company needs is to have their good employees become disgruntled. Certainly their efficiency will fall off if they do not outright quit, going to work for a competitor who *does* provide health benefits.

In one way or another you will be affected by rising costs if you fail to do your part in monitoring medical expenses. You can:

Insist on seeing the costs in question to ascertain if a better deal is to be had by "shopping around."

Get a direct read out on hospital bills to find out what areas have been padded, what medicines or procedures paid for but not delivered.

Question your doctor to determine if additional procedures are being performed in good faith or if ordered up simply because "insurance is paying for it anyway."

Brush up on basic medical terminology to become cognizant of what methods, medicines and techniques are being applied to you.

Only when we as consumers do our part to keep costs down as we do in every other aspect of our lives, will we begin to get a handle on the price of medical care, and/or insurance.

Now On To The Hospitals

About thirty years ago when medical costs were far more reasonable, nearly every item used on a surgical patient was sterilized in an autoclave. This was a bothersome but necessary step to ensure that contamination wasn't spread from one patient to another. The advent of inexpensive disposable syringes, scalpel blades, and many other items made sterilization and reuse largely obsolete.

Unfortunately as often happens we have outrun our technology. Today the percentage of items which have become disposable for the sake of convenience, is significant. But forgotten is the original objective. No longer are these disposables the inexpensive substitutes they once were. In many cases their cost rivals that of the corresponding item which was formerly sterilized and reused. It is now time for the medical profession or perhaps an outside consulting agency to take a hard cold look to determine which instruments and supplies might properly lend themselves to a return to the autoclave or other sanitizing processes. I am not for a moment suggesting that in this age of AIDS that items such as syringes, scalpels, and other things used for invasive procedures be included in that group. But there is much room for modification in this area without endangering so much as one life.

The High Cost of Medical Care

Next on my list is the need for hospitals to clean up their act. For various reasons, none of which hold any water, efficiency in certain areas has been caused to deteriorate. If you were to review a printout of your hospital bill you would find many surprises. You may find for instance charges of two or three dollars for a pair of Tylenol. Why?

This nonprescription substitute for aspirin is no longer kept on hand in large bottles. In a hospital setting one might expect to find it dispensed from five gallon pails, its usage is so common. Instead, when you are in need, the nurse will show up with two Tylenol provided in individual pairs in the always beloved blister pack. The cost, the additional trash created by thousands of blister packs discarded daily, and the inefficiency is ridiculous just on this one small item. To make matters worse you will invariably wait with pounding head (or other body part) for approximately twenty minutes. For whatever reason, Tylenol and other such medications are usually kept on only one floor of the hospital and the nurse will be necessarily delayed in retrieving them.

Items of a similar nature, like Vaseline for chapped lips, are provided in this same manner. Individual portions kept in packages quite like fast food restaurant ketchup, are more often than not, kept on only one floor of the hospital and of course that floor is never the one you are on. Like the Tylenol, a faint smear of this substance will cost two to three dollars each time.

Imagine a serious illness necessitating a lengthy hospital stay of a few months. The bill when tallied up will of course be astronomical. Simple things like Tylenol, Vaseline, bandages, and the like could easily come to several hundred dollars. Ludicrous yes, but it happens every day.

Because the system has come to rely on the majority of its consumers (patients) to be covered by insurance, nothing has ever been done to regulate hospital efficiency. Generally speaking, you go into the hospital which is rather nearest you when you have the need. This type of spontaneous "purchase" or lack of consumerism has effectively placed hospitals as a whole, outside the normal laws of competition.

You get sick. Without looking around for competitive prices you check into your local hospital. After a few days of care you are sent home, having neither seen nor questioned the bill. Said bill (the sky's the limit) is forwarded to your insurance company who without investigation or question pays it. Each month (or other period of time) either you or your employer pays a premium on your health care policy to the above insurance company. Everybody's happy.

Not Quite...

Who isn't happy? Well some people aren't covered by insurance and so either pay for their medical care directly from their savings, or lacking savings are forced to go into debt to do so. When they peruse their bill they become aware of each little item (like the Tylenol I mentioned) and just how overpriced these items have become due to a total absence of controls. By controls I do not mean those which might be placed there by government, (which through Medicare has long been a major part of the problem), but rather only those which you would normally expect to find in place if an enterprise were at all concerned with the financial well-being of its client, or if it were forced to compete on the open market as is the case with most any other business.

Also not happy are those small business owners who have traditionally provided their workers with health care coverage in the past, but are now faced with premium payments so high as to rival the payroll. Small business owners like these are faced with a dilemma. As I mentioned earlier in this chapter, but it bears repeating, they may have to make the tough choice between laying some workers off or dropping all or part of the health plan they can supply. The third option of asking the employees to shoulder part of the burden is never a popular one. All this on top of the recent tough economic times makes just staying in business a difficult proposition.

The best way to control costs at the hospital level is to set up a recommendations board. This board would be primarily comprised of accountants who have certain backgrounds and insights into the medical profession. With pen and pad in hand the group could tour each hospital dissecting both existing bills and ongoing procedures. They would be a form of "medical facility efficiency experts" and would most probably be paid by the insurance companies who do have a vested interest in keeping costs down so as to be able to offer a more attractive package to their clients.

Similarly, if we can convince both insurance companies and individuals to shop around when it comes to doctors, it may be the doctors themselves who will invite the team of efficiency experts in to help them keep costs down and remain competitive.

The Doctors

The U.S. could well do with half as many lawyers, and twice as many doctors. We are the most litigious society in the world, due to having the highest number of lawyers per population of any country. Our nations law schools have steadily cranked out graduates at a pace far beyond any hopes of being able to find employment for them all. Can you see how this has caused the profession to become perceived as being nothing more than a bunch of ambulance chasers? There is simply too much competition. This has created the flurry of distasteful commercials along the lines of "1-800 let's sue your neighbor" you see smattered all over television lately.

With doctors the situation is quite the opposite. One of the best and easiest ways to bring down the cost of health care is to increase the number of doctors, creating competition, as there is little competition now.

Excepting emergencies, when was the last time you were able to be seen immediately? The standard wait is usually three days and often a week or more. After booking an appointment, are you seen on time? No? How long is the wait? More than half the doctors I have known often keep patients waiting over an hour.

Most physicians will tell you that they put in between fifty and seventy hours per week. This is necessary in order to see the huge volume of patients which arrive at their door.

We need to increase the number of physicians to nearly double. And we can do this while *improving* the quality of the doctors turned out.

Rather than restricting the number of doctors produced as is currently the case, let us blow wide open the doors to our medical schools. We must start with an influx of candidates so large that they will comprise fully four times the current number. By quadrupling the number of people entering the process but doubling the outcome we will filter through this much larger matrix, retaining the very best to pursue the profession.

How can this be accomplished? By restructuring medical school as it exists today, we can put a greater emphasis on premed, which can take place at any existing college. A few more medical schools will have to be built in addition to the conversion of existing facilities on other campuses.

We must also tap more heavily into foreign medical schools. The standards may be somewhat lower but the costs are only a fraction of what we have here in the U.S. Already some of our best and most promising physicians and surgeons are coming to us from outside our borders, but this resource continues to be underutilized.

The High Cost of Medical Care

By seeing to it that a larger number of foreign-trained doctors are only required to boost their background with a year or two of additional training in this country, we can make full use of heretofore uncertified doctors who have gained their education abroad.

By doubling the number of doctors while starting from a proportionally even larger base, natural competition will reduce the price of care while improving the quality of the average physician.

But I do not wish this added competition to destroy the income potential of those very doctors on whom we wish to rely. In order to guard against this, a very important move must be made at the same time. We must put an end to frivolous lawsuits that have raised the cost of malpractice insurance through the roof. It has become the largest hidden cost in medicine.

It is no secret that the multimillion dollar awards being passed out in the courtroom like just so much candy, have negatively impacted the cost and quality of medical care. The magnitude of these rewards is quickly reflected in increased malpractice insurance premiums to the physician which you, the consumer, must pay in the end.

If we can offer the doctors relief from burdensome premiums by eliminating frivolous lawsuits it will be to our immediate benefit. It is indeed these very court actions which are killing the industry. I am not arguing that people who are injured by careless physicians should not have the right to be properly compensated, but in too many cases the amount awarded is all out of line with damages suffered. Also awarded are lawsuits where the doctor is clearly NOT at fault, but the physician or his insurance is made to pay anyway on the ridiculous presumption that "he can afford it." It has in fact become quite profitable to sue physicians. It is so easy for a judge sitting on a bench or a jury comfortably insulated from the results of their action to make an award of five or twenty-five million dollars when a just and appropriate sum may be closer to half a million dollars, or in some cases nothing at all. The results of such excessive awards are leading to the destruction of good medicine. Justifiably fearing confiscatory lawsuits, doctors have little option but to order a barrage of often unnecessary tests in order to protect themselves. In the event of litigation they can then prove that they went to the extreme in providing the best care possible. But these extremes come with a price tag and the consumer, the patient, is the one who will pay that price for these additional tests. And again he will either pay it directly or his insurance company will, with the cost soon being passed back to him in the form of increased premiums.

The imposition of these excessive awards to litigants increases the cost of malpractice insurance and hidden in the doctors fees, you pay that as well. As I said earlier people who have been damaged by physicians should of course be entitled to compensation. But the degree of that compensation should be fixed. Under my system you would still have to take the doctor in question through the court process in order to prove liability, but any award would be a set, determined amount.

By setting up a schedule of appropriate fees the temptation to sue for large sums over some trivial injustice will be gone, as the possibility of collecting will no longer exist.

Boards will be set up similar to those which have worked with workman's compensation, and substantial but fixed amounts for each type of damage will be arrived at.

Litigation will also be reduced, as only accessible blame will have to be determined, not the amount of the award.

By taking this action we will also gain the advantage of moving our doctors out of the courtroom and back into the medical field where they belong.

Million Dollar Machinery

In the future the government should buy up the patents on big ticket items yet to be developed. Those which are like the C.A.T. scan, M.R.I., and dialysis machine have become too costly for the consumer to afford treatment thereof when filtered through the existing channels of our free enterprise system.

Many of the machines of which I speak cost from one to several million dollars. In order for the owner/physician to amortize the cost he must charge the patient for the "mortgage" on the item, carrying charges, interest loss adjustment, reasonable profit, and his own fee. Although this is only just and proper compensation for assuming the risk of purchasing one of these machines it nonetheless leaves the patient with a bill of between four hundred and one thousand dollars per use.

We must grandfather in all the existing apparatus of this nature so as not to step on the toes of those who have already made the sizable investment in that machinery. It is only my desire that future inventions of this sort be held in the public sector. These could then be leased to individuals or groups of physicians who would not have the need to dramatically mark up the price of the usage of this equipment, never having paid to own it. Costs could be fixed so that the patient pays a known fee for each incident of use.

Market forces still come into play for if the government pegs the fixed rate too low for the physicians to charge and still make a living they will find no takers.

The giant and expensive machinery of the future should also be housed in community centrally located facilities and since owned by the government but used by private physicians, its use may extend around the clock. The advantage here is that more use is gotten out of each machine so the per use cost is reduced while the time it takes to fully amortize the equipment is notably shortened, reducing greatly the carrying charge period and thus the total interest charged.

The aforementioned idea is one of the few instances where I stray from my ultraconservative core philosophy, that part of me that wishes to keep government out of the picture as much as possible. I must report however that in sharing this idea with colleagues who are every bit as conservative minded as myself it has met with enthusiastic acceptance. Still it is imperative that we, the people, retain the greatest control possible over the process. The government is to be made to own the machinery, nothing more. Government must not be allowed any further incursion than this or as is usual with everything else they touch, it will become so screwed up as to no longer function properly. Let us not hand over to the public sector that which was formerly held privately only to have them mismanage it to the point where it costs more than if we had left things alone. Fair warning given.

Let me now briefly recap my plan for reducing medical costs.

1. Personal involvement by all of us in the procedural and billing process.

2. An oversight board to stop wasteful hospital practices

3. A doubling of the number of physicians so that free market competition will bring down the fees charged

4. Malpractice relief in the form of a fixed damage awards schedule to eliminate frivolous lawsuits and unneeded tests

5. Government ownership of future large ticket items like M.R.I.s, C.A.T. scans, etc., which do not yet exist. This in order to reduce the astronomical cost of the use of this type of machinery.

All of these steps taken together will send medical care in a new direction. It will become more responsible to the patient while reducing costs considerably.

This will accomplish one of the most important tasks of all, providing quality health care at an affordable level while keeping government out of the system to the greatest extent possible.

We will have no need for socialized medicine as it is envisioned by the likes of Hillary and Bill Clinton. Their way is the fast road to disaster and it works directly against the principles I have shown you here.

The more you know about the Clinton health care plan the less you will like it, this I promise you. For the sake of America, for the sake of the future of quality medicine, go with my plan.

TAXES, TAXES, TAXES
(or, your money or your life)

First A Perspective

Americans, as a whole, pay an enormous amount of their income to the government in the form of taxes. For all this great expense they receive very little in return. Many of the taxes paid are disguised in different manners as well, sometimes being referred to by that wonderful catch-all phrase "user fees."

When you catch on to an approximate idea of how heavily taxed we are, the government will reassure you that (according to them) we are among the lowest taxed nations in the world. Unfortunately for us, far too many of our fellow citizens have bought this statement either because they lack the essentials of pencil and paper, or the ability to add.

Those few countries which do tax their people more than us fall into two categories. Those who provide extensive services such as socialized medicine, subsidized housing, government paid transportation, old age homes, et al. In the second category are the very oppressive governments such as Idi Amin's Uganda, where the citizens were stripped of all wealth and dignity so as to provide an excess of the same for their dictator. Old Idi by the way was said to have executed over three million of his own people including a wife or two. Not exactly a role model.

Let us assume for a moment that you, reader, possess both the pencil and paper, and the ability to add with a fair degree of accuracy, and let's have some fun with figures.

At the top of the paper put your income for the week. Include any overtime but don't forget the hours you put in to get that overtime. After all, you earned it.

That figure, whatever it is, is as good as it gets. It's all downhill from here. In a separate column we'll start listing the taxes. First, write down your federal withholding tax. This will vary between fifteen and forty-one percent, depending on your income level. Next, your Social Security tax. This may or may not include the new Medicaid tax. Add that too, if separate. You'll have to double that figure, for don't forget that your employer is forced to kick in an equal amount to your "contribution." Money which could have been added to your salary if your employer didn't have to send it in to Uncle Sam. Those contributions together come out to about another fifteen percent. Next, add in your state, city, and local income taxes if any. There is a small disability payment also taken out of your check. Add it. What you won't add here is the workman's compensation. That is paid by your employer and is based upon (but not taken from) your salary. Remember however that you would likely have received at least a portion of that, had our government not squeezed it out of your boss. The amount varies, depending on the type of work you do, from a couple of percent for work like clerk-typist, to around fifty percent for those employed as loggers and coal miners. So keep that in the back of your mind and let's go on.

Take a look at your pay stub and see if there is anything I left out and add that in as well. Now add all that up. Subtract the sum from your pay and you have, of course, your take home, or that is to say what the government allows you to leave for home with on a Friday afternoon after having removed "their share."

There are yet many more taxes to come, but at this point I'd like you to note one important thing. These taxes have been taken out of your earnings (remember that word and its implications—"earnings") in the form of withholding before you get your check. The government's share comes out first. Some priorities. Could it be they don't trust you?

This, of course, makes it quite difficult to lodge any meaningful protest, once they have your money that is. You can't refuse to pay it in order to make a point, or because you don't like the way they are spending your money. (Please remember the terms they, and your. They'll come in handy later.)

So now you head home with what's left of your money, and you'd like to spend it. Let's say you'd like to spend all of it, and on yourself.

Can't.

That's right, you can't. Because we haven't gotten to the point that all of it is what can be referred to as "your money" yet. Some of this now dwindling pile of cash must be set aside to pay the semi-yearly property tax.

If you own your own home, each year you must pay anywhere from several hundred to several thousand dollars in property tax, otherwise known as real estate tax.

This tax was instituted because it was felt at the time that only the wealthy owned property, and that it would more fairly spread the tax burden to implement such a tax. In fact, the term "real estate" meant that it was a measure of your "actual worth," and thereby your ability (and assumed responsibility) to pay tax. Oddly, it would be hard to show that tax in this area gained us any relief in the realm of tax on income.

For those of you who are not fans of the rich, I might point out that although they live quite comfortably in their mansions, they might easily be paying forty thousand dollars a year or more in real estate taxes alone. Far out of proportion to "their share" for goods and services provided to them. But I digress.

Some of you do not own your own home but rather rent. You may think therefore that you escape paying property tax, that this part of the chapter has little to do with you. Nothing could be farther from the truth.

Your landlord pays tax on the property, and perhaps at a higher rate than normal, for it might be considered commercial in nature, not being his residence but rather an investment property.

This he pays, not out of the kindness of his heart, although this may surprise you, but because he is constrained to do so. As I think you are beginning to catch on, this cost he passes on to you as a portion of your monthly rent bill. Along with it are various accounting costs for handling this sordid transaction. It's quite simple really. If there were no property taxes, your rent would be much lower.

By the way, this tax is also one of those which you have no way to protest. Pay it, and every penny in full, or the government will find it sad but necessary to take your house. You may spend twenty or thirty years paying for a house worth, say, two hundred thousand dollars. But miss the tax payment for only three years, and your house, along with all your hopes and dreams goes on the auction block on the county courthouse steps for as little as what was owed in taxes.

Should the bidding bring a higher price, you get the difference. If not, not a penny. Although not a conspiracy per se, it would be difficult to formulate one which would more efficiently deprive you of that which you have worked a lifetime for.

So out of your take home pay you remove whatever is appropriate for this property tax. Fine. The rest is yours. Uh, no.

Just in the course of living you use various utilities. Whatever you use in this area: water, electric, heating, and even your phone, check the average bill. You'll find it not difficult to decode what portion of it goes to tax. Figure out what amount you average weekly, and subtract it from your remaining pay.

By now you are probably getting pretty mad, so you hop in your car and, oops. Your car!

Talk about a burden. Forget about its actual sticker price for now. That's the only part that's halfway fair. After all, you paid your money, you get a car to whatever extent it's worth. It's the rest that bothers me. Upon purchase, you paid sales tax. I'm not going into detail about that at this time, for I will be covering sales tax later. I do want you to note, however, that in regard to automobiles, the tax goes on as long as the car does. When you buy a car second hand, you also pay sales tax on that purchase. But why is this? Didn't the government take its bite out of the car when first sold as new? Don't dismay, when you resell your used car, the third hand buyer again pays tax upon his purchase.

As many people as there are who will own that car throughout its entire life, will pay tax on it. Were you to add them all up you would find the real sales tax levied on a car. My guess is that in New York it probably works out to about twenty percent. Not a bad scam if your name is Uncle Sam. No wonder the government is in such a tizzy about our failing auto industry. And all along we thought it was a concern for the loss of American jobs!

Well, let's move along, shall we? I'm sure you've got some money left that we can piss away.

While still on the subject of your car (though you would probably prefer a horse by now), there are a few states like Florida which possess a unique approach.

Knowing that most people who move in are retirees, Florida has decided that if the old geezers coming down have the audacity to wish to bring a car with them, they should have to pay a penalty. That will teach them to not have walked in, luggage in hand and purchase their car within the state, having disposed of the old one at home.

Anyway, you hop in your car, a bit more pissed off than you were before, and head off down the highway. As the needle is starting to nudge the "E" on the indicator you pull into one of those wonderfully convenient stations for gas.

What does it say on the pump? $1.25? No. Under that. Various state and federal taxes are often listed under the price. According to the owner of the station I use, the total tax in New York comes out to forty-six cents per gallon. The gas itself is relatively inexpensive. Find out what the total tax (federal, state, etc.) is in your area.

How many miles each week do you drive, and what kind of mileage do you get? Write it down, deduct it from your pay.

As a little aside while we are talking about gas mileage, it must be mentioned here that there is now a gas guzzler tax placed on new automobiles which don't produce the best efficiency. This may or may not affect you. Suffice it to say that if you buy a particularly large, or sporty-fast car, you will be penalized twice—once at the pump, and once again at the other pump we call Uncle Sam.

Another little aside while we are at it. As of this writing we have (or that is to say, about forty-three percent of you have) elected a new president. Hillary, I mean Bill Clinton, has pledged to institute a new energy tax. Placed on gasoline and graduating to a level of fifty cents per gallon, this tax would go on top of all that we are already paying and would supposedly help chip away at the deficit. Wanna bet? Fortunately at this time it appears that he has backed off, and is willing to settle for only a nickel a gallon, at least for now. Lucky us.

Yet another slick politician who never met a tax he didn't like, he reminds you of a modern day Huey Long, but without any vision. I wonder what he thinks this will do to the auto industry? Well, no matter, but again I digress.

Still on your car are we? Don't forget that it must be registered and inspected, and that you, the driver, must be licensed. These are all what might be referred to as "user fees." But what are these fees anyway, other than a different way of saying tax? Would a rose by any other name…

Write it down, take it out.

Disgustedly, you head home. I've ruined your drive for today. Sorry. Looks like a great deal of traffic up ahead. Better take the turnpike. I forgot, that's a toll road. You open the ash tray and get ready to start slinging quarters into the gaping maws of the collection cages at each toll booth. Your quarters are kept there because it became such a handy spot since you gave up smoking. No health nut, you just couldn't afford it anymore. Because cigarettes are mostly what? Tobacco? No. Tax.

If you do smoke, keep the ink flowing in your column.

From the turnpike you look over to your left where there is a very old bridge crossing the river. You guessed it, it's a toll bridge.

When built in your grandfather's day, the fee for crossing it was a dime. That fine was to be done away with once the project was paid for. That bridge was paid for decades ago, and still the toll booths remain. Toll booths that see to it that you not only part with your money, but that you are delayed in getting to where the bridge is supposed to take you as well. With one difference, however. Unlike in your granddaddy's day, the toll is no longer a dime. It's a couple of dollars or so. Incidentally, the toll on the Verezano Narrows Bridge, linking New Jersey to the city of New York (or almost) is now six dollars each way. I say almost because it only gets you so far as Brooklyn. To get to Manhattan you'll probably take a very short tunnel, leaving you short another three dollars, again, each way. So let's see, to go about a dozen miles from New Jersey to Manhattan and home again (we do want to eventually go home again, don't we?) will cost us in tolls alone around eighteen dollars. But that's only right, now isn't it?

As to the toll roads and bridges in your area, you know the drill. Divide it out, write it down, subtract it.

Hey, walking's better for you anyway, right?

So you walk down to the 7-Eleven for a cold six pack and some Fritos. You don't buy a lottery ticket, remembering who gets that money. I can't give you the figures, but alcoholic beverages are very heavily taxed. They call this a "sin tax." Odd how the words sin and tax go so well together. On to the Fritos is tacked on the prevailing rate of sales tax in your area. This may vary from zero percent in some places, to over eight percent like it is in New York.

Eight percent? Yes, that's right. Now don't get so upset. Put your feet up and pop open one of those brews. No, I mean it. I'd like you to try to relax. Put the book down, stare out the window and try not to think of anything for about five minutes.

Back already? Now, isn't that better? Forget the percentage I just mentioned, it isn't important.

What is important is the principle. Except for those who live where there is no sales tax, there is something morally quite upsetting here. The fact that you can be taxed on purchases means that you are not entitled to, that you are legally restrained from purchasing anything unless you have more than enough money to do so. The tax added to your purchase is in no way an option.

The second morally repulsive item in this, is the concept of double taxation. Our forefathers fought and died to form a country with a constitution which would guarantee us relief from this. What has happened?

Most municipalities are not happy with a sales tax. It's simply not enough. So they have broadened its scope to include all services as well. Call a plumber, auto mechanic, (there we go again), tree surgeon, what have you, and you must pay a sales tax upon their services.

To make matters worse, (yes, it can always get worse), most states are now trying to collect from you sales tax on purchases you made in other states. Certainly this must be unconstitutional. That was never the intent nor purpose of a sales tax.

Figure the total portion of your money you spend on taxable sales and services each year, divide it by the weeks, write it down, deduct it.

Well, we've still got a little ground to cover. So you open your mail. Good thing you picked up those brews, you're going to need them.

Along with the other junk mail you don't want, is a traffic summons and a parking violation. There I go with the car again.

You had put a couple of quarters in the parking meter when you went to get that haircut that you're still unhappy about. After paying the barber (including the tax), and tipping him nonetheless, like a fool you left his shop an entire seven minutes too late, to find a parking violations ticket on your windshield. Its bright yellow color offset by the beautiful red "expired" wand on the meter which seems now to be silently laughing at you as you fish for your keys. Only briefly do you reflect on the fact that the original coins thoughtfully placed in the meter earlier, were in their own right a tax.

Too much trash remains on your mind as you carelessly pass that radar trap at Norbert and Third. Yes, there's no sense denying it, I saw you.

With the needle on the speedo approaching forty-two, you remember only too late that this is a thirty-mile-per-hour zone, as the high-pitched scream of a siren fills the air.

All this now flashes back in your mind in much less time than it takes to pop the lid on yet another beer. Don't you wish that you had remembered to pay those tickets on time? It would have been preferable to the new fine which now includes penalty and interest. Don't you wish you had refrained from saying "your mother" to the nice officer?

Lest you think you are an isolated case, most of us get some of these kinds of tickets sooner or later. And when fines like this become broad based enough, what are they? That's right, another tax. No, we are not all Charlie Manson, but yes, most of us do get a few tickets. It's just a round about way of squeezing a few more bucks from you. Average it out, add it to your list.

Just one more thought on this subject. At forty-two miles per hour, did you ever feel you were truly a menace on the road? Are you beginning to feel that the thirty-mile-per-hour limit is more of an arbitrary and low speed selection designed to encourage exceeding said limit so as to improve on ticket revenues?

By the way, did any of those past tickets ever raise your insurance rates? You know what to do.

I know I'm getting you down, but at least you can rest in the comfort of knowing that your dog still loves you. How much was his license? Deduct it from your money.

The democrats, in general, do not want to see a cut in the capital gains tax. Actually they don't want to see a cut in any tax, but proposed capital gains tax cuts in particular, really bother them. They claim such a cut would only benefit the rich. Think of it. As if the rich were some horrible group that we must make certain never to grant anything to.

Actually, it isn't the rich at all who would be the main beneficiaries of a rollback in this area. What kind of a tax do you think you pay when the day comes to sell your house? Are you rich?

You sell your house to retire. You are taxed on its sale. You can't stay where you are because the real estate tax is too high. You move to Florida. They punish you for bringing your car. You will live out the rest of your days on your meager savings, and a small Social Security check which the government is trying its damnedest to reduce. But that's okay, for with any luck at all you'll be dead before dog food becomes your meals. Your heirs will pay a large tax upon your estate, the government again being somehow entitled to its share. Your heirs will not have life as easy as you did. Taxes are going up, because during your life you weren't taxed nearly enough, or so you are told.

This just in: some places are instituting a birth tax of around seventeen dollars per baby. My prediction: 1) it will soon catch on everywhere, 2) it will quickly rise and, 3) it will extend even so far as home births and yes, the stillborn. I hope you've noticed a trend. They take from your paycheck before you receive it and then spend all their time and energy trying to figure ways of robbing you of each cent of the rest of it, ever complaining that it just isn't enough. As to how you'll survive on what little is left—that's for you to figure out.

Add it all up, and don't forget that I've missed a few things, some by accident, some by design. I did not include any taxes or fees should you decide you'd actually like to *do* anything. Go on vacation, pay fifteen percent airport tax and a motel tax. Build a deck on your house, filing fees and a permit from the town and county. You get the idea.

Add it all up and tell me, what is left for you? I know the government will try to convince you that you are greedy, but nonetheless try to start thinking of your own self. Did you get a salary minus a small bit for necessary government, or is what you take more like a small finder's fee?

One of the least taxed countries in the world? Please spare me the insult. And the neat thing, the really neat thing is that the Clintons and the Gores, the Cuomos and the Florios, the Dinkins and well, hell, most of our esteemed politicians have one thing in common. They don't think we're being taxed enough.

Apparently, their personal budgetary constraints are such that a paper, pencil, or simple calculator are out of the question.

The saddest and last insult is that if cornered they would find it impossible to tell you just at what level it would be enough. Because it never will.

And just what is it that we get for our money? The roads are paved. Sometimes. The snow gets plowed. Sometimes. The bridges are maintained. Poorly. Our educational system is failing our children despite the ratio of B.M.W.s driven by our teachers. You could fill a book with what we don't get for our money. But that will have to wait perhaps until my next book. You know as well as I (or nearly so) what kind of waste, graft, incompetence, and corruption gobble up our tax dollars by the tens of billions, leaving us with nothing in exchange.

I want to ask you something, and I want you to think long and hard about it before you answer. At what point in your life did you agree to this system? That they could make up whatever rules they want, and that you would dutifully obey? That they could raise and raise and raise taxes all the more, and that you would pay?

When did you sign on to a system where those "in government" decide what to spend your money on, and that your job is to pay the bill, whatever it is? Do you remember ever signing anything to that effect? I don't.

Understand that we were not put on this earth, created in the image of God, to have our necks stood upon and to act as servants, slaves if you will, to man, and to serve a morally bankrupt system. We were destined for higher things than that, but only if we do not hand over our birthright to those who would gleefully destroy us.

The Constitution of the United States, that great iron measuring rod forged between man and God claims "that we are endowed by our Creator with certain inalienable rights…that of life, liberty, and the pursuit of happiness."

I tell you true, you do not have a life, if the majority of it is spent serving an ever hungrier government, a government which was originally designed to serve you. You have no liberty if being bound so tightly to a system of taxation leaves you barely able to wiggle your toes. And you have no happiness if you already forfeited the first two, the only exception being if you qualify not only as a socialist but a masochist as well.

What Can Be Done

Let us instead think of this as what should be done or what must be done. That is, if there is to be any future for this country.

First, visualize the role of government as what you would like it to be. Small, efficient, hard working, and in touch. People in the public sector forced to perform their jobs properly, otherwise facing dismissal. No slothfulness, nor cover-ups here. Penalties too high when you get caught. Being held accountable for their actions and acting accordingly.

A government whose employees are perhaps slightly underpaid, a fair exchange for the type of job security and benefit package that generally isn't offered in the private sector.

Picture these employees always working just slightly undermanned, not enough to harm efficiency, but just enough to operate lean and mean like a highly trained athlete. No fat. No waste.

The offices are adequate and no more. The officials do not sit behind walnut desks whose value exceeds that of a small home in the country. None of them. Not even our president. Picture the perks to "our" officials cut to the point that anything which is at all beyond the purvey of their exact office comes out of their own pockets. Start to look at them as what they are supposed to be: public employees.

Stretch your imagination a little till you can see the salaries of even the highest officials at a level where even for them the purchase of a new Mercedes is a bit of a squeeze, not undertaken lightly.

Try to see a government where Mr. Average Guy, Mr. Harry Wage Earner has not good reason to be jealous of the working environment, the salaries, and the frills of those who are purportedly there to be of service to him.

Picture further still a government who does not try to take on all of the problems of the entire world, and this at the expense of its own citizenry.

Envision if you will, a world where bureaucrats would find it difficult, exceedingly difficult, to add to their numbers, and where their concern is for the common man, for they are the common man.

Where every woman who desires one, owns a fur coat, easily purchased with paychecks which have not been stripped of their substance by an ever greedy and uncaring government.

In this world your pay check after taxes would look very much like it did before taxes.

The government would be placed on a strict diet, neither allowed to spend over a certain carefully regulated amount, nor to grow itself of its own volition. A diet nearly as spare as the one it has placed you and I on in the present. Note, what I am not talking about is a starvation diet. We will never be made to look like a third-rate power to the rest of the world. The money will be there for whatever it is determined (by us) that the government needs. But the operative word here is needs. It shall get that which it in fact needs, and no more.

This is not just some far fetched idea of what the government could look like in the future. It is a picture of what our beloved government did look like a scant one hundred years ago, and should look like today.

We have missed the Industrial Revolution. Its benefits did not benefit us. Instead, the profits which should have fattened our wallets and insured a golden retirement for each of us, have gone to fertilize the growth of a system whose very purpose, whether by accident or design, has been to enslave its people and strip them of every last penny. The burden of the national debt is just one of the weapons in its arsenal used to accomplish this goal.

Breathe deep, stretch out. Dare to imagine a country, a government, a system, where you pay only ten to fifteen percent in income tax, and no other taxes. Imagine the free enterprise system no longer starved of their rightful profits, the new found cash flow permitted to go into the employees, the stockholders, the executives, and to ever rebuilding the structure of the company. Where we look at prosperity as coming from the industriousness welling up from within ourselves, not as something we seek the government to hand us like crumbs to a beggar, or a beggar's dog.

Can this really be accomplished?

I answer with a resounding yes! How? If and only if we the people (where have we heard that phrase?) set hard to work at a program designed to gut our government of its power over us. To relegate it back to that small corner of our lives where it belongs, only then will we prevail.

You were meant to run this country. I was meant to run this country. This country's government was not designed nor envisioned by our founding fathers to grow to the point it has, and with the intent to oppress its people.

Only by instituting the ideas in this book and considering the rights of the individual and not that which is foggily termed "the state" to be of supreme importance, can we start out on the right track.

I know that what I ask of you is a very difficult thing because it goes against everything that you have been indoctrinated to believe, but please get it through your thick skull that it's your money. They have no legal claim to it, no moral claim to it, nor do they use it with good intent. You must go on the offensive and not ask, but demand back control of your country. From day one, true self-rule was meant to be your destiny. When you napped but a little while they have stolen your birthright. You must snatch it back out of their closed fist!

Otherwise you will have doomed yourself not to a life, but to a mere existence where your sole function, your sole purpose is to earn a wage, only to turn it over to your "betters" to do with it as they please.

At the rate of natural progression we are now experiencing, it will only be one generation or possibly two at the most, before the spoilers will have transformed our entire society into one giant model of Auschwitz, complete with the "work makes you free" sign, and the cold, rancid cabbage soup for your one meal. And we? We will all be the Jews, but with no one to liberate us. No "America" outside our walls poised to rescue us.

Your choice.

The Economy

Every once in a great while you come across an idea so good, so unique, that you would find it difficult to counter with a superior idea, or even substantially improve upon the one which has been put forth.

In my home county of Rockland, New York the residents recently made the mistake of agreeing to add yet another layer to our already bloated government. A new position was created, that being the County Executive. The predictable happened and within a short time the newly elected county leader found more problems than anyone ever knew existed and of course found it necessary to markedly increase taxes.

Two terms later he is now faced with not one but three opponents, each of whom has a number of good points as well as his share of flaws.

Remarkable among them is a certain Rabbi Eidensohn who was the only one to offer a creative proposal for dealing with our lagging local economy on a long term basis. The plan is called Universal Capitalism and is presented here in capsule form.

Universal Capitalism

Due to the direction and pace of a changing world, Americans must be trained to work for themselves rather than for others as has long been the practice.

Because most of the largest companies are rapidly downsizing, yet their very survival is still in question the marketplace for prospective employment has become uncertain at best, no longer the bedrock place of security it had been in the past.

The person however who starts his own business puts his heart and soul into it and as a result has a vested interest in its health, prosperity and survival. It is these people of whom their own personal job performance is most likely to be pursued as an ideal worth striving for.

Large corporations are often out of touch with the individual and not in the best position to press to fullest advantage their talents. Commonly they are unable to properly focus on the strengths and weaknesses of the on line employee, while small to moderate size companies find it easier to retain control of these pluses and minuses in the day to day running of the business. Once properly capitalized a reasonably sized company usually is capable of extracting the utmost efficiency from its operation due to utilizing the hands on approach necessarily missing from a larger concern.

Similarly, the larger companies (no longer employing the majority of Americans anyway) are finding it increasingly difficult to readily change in order to meet different market demands, while smaller outfits can effectively "bob and weave" in the new battles which have become American, and indeed today's world commerce. It is the young spry David with the sling and rock who is now capable of bringing down the overconfident and slow moving Goliath of business.

Starting in our educational system, we must begin to promote universal capitalism. Anyone so inclined will be encouraged to make it on their own. Rather than the emphasis (as it is now) being on turning out workers only capable of chasing after and competing for quickly disappearing jobs, we should seek to turn out entrepreneurs. Each student would learn the basics of business, and good business sense.

Even in grade school it could be implemented as simply as setting up small business projects like bicycle repair or lemonade stands or others such that the pupil is capable of grasping. Within the upper grades actual hands on training could be provided with regards to a myriad of American business enterprises.

The short term goal would be to give every child a taste for and understanding of business throughout his or her schooling. Even the negative aspects can yield positive results. Let our youth early on see what it is like to deal with the hardships of business, being cheated, shortchanged and lied to, addressed by rude customers, and learn the proper degree to which they can afford to extend trust to their fellow man. And all of this within a classroom setting.

What we currently do is quite the opposite. We encourage kids to be overly trusting, painting too rosy a picture of the world outside, and upon graduation they are often crushed by the realities of the world of competition, and in fact life in general. It is often difficult to recover from this late awakening.

In today's America most businesses fail very shortly after their inception. This most often is from poor training and a misconception on the part of the new businessman as to what can work, and what by its nature, cannot. It is the early training that we can provide which will make it easier for each individual to avoid the most common mistakes and pitfalls.

This system would embrace all people who wish to be the leaders rather than the led. It would become an integral part of the educational system, and in fact one of its central goals.

The students would experiment with various fields in earlier classes, and then aided with computer testing etc., eventually choose a business to pursue, and all of this coupled with hands on application of learned skills such as actual selling.

The system would encourage free thinking while providing the basics of enterprise structure.

In all areas public funding would make the realization of the eventual goal possible, and the manner in which this funding would work is as follows: the public would be allowed to buy shares in the fund with all shares to be governmentally insured against failure. The monies thereof are then lent to the commercial private sector, builders etc. who pay interest or a profit share back to the fund. From this the public investors are paid their dividend.

Those students who have been properly exposed to business and wish to start companies of their own would approach a governing board installed to represent the funds interests. They would present to this board a well outlined plan of their idea, complete with supporting data to show that their idea is sound and worthy of being underwritten. If the board decides a plan has merit loans from the fund would be made to the aspiring entrepreneur.

With a strong and deeply ingrained background in business the candidate is much more likely to succeed. Having been tested in school the second and truly acid test is the ability to gain approval from the board. These early successes coupled with proper funding will yield a much higher opportunity for the candidate to start a profitable venture than the hit or miss, pull yourself up by your bootstraps way things are currently done.

The loans are to be paid back not with mere interest but rather with a share in the profit. If the project is done properly the upside could be very interesting indeed, while the downside potential is limited.

That was the core of the Rabbi's plan. It was designed by him to apply to the revitalization of our local economy. As you can see it is only one small step to apply this concept on a national level so that the whole country may benefit.

Quite naturally the majority of students will have not the desire, the courage, nor the confidence in themselves to take advantage of what will be offered by this system. Their role in many cases will be to work as employees for those who do. At the very least they will come to the workplace with an enhanced appreciation for what it takes to make it on ones own. And the system benefits them as well, as their range, scope, and opportunity for employment will be much improved.

To this proposal of universal capitalism I would add only two things.

The government must provide the framework for a "business information clearing house." This would be a place where aspiring businessmen could go within their local area to get all the facts about his or her legal responsibilities under the law. Workman's compensation, liability insurance, disability, withholding tax, local and other governmental licensing, social security, the list goes on and on. This is a quagmire which each new enterprise is forced to wade through, uninformed and at times misled. It should not always have to be done by trial and error on the part of each new businessman. A clearing house providing this type of information would smooth the way for those willing to take the plunge.

The other thing so sorely needed is a theme I harp on throughout this book. Government must not only encourage new business ventures but to a large degree allow them to flourish by getting out of the way. The impediments they present to the growth of our economy through ridiculous and unnecessary regulation have reached the point where they are immoral. If you are viewing a sick economy you have no farther to search for the causative force than our own government.

Prior to any system like the good Rabbis being attempted, America itself needs one large and basic change. A change of heart. Business must no longer be looked at as antithetical to American life as it is so often viewed today.

The prosperity of business *is* the extension of trade *is* the success of America. The Liberals, bless their little hearts, cannot have it both ways. Discourage business, look down on it, attempt to tax or regulate it out of existence and consider profit a dirty word. Then you have the gall to wonder what happened to all the jobs?

Business and enterprise, even ambition itself should be considered something laudable, that which is worthy of admiration. Until this change of heart is evident no plan of any value will be given a chance, and without it the resurgence of our economy has no chance either.

Immigration

"We are a nation of immigrants." The same old tired refrain will always be heard anytime someone brings up the possibility of being more restrictive with our immigration policy. It is as if there were some moral imperative to forever keep our welcome mat out to the entire world, simply because at one point in our history it was the major way we experienced population growth.

Let's face it, at the time of the formation of our country, we gained this great land at horrible expense to the Indians. I am not at all trying to justify that, but that is just the way it happened. Shortly thereafter, huge masses of people were needed (from our standpoint) to conquer an untamed land. The Chinese were allowed here only because we needed railroads. The Irish in order to mine coal. The Polish and others to work the meat packing plants in the Midwest, and the Blacks as slaves to provide cheap labor in southern agriculture. Most of our past immigrants were permitted in, not to fulfill their needs (which it coincidentally did, nonetheless), but rather to meet the needs of a developing nation. Couple that with the fact that everyone was brought here in order to work, for there was much work to be done, not as political refugees or because we felt sorry for their plight.

Several of the dynamics which were in place during the creation and early growth of this country have changed dramatically or disappeared entirely. This is not the America of the early 1800s or of 1910. When you come right down to it, we are so far removed from even the America of 1950 as to be unrecognizable.

We are now a nation of some two hundred and sixty-five million people. The industrial revolution has come and gone. The technological revolution is upon us and in full swing. Agriculture and mining are no longer the big draw. Jet engines, computers, and telecommunication are this generation's playthings, and a need for masses of raw laborers has disappeared, undoubtedly never to return.

Our nation has probably seen the last of the days when unfilled jobs went begging for immigrants. Those days were the cause for the birth of labor unions. The decline of unions can likewise be blamed on the inversion of that situation. Too many people are chasing too few jobs.

It is now too often the case where someone new to our shores immediately goes on public assistance, a scenario never desired nor envisioned by the framers of our Constitution. Where else in the world can even an illegal alien give birth while on the nation's soil, automatically making the newborn a citizen and then stay on legally to care for the child, and in fact be eligible for welfare? Food stamps and medical care are also provided along with a lifestyle that she never would have enjoyed in the land from which she fled.

Due to the high unemployment we experience now in the modern age, it is irresponsible of us to continue to pursue the same immigration policies which may have had merit in the past.

Can we morally continue to take in the flood of additional immigrants despite what we know it will unquestionably do to our own current citizens? If we insist on progressing down this poorly chosen road, one or more of several different things will happen, all of them bad.

The first possibility is that the immigrants will take the jobs as they become available, jobs which would have gone to citizens who have already waited too long, and who now will have no choice but to wait longer.

The second is that no jobs materialize and so the new immigrants are simply added to that burgeoning number of people searching for work. A sort of doubling of the misery index as it were.

The third is that they create job situations for themselves either by working illegally below minimum wage, or above the minimum legal wage but below the traditional market level long since established. In either case, this move lowers the work market for all related labor as the shift in supply and demand sets in. While this will have a short term positive effect for business which will enjoy increased profit margins due to reduced manpower costs, there will be lasting and painful effects upon the work force. Labor will suffer both from job displacement and wage rollbacks, often beyond the point of survivability.

The fourth is what usually happens. The new immigrant either searches for or perhaps doesn't search for work. After a time, he may either opt for or be forced to go on welfare. Who pays the price here? We all do.

As the number of those on welfare starts to increase in proportion to those who are footing the bill, the burden of the privilege of paying for the nonworking becomes unbearable. In a socialist system like the one we are fast approaching, the needs of the people providing the tax base are never allowed to be considered, only the needs of those on the receiving end are of any importance. You can easily see how a continuation in that direction could well lead to a situation where those who are being provided for might eventually have a better quality of life than their providers.

Given our present set of circumstances; swelled welfare rolls, high unemployment, a faltering economy, and little reason to anticipate dramatic revitalization, it only makes sense to close our gates and pull in the welcome mat.

The current flood of people relocating to our society should be slowed to a trickle. Those who we do let in should be of such mental and moral caliber as to be considered an asset rather than a threat, as well as being self-sufficient instead of looking for a handout.

I know that there are certain individuals such as Mario Cuomo who will violently disagree with me. I caution the reader to remember that Mr. Cuomo is secure in his position and has an income of such a level as to insulate him from most of the common man's problems. No matter how large the influx of foreigners, he and others like him cannot be impacted, but most of you reading this both can, and will be. Your pain and diminishing quality of life are, of course, none of their concern.

Our nation is like a lifeboat which has nearly filled to capacity with survivors. There are still a great number of people outside the boat bobbing around in the water. The number of those inside the boat is such that each additional person pulled aboard jeopardizes everyone who is already in, and to an ever increasing degree. The time will come where we will bring in that one person too many. Our "compassion" will be the very thing that ensures that all who were safely aboard will join in the fate of those who were not. It's sort of like some insane game of Russian roulette, where all the chambers of the revolver are loaded. Everybody loses.

Recently a great deal has been made about our excluding hundreds of thousands of Haitian refugees from immigration. Those of the liberal persuasion say that our policy of exclusion is racist, that were these people white our opinion and policy would be different. Nothing of the sort is true.

People of ill intent, such as former mayor David Dinkins, call this a racist country, this despite his being a black man elected by popular vote as mayor of one of our largest cities.

He and others of his ilk conveniently ignore the fact that we have millions of Haitian citizens whom no one tried to stop from coming into this country. They also ignore the fact that ten percent of the current Haitian refugees have AIDS, a disease that at least some of us have no desire to purposely import. We already have enough of this always fatal disease in our own population, thank you.

Those of us whose pocket books are already stressed to the max have another reason to keep bearers of the AIDS virus out. We know beyond any doubt that it is us who will somehow have to find a way to pay for the hospitalization and eventual burial of this very group, and simply haven't the resources nor the desire to take on the additional burden.

This has nothing to do with race at all, it's just a matter of practicality. Anything we offer to outsiders from our no longer growing economy must by definition come at the expense of our own citizens.

When I said to close the gates and bring in the welcome mat, I did not imply that this would necessarily be permanent. Quite naturally, if I am wrong in my prognosis of our future and we find ourselves experiencing unprecedented growth, full employment and a thriving economy, our borders could always be relaxed again.

Until such time, we must change our policy on immigration so that it is based not on some perceived need of those who would like to relocate here, but rather on the very real needs of our current citizenry.

There isn't a country in the world outside of the United States that wouldn't see the wisdom in this.

ILLEGAL IMMIGRANTS

The term alone rather sums it up, doesn't it? While there are many politicians currently in positions of power who would champion their cause, allow and at times even encourage the problem of illegal immigrants, this author will tell you that it is high time we dealt properly with this cancer to our society.

If you think that our nation, our economy, or even your own personal earnings can much longer withstand the additional burden of the hordes of people illegally making their way into this country, you lack a great deal in the area of common sense.

When you go to the hospital, in addition to paying for the cost of your stay, you must also help pay for care given to those who do *not* pay their bills because they are illegal aliens. When the job market is tight let us not lose sight of the fact that many positions are filled by those who are not citizens. The liberals among us would tell you that these people only take the bottom line jobs, the ones that you would never be interested in. This simply isn't so. Suppose for a moment that it were. What do you think happens to those who they will displace? There is of course a ripple effect translating itself up the job ladder into every level of available work. The next time you feel that the minimum wage is too low to properly live on, I remind you that it is caused by those who are willing to accept any pay and conditions, no matter how low they are. Had we no illegal immigrants it would open up just that many more jobs to Americans who are in need of them. Whether you know it or not, whether you wish to acknowledge it or not, the presence of illegal aliens impacts us every day and in every way. Lest you feel otherwise I must tell you that yes, it is just that simple.

Recently the man we have in lieu of a president, Bill Clinton, tried to appoint to the office of Attorney General a Ms. Zoe Baird. Because of his contempt for you, the American taxpayer, he did not so much as check her background to see if she had employed any illegal immigrants. Even at the outcry of the American people that "it just wasn't right" that the person to hold the highest law enforcement position in the country should herself be considered above the law, the administration and the congress both down played the importance of her action.

Let me pose to you a simple question. Had it not occurred that a soon to be high official *knowingly* hired an illegal, how do you think you might be treated by this same governing body had you done precisely the same thing?

I'll tell you. In your case it would no longer be considered "no big thing." You would be tried and convicted by the courts, and again by the press for "flagrant violations" of both immigration and employment laws. You would be openly castigated for giving employment to a noncitizen, particularly at a time when so many of your fellow Americans are out of work. You would be further vilified for having evaded your responsibility to pay social security, disability, workman's compensation, and federal withholding tax on that individual. Since I mention the press I would like to point out that had this been a Republican administration, the news media would never let us hear the end of it.

I make note of these things only to bring to your attention that there is a great deal of difference in how our government (and particularly the democrats) feel about illegal immigrants and how the majority of American taxpayers do.

This can be seen in the way that the government and the media employs a clever little device called TERM SWITCHING.

By now you must be used to the fact that the government would prefer that you no longer view things in terms of there being higher taxes, the word taxes according to them carries an unnecessarily negative connotation. That is why they wish you to use the word "contributions," a term which somehow sounds more noble and less noxious.

Similarly you are no longer to consider that the boys in Washington are continuing to spend more of your hard earned money. These are now "investments." And you know that our beloved government no longer takes "contributions" from its working citizens and gives their money to those on welfare. No, that is now an "entitlement." Don't you see? That person who is on what was formerly thought of as the public dole, is now "entitled" to your money!

Likewise, heaven forbid that you continue to think of people who have entered our country in violation of the law as illegal immigrants. They are now to be referred to as "undocumented individuals."

See how nicely term switching cleans up a problem?

There are those of the liberal persuasion who would extend to these "undocumented individuals" the right to receive welfare, food stamps, and yes EVEN THE RIGHT TO VOTE.

I would not.

Frankly I don't think you would either or you wouldn't be reading this particular book right now. If you are like minded with myself you see that there is a limit to how many illegal, and might I add quite often undesirable, immigrants our nation can absorb. For the survival of our nation, our way of life, and our standard of living, we must set out to reverse this flow.

Our country has in place an immigration policy. I, for one, would tighten up restrictions even there, but that is both beside the point and the subject of another chapter. Point being that since we have an immigration policy we should let *no one* enter our country outside of the workings of that policy.

I propose that we first start by getting serious about applying the existing laws which are already on our books. No longer is illegal immigration to be tolerated. When intercepted they must be deported immediately, and deported in a dramatic manner. What I mean by a dramatic manner is as follows. As an example with regards to those who have been slipping across the Mexican border, it has proven futile to merely return them. We find ourselves returning the very same people day after day.

I propose that we instead fly those who we catch crossing into America, several hundred miles into Mexico, dropping them off there.

I am aware that this will initially cost a great deal more money, but very quickly it will cost less as we will no longer be returning the same people to their native soil over and over again. Also reduced is the risk that one of those times the individual in question might slip through our security, which is the real problem after all.

In conjunction with this idea, those who are detained as illegals should be heavily fined if found to be in possession of any money. This will help pay for their transport back, but this should also contain a fine for punitive purposes as well. It would not take long for word to get out that it is no longer profitable to attempt to enter the United States illegally.

As to our borders, how can we more effectively patrol them?

We are about to institute severe cutbacks in our military. I propose that we make these reductions not quite as dramatic as originally planned, and dispatch a portion of those soldiers we might have fired, for the purpose of making our borders more secure.

Not only would this properly address the situation in question, but at the same time it will soften the blow which will soon be coming to our unemployment rolls. And lest we overlook it, each time a border guard is successful in stopping an "undocumented individual" from entering our country, that is potentially one more American job saved. Looking at it this way, if each soldier so engaged captures but a handful of illegals each year, the cost of retaining him is inconsequential.

There is another side benefit to be derived from this use of our soldiers. This move leaves us with a strong standing army which can readily be dispatched elsewhere in times of need or military crisis. A sort of active reserve as it were.

In our harbors, at our airports, the human wave illegally coming into our country daily *by the thousands* must be turned back. It is estimated that the problem has grown to the point where in excess of one million people enter this country illegally each year. Bear in mind that this is of course in addition to the close to one million who add themselves to our numbers through normal legal channels. Only a small fraction are apprehended and sent back.

Foreign countries willing to cooperate should be encouraged to enact legislation calling for jail terms for their citizens who are returned as illegals. The very threat of the possibility of serving jail time in their own country will be enough to discourage many from attempting to enter here illegally. Mild but adequate pressure can be brought to bear upon these countries simply by imposing upon them the bill for the cost of returning those who have been intercepted. Cooperation from these countries will go along way toward solving our problem.

Many will think that my approach to this situation is rather drastic, but I must point out a very important fact which should be obvious to all who are willing to examine things properly. While it can be argued that many illegal immigrants turn out to be otherwise decent people, as a whole they suffer a disproportionate number of undesirables. Are you aware that approximately seventy percent of those arrested during the 1992 Los Angeles riots were illegal aliens? As might be expected from L.A., *none* of them were deported even after having proved themselves to be less than pillars of the community.

The news media chose not to draw attention to the fact that a number of the conspirators in the world trade center bombing were also illegally here. As this was our countries first major brush with domestic terrorism, you would think that this might be considered with some gravity.

You would also expect that one who is here without the advantage of proper documentation would wish to maintain a low profile. For reasons which escape me, this doesn't seem to be the case. Could it be that our country is perceived to be so ridiculously tolerant in this area that there is a notion even among illegals that anything goes? I wouldn't doubt it.

It is for these reasons as well that we must become vigilant, sending back to whence they came, all those who have already slipped in here illegally I hope you realize that it is these very people who have established themselves here, who have set up the networks, and created the mechanism for bringing in many more of their own kind. This is one of those problems which tends to snowball if not dealt with properly, and up to this point it has not been.

We must formulate an ongoing system whereby we might continually purge from this country those who have not seen fit to enter through proper channels. This is *our* country and it is we who must determine who is allowed to relocate here, in what numbers, and according to what guidelines.

Once we get serious about protecting our borders in the same manner in which all other nations protect theirs, once we get serious about sending back those who have managed to sneak through in the past, then we can truly move forward in bettering our society.

There will be a reasonable and perhaps even a dramatic impact on our health care system when we have stopped paying for all of those who should not be here in the first place.

Our homeless problem will be enormously reduced as soon as we have stopped insisting that the poor among our own citizenry compete against the rest of the world for our limited resources and jobs.

It may sound selfish of me, but I am bold enough to be honest with you. My overwhelming concern is for the citizens of THIS country, their well-being, their future. I wish for my children and their coming generations to live in a country which still has a great deal of potential, and a lot of freedom to offer its people. This will not long remain available if we do not in some way start protecting our own interests, and yes, at times without regard to the problems of outsiders.

Those who would encourage you to go to the farthest reaches of altruism, to "think globally" would accomplish their goals at the expense of your substance, your hard-won earnings, and your security.

It is up to you to stop them.

Foreign Aid

The time has arrived to become selfish. Not selfish in the sense that a stingy miser with an enormous wealth denies the crippled boy on the corner a few coppers for sweeping his stairs.

Rather, selfish in the way that anyone recognizes a responsibility to care for himself before all others in a time of need and as a matter of survival.

"But then who will help the needy nations?" The cry goes up. "Who will help them indeed," I answer, "if in our generosity we perish from the Earth?"

In recent history, then President George Bush, forgave Egypt a debt of several billion dollars. A debt owed to us, the people of the United States. Within one week he balked at the opportunity to give the same amount of money to our own citizens when a request was made to extend unemployment benefits, a very real need right here at home. It is my desire that we cut foreign aid in half, saving us billions each year.

The countries which we would continue giving support to must meet one, or more preferably, two requirements.

In the first, the need must be immediate and of such magnitude that if left unmet, catastrophe would result. Additionally, it must be that if we did not provide this aid, no one else would.

The second requirement is that the aid given would in some manner be for our own best interest. Helping a trading partner, an ally, or a nation that helps keep our productions secure would be examples.

Most importantly, the decision to give such aid, and the ability to do so must be removed from the power to the Congress and the President. They have proven themselves incompetent in this area time and time again.

Make no mistake. I wish the cuts to foreign aid to countries in need to be only on a temporary basis. They should be returned again (although with more restraint than in the past) when the day arrives that we have returned to our former economic strength, when we are once again a major superpower with a strong economy. Only when homelessness, starvation, poverty and underemployment are strangers to us, will we again be in a position to care for those less fortunate than ourselves.

Until then our focus must be on the needy here among us, *they* are our brothers and sisters. As such they must remain our prime concern.

Let us now make the commitment to caring for ourselves, so that someday we may again be strong enough to care for others. They were meant to be helped out of our excess, not by draining our blood.

THE TRADE BALANCE

The strength and health of any country's economy lies in its exports.

While it is imperative to maintain a healthy internal economy, it has often been discarded the importance of cycling fresh currency through the system. This new money must necessarily come from revenue gained from the export of products, services, and technology.

When the trade balance is such that more is imported by a country than exported, you are faced with a trade deficit. The United States has been operating with this deficit for the past several years. We, who were once the worlds premier supplier nation, have become one of its largest consumers. This big switch came about in a very brief period of time, but why?

Allow me to backtrack a bit.

World War II and the defeat of Japan and Germany spawned a new style of imperialism in both these countries. Resolving themselves to shifting their method of attack from one of military exploitation and extension to that of domination through technological and economic superiority, each waged the new battles not with weapons of bloodshed, but rather tools of commerce and marketing competition.

Forbidden from rebuilding their military to any meaningful level, these countries benefited from the U.S. bases stationed in their lands which not only provided a measure of protection but produced an additional income source as well.

Unencumbered by the need to build a strong defense, Germany was able to pour a larger portion of its energy into accomplishing the goal of producing tools, machinery and other hard products, unsurpassed in quality. Mercedes Benz cars, Leica and Leitz cameras and lenses, Heckler and Koch weaponry, all top shelf items generated at new higher levels in post war industrial Germany.

Japan took another tack. Using inferior, but incredibly low priced items to break into new markets in the U.S. as well as around the world, they were able to gain a foothold into territories where they previously had been left out. With time, quality improved immensely, and the price increased commensurate with that quality. The first Subarus imported into America in the early '70s were air cooled contraptions about half the size of a V.W. bug, if you can picture that. They had the same sleek lines as an outsized baking potato, and a limited life expectancy, but the price was about twelve hundred dollars. Not quite pocket change but far below the least expensive American car available, which went for around three thousand dollars.

Today's Subaru is now a top quality automobile, no longer the disposable item of twenty years ago, and some models sell for upwards of seventeen *thousand* dollars. Not bad for only two decades in a new market.

The primary reason that our country experiences yearly trade deficits can be explained by the fact that we as consumers find it all too attractive to purchase foreign products of excellent quality, at prices far below that which we could produce those products domestically. Our competition has caught up, and surpassed us.

It isn't so much that labor costs are less in other countries. This certainly isn't the case in the examples I have chosen with Germany and Japan. It is their manufacturing and marketing techniques which have us beat.

Were we able to produce a good quality VCR that could retail for two hundred dollars, is there any reason our people wouldn't buy the product?

In production we have made a double mistake. The producers of material goods have often taken a bit too much profit out of their companies at a time when some should have been plowed back into modernization. The second and more glaring error is that in many cases the very technological advances which are being leveled at us are ones we sold to our foreign competitors in the first place!

It is a foolish thing when the only edge you hold over other countries is your technology, and yet you sell it anyway. I am well aware that had we not done so it would only have been a matter of time before the opposition would catch up, however the time lag itself is an advantage as is the necessary expenditure for R.&D. which we have saved them. Trump cards too hastily dealt away.

But make no mistake. I did not say there is no difference in labor between our countries, there certainly is, however more in the area of labor/management relations than in an hourly wage discrepancy.

In Japan each employee feels himself to be more a part of the company than is true here. More a member of the team as it were. And interestingly so does management.

When production quotas and quality levels do not meet acceptable standards it is those in middle management who take it the hardest, considering it a personal failure when anything less than excellence is achieved.

Our esteemed left in this country, has spent the last several decades convincing Americans that business is the enemy of labor, while the reality is that both exist in a state of co-dependence. Of course it is only in the U.S. that industry is saddled with racial, gender, and citizens with disabilities quotas, sensitivity training, sexual harassment suits, antitrust laws, and a myriad of other roadblocks to top production output. Pity we can't export to our competitors a bit of that misery!

Our nation is expected to compete in the battle for commerce with one hand tied behind it's back. To put it bluntly, our competitors are waging war in the marketplace while we are playing at it.

Do we have any cards left to play, and what is the best manner in which to play them?

Yes, we do hold a few.

The biggest advantage we have left over other countries is what little is left of the American spirit. When unfettered it has proven itself time and time again to come to the forefront, solving problems as difficult as these and more. But even a heavyweight champ cannot win a boxing match if he is first tied down or drugged.

This spirit of enterprise requires nurturing and incentives. The nurturing must come in the form of the removal of impediments to manufacturing and export sales. The incentives in the form of tax relief. Throw aside the barriers and American creativity will find the way, as it always has.

I propose the following. To any manufacturing concern which increases it's level of exports by more than twenty percent, we should grant a corporate tax reduction of fully one half on those sales over the threshold amount. Any lost tax revenues would be more than offset by the increase in employment, in overall revenues (remember, we just increased the base) and the part that company plays in returning our nation to economic health. Likewise this tax break should be extended to any new companies (not subsidiaries of existing ones) going into export, or to existing companies breaking into new territories overseas.

Similarly, any American business which makes serious inroads into market shares in our domestic markets which have till now been dominated by foreign competition, should get the same reward.

A perfect example of this is the two hundred dollar VCR I spoke of earlier. Any American company who can help us win these markets back deserves to be rewarded.

Should an American motorcycle company spring up which can start to displace those machines made by Honda, Kawasaki, and Suzuki, again it should not go unrewarded.

The incentives in the form of tax relief would in themselves make our companies more competitive, increasing the ease with which this can be accomplished.

Beyond this, our government must also be ready to take action in international matters. While we can in no way force the people of other countries to buy our cars or any other product, we can at least see to it that they are not forbidden to do so by law. Any country exercising the principles of the mercantile system against us should be shut off from trade altogether. The countries which happily ship us their products while holding it illegal to purchase ours, a total import ban, should no longer be traded with. They will then see that they need us as much as we need them.

There are also a number of countries, most notably in South America, which deal in another form of unfair trade. In order to see to it that much of their generated wealth remains within the country, they have placed stiff tariffs on any products imported into their land. At times these tariffs go as high as one hundred percent, effectively doubling the price paid for the item. This accomplishes two tasks. For each dollar expended on any item imported, the government gets one as well, reducing the "lost" dollars by fifty percent. And quite naturally not too many of its citizens will purchase imported goods with such a high tariff, if a serviceable replacement is produced locally. This again reduces the flow of money out of the country, as few imported goods are purchased.

Ah, but when it comes to these country's exports, its another story. Generally we do not at all play the same game, as we consider the products from these countries too valuable to jeopardize the availability of. Therefore we place few if any import restrictions and tariffs on their goods.

Something must be done in this area.

We must approach these countries and let them know that we will no longer stand for these unfair trade practices. With a five year phase in (at twenty percent per year) of the elimination of such tariffs in order to achieve parity, we could again be importing and exporting with them on a level playing field. This move provides us with considerable leverage. Faced with the possibility of totally lost markets it is of course hoped that the nations in question will enter into truly free trade. Due to the fact that there are any number of emerging nations waiting in the wings to take their place, it is most likely they will not be so foolish as to loose their position. But should they pigheadedly stick to their policies of stiff tariffs, our emphasis would then shift to gaining new trading partners, those who welcome free trade and in fact welcome anything as long as it opens new markets up to them. This as I'm sure you've guessed, opens new markets to us as well.

We must address all these problems and get our trade balance back on an even keel. To fail to do so will be to have missed one overriding consideration.

Our largest danger in not addressing this deficit lies not in the exiting of our wealth, but rather in the transinternational political arena.

The Trade Balance

Once, due to unfair trade and the resulting trade imbalance, foreign nations have "bought up" too large a share of Americas companies with dollars which we have supplied them, they come into a position of being able to determine and dictate policy. If we are to survive as an autonomous nation we must put a stop to this.

By the unleashing of our production community, added to an insistence on equality in trade regulations with other nations, we will quickly reach a point where large quantities of American money no longer flow on a one way trip out of the country.

It is not likely that we will again return to our former position of being the worlds largest supplier, but we can make the patient healthy again if we first stop the bleeding.

THE NATIONAL DEBT

Deficit spending, something you could never get away with at home for very long, seems to be the private little darling of democrats and republicans alike. Even though both sides readily agree that something must be done soon, oddly they are unwilling to take even the first step, and sign a balanced budget amendment.

Just what does this mean?

Its true meaning is that those who we have elected to watch after the farm, are horrified at the thought that their mathematics should have to live in the real world. They wish it to remain their sovereign right to spend more money than they have any hopes of taking in. And we elected them?

There are many things we could do to get rid of this massive debt, now hovering around the four trillion dollar mark. Only the last one is A) ethical, B) fair, and C) workable, hurting the least. And that solution is to pay it off. A concept like this being far too difficult for our congress to grasp, they will instead try anything but. Don't forget it was they who got us down this deep hole to begin with.

One attempt might be to encourage inflation to run wild for a time. If we again saw those peanut farmer days of twenty percent inflation for a few years, we could then pay the debt off with greatly devalued dollars. If we could count on Congress to balance the books for a change, as unlikely as that seems, this just might work.

Ah, but there's a very heavy down side to this solution, a great deal of suffering all around. Everyone suffers during inflationary times as they scramble to keep up with rapidly rising costs. Additionally, your tax bracket shifts although you've made no real gain monetarily. Worst of all is the effect it has on those who are living on fixed incomes. The monies they receive on which to live remains frozen, while everything they need to buy may double in just a handful of years. The largest percentage of this group are retirees. That small social security check will quickly dwindle in its buying power.

Solutions like this usually hurt the most, those who have had the least to do with creating the problem. Hence it's probably what the democrats will go for.

Another cute approach first involves looking at just who it is we owe this money to. Well guess what? It turns out that most of it is owed to ourselves, with a secondary amount owed to foreign investors.

What we owe to ourselves is in the form of long term bonds, municipals, and other devices by which we have encouraged our citizenry to invest in its future, for schools, roads, bridges, etc. An answer might be to just cancel the debt, or in other words, default.

Only one problem here. What happens to the people who were relying on the pension fund which you have just caused to become insolvent? How about that business tycoon who you've just stripped of his future wealth, who now has no choice but to liquidate his company, firing hundreds of employees? And that foreign investor? Will he ever again be so foolish as to trust us as he did in the past? Why should he? The small time investment by the blue collar worker? That was for his old age.

And who do you go to the next time you wish to float a bond? There is an old saying up in the hills: once burnt, twice learned. No one in their right mind would again invest in this country either from within or without should we take that direction. Again, that probably makes it quite tempting to congress, and again I mention it was they who got us into this mess. They therefore should never be trusted with its solution.

What has escaped most peoples attention is the fact that we are morally corrupt to defer the payment of our debt to future, and at that, unborn generations. It is said that the interest alone on this debt gobbles up twenty five cents on each tax dollar, without ever touching the principal. What are the implications should the debt go to eight trillion? Or sixteen trillion? At sixteen trillion, all tax dollars would go to paying the interest on the debt, and forever it would go on. The result is that the children we may be planning on bringing into the world and their children would be born into slavery. Their entire toil going into the futile attempt at paying off a debt they had nothing to do with the creation of, on things they never enjoyed the benefit of.

Our Congress spent the money (which they are so good at), and cackling like witches at a cauldron, are even now forwarding the bill to the unborn.

As I am so fond of saying, there has to be a better way, and there is. My way.

The only practical solution is as follows. First, muzzle Congress. Never again allow them to spend so much as one penny more than we can afford to. Only in this way can we start to chip away at this four trillion dollar mountain of debt without finding it growing at the same time.

There is much fuss made about a rolling light sign in Manhattan's Times Square area, which purportedly gives out an up to the minute report on how much the debt will cost each of us. Last I heard, it was hovering around the seventeen thousand dollar per citizen mark. Only one thing wrong here. As that figure was derived by dividing our population into the total debt, what is shows is the share each man, woman, child, and even baby will have to pay.

But who really pays for things anyway? You guessed it, the American taxpayer does.

So now you can see that a much more realistic way to look at this would be to divide this four trillion dollar debt by the one hundred ten million taxpayers who would be in any sort of position to pay it off.

This figure rounds off to about thirty six thousand dollars per taxpayer. Quite a chunk of change, but if we go about repayment properly, and soon, it is not insurmountable.

Here's the concept: Let's pay it off now, after refinancing portions of it at today's lower interest rates, so that no amount of it is paid off at a rate above today's prime. It would be paid much like a mortgage over a twenty year period. This time frame would serve to make the size of the payments as painless as is reasonable, while allowing the length of the term to be short enough so as not to extend the burden to future generations.

This works out to about three hundred dollars per month, per taxpayer. That's how deep Congress has dug us in.

Where will we, the taxpayers, come up with this kind of money?

There is only one way to do this without further stressing the already overburdened taxpayer. That is to implement many of the other controls that I have outlined elsewhere in this book, at the same time.

To recap just a few of these:

1. Cut congressional salaries, powers, perks, staff, and spending.

2. Take a broad based axe to most government programs.

3. Reduce welfare spending by twenty percent, and break the vicious cycle.

4. Cut foreign aid in half.

5. Reduce crime—a hidden tax.

6. Destroy the drug trade—another hidden tax.

7. Shrink government in its entirety, both in size, and in the scope of its powers.

8. Vigorously pursue zero unemployment. We could add ten percent more taxpayers to our rolls.

9. Stimulate the economy as I've outlined in that chapter.

10. Cut back on immigration, and eliminate illegal aliens.

11. Make the trade balance live up to the definition.

12. Adopt zero base budgeting and wipe out government mandates.

Add all these programs together, and the savings we could realize in no longer supporting the unnecessary and irresponsible government would be phenomenal. These savings go a long way toward approaching a total ten or fifteen percent income tax I've alluded to in the chapter on taxes. With that accomplished, we could easily address the deficit and in one generation when it is paid off, truly be a country enjoying prosperity.

It would be a considerable bite right now, but the feeling provided once finished some of you know quite well. It can be likened to when you pay off the last of your credit cards, and then pass the scissors through them. Only on a much grander scale.

Yes, we could do it my way as outlined above, or we could continue to trust in the President and Congress as we have in the past.

I think you know what they'll do.

OUR FAILING AUTO INDUSTRY

When you've made bad cars for so long and managed to get away with it at the expense of a gullible public, it must come as quite a shock when you finally find yourself losing a large market share to the very competitor you used to laugh at, Japan.

The hideous rat traps produced by this country through the seventies were quickly replaced by the hideous rat traps of the eighties.

There was one major difference by the mid-eighties, though. It became apparent even to the stubborn leaders in the industry that their hold on the American public was slipping badly. Nearly as badly as some of their transmissions.

And so they responded appropriately. Money being no object, enormous quantities were poured in to where they would do the most good. Into a public relations campaign to convince you, the consumer, that American cars were now much improved over those of the seventies. A wise move. After all, just look at the time, effort, and most of all money it saved them over actually doing something about the quality of the cars.

This method was just a bit short sighted however.

As even a mighty oak learns that it must bend in order to survive a wind storm, those who head America's car corporations finally had to acknowledge further inroads by the competition. Having exhausted all their preferred options, they sadly and begrudgingly took the only one left, and found they had no choice but to start building better cars.

The vehicles our factories produced in the late eighties and early nineties were truly a vast improvement over past efforts. There remained only one problem: There was no market for them. Now I don't want you to get the wrong idea and have you believe that I think the average American is overly bright, but the fact is that you can burn the American consumer just so many times before he makes a permanent switch to a foreign, and as proven, better product.

All the "buy America" and "you're not being patriotic unless you do" campaigns no longer have the effect they once did. Consumers are lining up with one answer to that: "Make a better product and we'll gladly buy it, until then, sayonara."

So now the producers of American cars are facing real problems. They are finally making a better car, but much fewer Americans are willing to listen than they had expected.

All their marketing techniques, all their advertising strategies are for naught. The fact is, if they wish to recapture a decent portion of the market that they once called their own, there are but two things they must do. First, continue along the lines they had recently adopted, refining and improving the product so that it never again will earn a bad name. The second is much harder than the first. It is to wait. Nothing other than the passage of time, while continuing to make a good product, will do the job of bringing back customers which were not merely lost but in essence chased away. To expect the buying public to respond with anything other than caution is to ask too much.

But what to do in the mean time while patiently waiting for the market to return?

The best cars, and the ones likely to produce the best markets are those in the twelve to twenty thousand dollar range. More expensive cars of an average price of thirty thousand dollars have two major drawbacks. Although the profit margin on each sale is vastly increased, the total number sold will be small compared with the mid-priced cars. The second drawback is our inability to compete in those markets. If one were to "invest" in a thirty thousand dollar car, he would probably feel it wiser to look towards those being offered by Lexus, Acura, and Infinity. If luxury is the goal, the "E" model Mercedes comes to mind and if sportiness is what you want, the B.M.W. or Mitsubishi 3000.

Looking at the other end of the scale we have the econo boxes. We have traditionally not pushed hard for this market for although we could sell a high number of cars in this category the profit margin is quite thin due to considerable competition.

The answers to the problems of the American car industry fortunately can be found within the industry itself.

If the quality of American produced cars has dramatically improved as they claim it has, they should have less trouble competing on many of the heretofore untested European markets.

Assuming first that we have managed to successfully push through legislation requiring fair trade as I've developed in my chapter on the trade deficit, and by this effort created a level playing field, we should have no trouble going head to head with any country's mid-priced cars.

You'll notice here that I am restricting my discussion on car sales to those which we should be selling abroad. This is due to my belief that while waiting for the American consumer to start buying our home grown product again, that these foreign sales are where we might most efficiently place our emphasis. There is simply no sense in sitting on our hands, nor is this the only avenue of approach which I would recommend.

As I pointed out earlier, I am quite dissatisfied with the quality versus price of our top of the line cars. There are few foreign competitors who do not go us one better. At this particular time I don't believe it would pay to put a great deal of effort into the attempt at expanding those sales overseas. This I say especially in light of the fact, as I have mentioned earlier, that the profit potential per unit may be high, but by its very nature the number of units the market can absorb is relatively small.

The other end of the spectrum does hold some promise however. I did not mean to lead you to believe that there was no hope for us in this bottom end market. There can be, but only if our auto industry makes some drastic changes.

What I am proposing is that the enforcement of antitrust laws be waived to allow for a joint effort of the "big three" to develop two different econo-boxes.

In the case of the first one, the target consumer would be low income Americans. The concept would be to provide a sub-sub compact at an equally sub price, and draw millions of Americans into the new car market who have never been able to enter it in the past.

This car would be much along the lines of the old Renault Le Car or the Yugo. But better. And cheaper.

Built with the combined technology of our entire auto industry, and very much mass produced, I have no doubt that we could accomplish these goals.

The car would be better in the sense that unlike the Yugo, ergonomics would be considered. No sharp edges protrude from the hatchback or front seat to gash the driver or passengers. Certainly not lusty, but adequate horsepower would be provided from its engine, eliminating needless downshifting.

The production price would be slashed in many ways. Again the fact that it is a joint effort will reduce many costs. Corners on certain things would be cut like they were never cut before. For starters, no options would be offered. The very ability to provide options, whether they are chosen or not, costs considerable money. This cost has always been passed on to the consumer, now it could be done away with.

As for a paint scheme, there isn't any.

Cars could be produced covered only in dark or light grey metal primer (your only choice) and if the buyer wishes, he or she may paint it any color desired later. Or not.

Please remember that you or I might have no interest in a car like this, but it is very likely that millions of other Americans will.

This would make new car ownership a reality for a large segment of our population for whom it was only a dream. Not the sort of car they would be able to show off, simply one they could drive. After all, isn't that the point?

If you've managed to digest that, let me frighten you with more cost cutting ideas. If appropriate, the front and rear windshields could be identical. One less part to process. Front and rear bumpers, front and rear fenders, likewise. This last idea was not my own but rather was actually used by the Checker Car Company which produced so many taxi cabs.

I have absolutely no desire to union bust, so please don't misunderstand what I am about to say next.

These cars as a new entity, not designed to compete with domestic models we are currently producing, and coming under the banner of a new car company due to being a joint venture, call for a new contract.

The people who would be building them would be either new employees or preferably those who had been previously laid off by the industry. Hopefully there would be little resistance to the idea of working for somewhat reduced wages and benefits, if there is the understanding that were it not for this heretofore nonexistent car there would be no employment.

I have every reason to believe that a deal could be struck to the utmost benefit of both the auto industry and the workers. The auto companies would have access to experienced workers at a reasonable cost, and the workers get a contract they can live with, especially when compared to their other options.

As a little icing on the cake, the factory might offer performance incentives in the form of these very same cars if production quotas are exceeded. What better way to advertise a product than to have your employees driving it?

My last major idea for cost savings in the production of this car is in the area of the manufacturing facilities. Again, due to the fact that this is a new car for a new market not meant to compete with existing models, it will require new factories. This opens up two new areas of opportunity for the car companies. They can either go about the process of reopening factories which they had recently closed down, or they might find it more feasible to move into new geographic locations, ones not traditional to the car industry.

The key to this question is tax incentives. Will the local governments of the municipalities which once contained working auto factories see the wisdom in granting tax breaks to the industry in order to encourage local production and employment, or will other areas of the country work harder to seduce this new segment of the industry? It all boils down to dollars and sense. What the auto industry should base its choice on is none other than finding a "user friendly" government. One which would look at the presence of a large car manufacturing plant as an asset, not as a cow to be milked dry.

Put all these ideas, all these concepts together and I see no problem in our ability to produce what was once our goal. Good, solid, reliable transportation, at an affordable price.

There is only one item which must be demanded from the auto industry. These cars must be produced here. Not Mexico. Not Canada. Here.

The American worker will be the one to purchase this car, the very person who this new market will be aimed at. He must not be allowed to be left out of the equation from the production end of things.

I mentioned several pages ago that I wanted to see the production of not one, but two econo-boxes. If your mental image of the one I have just described is, let us say, not your cup of tea, well you're really going to love the other one.

This other car that I recommend we produce would be much like the preceding one with just a few major differences. First they would, if you can imagine it, be *much* cheaper. Second, they would be intended for export only.

There is a whole new market out there just waiting to be discovered. The basic reason for this is that no one here has been looking.

Most third world countries have either poor, or no manufacturing facilities when it comes to automobiles. It must of course be remembered that these countries also possess little cash. In order to succeed at developing this market, we must be prepared to offer for sale a car which is so inexpensive that is would never meet any standards that our country has set for domestic consumption.

This car might have only two or three cylinders, it might be air cooled, and it would undoubtedly weigh only about one thousand pounds.

This would not be a car that the average American would allow himself to be seen in, but it would be light years ahead of the only alternative offered to those of the third world till now: the bicycle.

The use of such innovative ideas like these which I have promoted here, coupled with the necessary governmental cooperation could result in a revitalized auto industry, one borne up by the branches of new life and new hope.

It is also clear that if we instead stand by and do nothing that we will continue to witness a downward spiral in this area until this important industry along with large areas of the nation go bust.

Section II:
THAT WHICH STEALS OUR HEALTH

Red Bag Medical Waste

It goes like this. In most counties are hundreds of doctor's offices, dozens of clinics, and one to several hospitals. In each of these facilities are several rooms and in each room are produced yearly, several, to several hundred pounds of red bag medical waste. A network of companies has been formed across the country for the express purpose or routinely picking up, transporting, and finally disposing of the aforementioned waste. Pretty smooth so far isn't it? But then the kicker comes in. No one wants to pay more than necessary for said removal, and as there are numerous companies involved in what is a quite lucrative industry, competitive bidding quite naturally evolved. Of course, the lions share of the business went, as one might expect, to the lowest bidder. This understandably upset the higher bidders who in order to remain competitive cut a few corners and in turn they became the lowest bidders etc., etc. This unfortunately results in two undesirable conditions. In the first case price fixing evolves by which each hauling company gets an equal share of the market. Everyone is happy with the exception of the one paying the bill (which eventually is YOU, the patient.)

In the second case, competition continues perhaps a bit too far. More corners are cut and fees spiral downward until something "not nice" happens. Some hauling companies find that the final corner to be cut lies in the direction of disposal. Why pay an authorized facility when one can simply use a convenient dumpster, road shoulder or (my personal favorite) the shallow waters just off the Jersey shore?

And guess what? Again eventually YOU pay the price. And somehow the cost of cleanup always considerably exceeds the cost of proper disposal.

What to do? What to do? Such a difficult problem. One requiring a difficult and of course necessarily expensive solution. Not at all!

The solution is incineration. Where? Smallish incinerators on site at each place where red bag (which is to say infectious) medical waste is produced. The important key to notice here is that once produced in the form of bloody bandages, blood samples, used syringes etc., etc., the product never leaves the premises. It comes in, but it doesn't go out except in the form of burned gases expelled at a temperature which no dangerous microbes can survive.

The trade off? The slightest addition to already existing air pollution, far less than the pollution currently caused by improper disposal. Some of this could even be offset by the possible innovative use of cogeneration by which some of the heat produced in the incineration processes could be recaptured to provide part of the heat or light for the facility.

The cost? The cost of the incinerator will be offset by not paying hauling fees with a built in profit necessity, not to mention clean up costs.

Where to locate these incinerators on already built facilities? Probably the roof. In other cases the basement. Last choice, fire codes permitting, within the building itself. With the exception of in home doctors offices, or converted houses the majority of existing buildings used for clinics, hospitals, labs, etc. are commercial buildings with flat roofs already structured to take the weight of large air conditioning units and so forth. In the cases where this is not practical, it must be remembered that most places have their existing heating furnaces and hot water heaters already located in the basement. Sometimes the flue chase for these will allow for the addition of the flue pipe for the incinerator installation, which otherwise could probably be located close by. An additional upside is that gas or oil lines may be conveniently located, and sufficient stairs access is probably already there.

There will of course be the exception where installation of an incinerator is just plain impractical. In these hopefully rare instances, arrangements could undoubtedly be made to share other facilities for a reasonable fee including hauling. Said hauling would be at much reduced distances when compared to the way things are done today, and the shipments would be easier to keep tabs on. An interesting alternative would be a mobile incinerator to handle such problem places. A converted tractor trailer (or possibly smaller vehicle) shows up at the doctors office during off hours, medical waste is placed inside, and burned on the spot before the vehicle leaves the parking area.

Who stand to lose with the above recommendations? Unfortunately a number of honest hauling companies. But like anywhere else in the free enterprise system, when your job no longer exists, you move on. As a small consolation, those jobs did not even exist a few years ago. The only other losers are the bureaucrats who up until now have thrilled in writing more complicated laws which have caused the very mess we find ourselves in today.

Atomic Waste

In addressing the problem of the final disposal of nuclear wastes, that is the radioactive products no longer of a high enough energy to use as fuel, the U.S. has come up with any number of answers. Unfortunately none of them are practical or cost effective.

Spent fuel rods may find their tomb deep within the earth, stacked carefully in abandoned coal mines, or played out salt mines. This always leaves us open to the probability of future leakage and eventual contamination of ground water permeating the underlying rock strata. When a substance has an atomic half-life that is measured in tens of thousands of years, time itself becomes a medium in which things can go wrong. Ironic that it was less than one hundred years ago that Madam Curie first experimented with radium and today we have created substances bearing disposal problems which will last far longer than civilized man has so far walked the earth.

An alternative solution offered, was to encase these wastes in special concrete "coffins" and give them a burial at sea. Far beyond the continental shelf, where the ocean is more than three miles deep would be their final resting place. Supposedly, constant monitoring would go on to ensure against leakage. Both the costs and of course the risks involved make this plan unworkable.

If, during the tens of thousands of years that these items remain "Hot" just a few of them rupture (if not immediately, in loading accidents) what will the result be to our oceans ecosystem? There is an equal chance that after, say, the first few hundred years, a lack of concern, or budgetary problems of the generations then in existence, may cause the monitoring activities to cease.

Even the finest concrete will eventually succumb to natures erosive force. And were this idea to work properly, the cost alone would be staggering.

Perhaps one of the most imaginative answers to our problem, and one straight out of Jules Verne is the following: Load up rockets with payloads of this obnoxious stuff, and deliver them to that ultimate incinerator of all, our sun!

They would without question be totally burned up, and the cost is reasonable. Oh it isn't that the expense wouldn't run into the billions per launch, it surly would. But without the necessity of continual monitoring going on virtually forever we'd be getting off cheap.

Pretty neat so far. Just one problem though and it's kind of a biggie.

As we've seen with N.A.S.A. (Not *another* seven astronauts!), launches don't always go off as planned. The problems of Three Mile Island, and even Chernoble might pale by comparison to what would happen should one or several rockets fall a bit short and land, say, in New York, or with a bit more luck, Washington D.C.

Oh well, so much for an otherwise pretty good idea.

I'd imagine that given enough time and of course more of your money, the experts could come up with ideas even more fanciful than these. There seems no end to their imagination.

Ah, but for an idea that would work.

Actually the best I have heard so far, comes to me courtesy of my father. This idea is supposedly used by the French with great success (Although I know it isn't popular to learn anything from *those* people.)

It goes like this. The offensive matter (spent fuel pellets etc.) would be taken right back where it came from—the mines.

By carefully mixing the radioactive matter with the same amount of tons of dirt that it originally was extracted from, we will have returned it to a state no more (and perhaps less) noxious and dangerous than the soil was before it was mined. Properly placed back in abandoned uranium mine shafts it is now as safe as the day it was found.

Diluting these wastes should be the wave of the future.

Another simple and inexpensive solution involves placing wastes in areas which are no good for anything else.

Thanks to decades of nuclear testing, primarily in the Nevada desert and on certain Pacific atolls, we have rendered large portions of our earth rather permanently unsuitable for "life as we know it." What better place to use as a nuclear graveyard than that which we have already destroyed?

Both of these ideas have considerable merit, and will be met with enormous resistance from those in charge of such things. But the fight will be worth it. We will not only save the earth, but our wallets as well.

SOLID WASTE DISPOSAL

First A History

Hundreds and thousands of years ago when the Earth's population density was relatively low, solid waste disposal was handled much in the manner that it is today, but with quite different results.

A person would buy, trade for, or make something, use the item until it was worn out or broken, and then quite naturally discard it to a point just outside his dwelling. Occasionally, either at a specified interval of time or when the pile of such discarded items became of a certain size, the collection of trash was moved a moderate distance away to a less offensive location. There it was either burned or buried or in some cases just left to decay. As society evolved, groups of individuals pooled their resources as well as their liabilities and the second movement of the garbage was to a place centrally located and at a bit greater distance from the houses than it was before.

The reason that this system worked so well was twofold: man's numbers were small, and he tended to economize on what he considered as worthy of disposal. Many things were repaired, and repaired again. Those beyond repair were often made into something else still useful. Worn bedsheets were turned into pillow cases, pillow cases became handkerchiefs, and they in turn were used as cleaning rags, paper towels being unheard of. In the end even the rags made their way to the compost heap with the rest of the organic matter to be used to reinforce the garden soil. This type of internal recycling continues today in most third world countries.

Times changed, garbage changed, but over the years the method of disposal didn't. The volume of refuse per household became much increased. This was due primarily to an interesting combination of factors. More garbage was actually being produced at the point of manufacture: store bought food and supplies came wrapped in paper, plastic, or Styrofoam which often was wrapped again in the same. This in turn was placed in a paper bag or cardboard box. Toys, spark plugs, cereal etc., etc., all came in their individual boxes, or perhaps even in the ever beloved bubble wrap. At the same time, internal recycling slowed down dramatically or perhaps even stopped. Fireplaces and wood burning stoves in which anything that could be burned was, were replaced by central heating which brought with it it's own form of pollution.

The backyard compost heap went the way of the home garden. Items were no longer reused in other ways. Bed sheets no longer became pillow cases etc., as people economically no longer had the need, nor could be bothered to take the time to economize in this manner. Interestingly, at the same time that man actually produced more trash, he became less responsible for its proper care. And no longer was he even involved in it's eventual demise. Garbage was now placed in a can curbside (after first being placed inside yet another plastic bag drawn tight with a plastic or wire tie), for a fee a stranger would come and haul away the contents of said can to a location that the dwelling owner neither knew nor cared about. With the transfer of said fee the responsibility of getting the offending waste to its final resting place was also transferred.

In the evolution of the garbage crisis the two biggest problems were yet to come. A rapidly increasing and eventually exploding world population compounded the effect of the aforementioned problems. Nowhere was this more apparent than in the developed countries where the most trash was being produced, and at the same time the least room was left in which to put it. So far what we see is a natural progression in which each player does his or her part for the better or the worse.

Then the politicians got involved. Evil and greedy people can seldom be counted on to miss an opportunity. The more golden the apple the less likely it will be that it misses getting plucked. When the day comes that the last dump (euphemistically called landfill) is full, solid waste management will become a difficult and expense proposition. The more difficult and expensive, the more lucrative things become to those who are used to having their fingers in the pie.

To those particular vultures waiting for the victim (yes taxpayer) to expire so they could pick yet another carcass, there stood only one small impediment: How to fill the dumps all the quicker so that the day of feasting might begin?

As all good politicians do, they again reached into their bag of tricks and pulled out their two old favorites: laws and taxes (sometimes lovingly referred to as "Fees")

As confusing as it may sound to the poor fool who still thinks that politicians are working for the public's best interest, laws were passed to ensure that the landfills would be filled and thus closed as fast as possible.

Dump picking was no longer to be permitted. The excuse given and so foolishly swallowed by the public at large, was that the towns, counties and cities, did not posses the necessary insurance should anyone picking the dump get hurt. Interesting that no one was told that they couldn't similarly bring garbage *in* because of insurance restrictions, they just couldn't take anything out. This served to put people out of business who had up till now been performing a valuable public service. The swelling garbage pile was to a small degree being mitigated by the removal of some of its contents by an interesting group of entrepreneurs. Each reasonable sized dump facility had a few individuals who would show up daily in pickup and rack bodied trucks, to pick over yesterdays deliveries and see what they could reclaim. Many items referred to as "tin" such as washing machines, dryers, refrigerators and stoves were trucked off to be sold to scrap dealers. The removal of such bulky items from the growing pile was truly a Godsend to the public. Also of benefit was the small income derived to the picker, the increased business to the scrap yard, the public benefit of keeping just a few more people off the welfare and unemployment rolls, and the intrinsic value of making items worth something out of that which is thought to be worth nothing.

Of equal value was the citizen picker. On a day off he pulls into the dump, his car trunk or small trailer loaded with lawn clippings and tree branches from his yard. Upon emptying his trunk he spots a couple of plastic five gallon pails which he has a use for. Into the car they go. That handful of short two by fours is perfect for the home project he had planned and so he takes them as well, and a little to the left is a lawnmower with a blown engine that is the same model as the one he has at home. The handle will be useful to replace the one that he backed the car into last week. Pulling out of the dump said individual heads home. His car is nearly as full as when he had entered, and the landfill no fuller than before he arrived.

Solid Waste Disposal

Throw a few thousand of these practical sort of people together and you start to make a sizable dent in the burgeoning trash mountain we are all producing.

Unfortunately today in most municipality such trash picking has become outlawed. Garbage may come in, but it may never go out to be used for another purpose, with the aforementioned insurance excuse being given and too often taken for legitimate reason.

In some places the crafty and ever innovative officials have found another clever way to quickly use up space in the landfill.

Annual curbside leaf pickup is instituted, at of course great expense to the taxpayer. Rather than compost said leaves producing a valuable and usable mulch, the leaves are generally trucked to the dump and covered over with a layer of dirt like the rest of the trash. This not only uses up important space which should have been kept available for true garbage, but calls for the use of more of the costly cover fill, the soil which is hauled in from elsewhere, also at considerable expense to—you guessed it—you, the taxpayer.

In many areas the fee has been dropped for the car trunk or small trailer load of garbage brought in by the homeowner. In this manner we can cut off what was a legitimate source of revenue, thus making the landfill less cost efficient, while at the same time further encouraging the filling up thereof.

With the inexpensive landfill concept a thing of the past, the government can get on with their plan of making solid waste disposal very expensive indeed.

Two great ideas have evolved. The first is to build elaborate and naturally expensive incinerators. Thus we can burn what might have been used for other purposes as well as adding by a staggering degree to the air pollution problem.

The second is to continue to use landfills in quite distant locations. Someone else's backyard if you will. By this method large truck, transfer, and bailing fees can be applied as well as continuing to add to the air pollution via the trucks doing the long distance hauling. Trucks, by the way, always returning to point of origin empty, making half their round trip for no other reason than to return to base and using nearly as much fuel as they did while running loaded. It is my understanding that already in some cases, trash is being transferred as far as fifteen hundred miles away.

Incidentally, these distant landfills are being no more better managed than the ones closer to home and so will be filled up just as quickly, till the problem comes full circle and bites us on the rear.

Once *they* are gone, no alternative will be left than to build those billion dollar incinerators or perhaps to play that final trump card still hidden up the politicians sleeve: Shipping our garbage out of the country!

What better way to plunge us further into debt than to send our garbage half way around the world? And once we've gotten used to the idea and have no other avenue left open to us is it too much to imagine that the countries receiving this trash will jack the rates up several fold?

Perhaps the point will not sink in until you have bought yourself a candy bar for seventy-five cents, and found that you will need to pay an additional seventy-five cents to discard the wrapper!

The cost of many of the products we buy will often be outweighed by the cost of disposal of the refuse they produce.

I have a better way. What I am about to propose to you, although multi-leveled, is really quite simple. It's additional benefits are that it is cost effective as well as producing very little true trash.

To begin, at the point of manufacture companies would be encouraged to reduce unnecessary wrappings and boxes.

Financial incentives might even be proposed (notice I take this avenue rather than to propose fines for non compliance. I would rather not make government the enemy of enterprise). Less garbage produced is less to worry about down the line.

Next we get *properly* into recycling. At the home front people would separate glass, plastic, paper, cardboard, aluminum, other non ferrous metals, and iron and steel. Belly boxes would be built into the currently existing garbage trucks to hold these recycled items on pick up day. There would be no need for a fleet of separate pick up vehicles and an entire separate crew for recyclables. *Remember we did not produce anymore garbage, we just segregate its contents.*

All the contents of the truck would be brought to the same location. The recyclables to be further worked on in one area and the rest of the truck dumped in another. The main contents of the garbage truck would be placed in a hopper which distributes the trash onto various conveyer belts to be picked over by hand as it passes by the sorter. These sorters would be trained to pull out such things as should have been segregated to begin with. Additionally they would pull out items such as scrap wood, plastic bags, reusable objects etc. Further down the line other sorters would continue to divide the items still on the belts as compostables, rubber, burnables and non, etc. After final sorting of these other recyclables, reuseables and other by-products and some hazardous materials, the last conveyer should be carrying that which you could do nothing other than bury. That final pile should be very small indeed.

If the place where this garbage truck dumped its load is a still operating landfill, this last pile will be buried there. Even here however the pile will lay exposed for a day, so anyone so inclined may pick through it before burial. If this final stage garbage must be trucked to a new landfill, this dumping grounds must be new in every sense of the word. Now is not too soon to be seeking out the next generation of landfill sites. Properly selected and designed places to be filled at a snails pace with only true garbage, could be planned to last one hundred years or more. Several possibilities come to mind. Abandoned rock quarries might prove to be ideal with some further research, arid desert areas with no underlying streams or aquafiers present another possibility. The important thing is to start now, using all of the modern technology at our disposal. Computer imaging, satellite surveys, and sonic soundings might all come into play. An important consideration is that things like refrigeration compressors, solvents, unknown substances and hazardous wastes will no longer be buried. By carefully discriminating we can insure that leachate as we now know it will be reduced or eliminated as a threat to our water supply.

Now backing up on our conveyer belt a bit let's take a look at the burnables. As opposed to the incineration of all mixed garbage which calls for high heat, requiring natural gas or another fuel to augment the burning process, we will take quite another path. By burning only the natural burnables (organic matter, food scraps etc.), we could use a rather normal furnace to accomplish our goal. This would require little if any additional fuel. The heat thus produced would be used to run an electrical generating plant hooked into a grid to serve the very community that the garbage came from.

Another fine product of this great garbage sifting process is rubber. A prime example of often wasted rubber is the automobile tire. The main ingredient in today's tire is oil, and by a simple process which exists today, tires can again be turned into oil. From this, new tires might be produced again thus completing the circle, or it might be used elsewhere, and it sure beats landfilling them.

Compostables would be used to do just that, with the final product either returned to the homeowner for his back yard garden or to be made available for free or at slight cost to area farmers. In fact compost properly put up, turned and cured, might even prove a valuable export commodity once local markets have been satisfied. This again would serve to get the government out of the picture and free enterprise deeper in.

The metals, ferrous and otherwise, would be stockpiled. When the market is right the dump would accept competitive bidding by businesses who use such scrap products. We are all familiar with the fact that it takes only a small percentage of the energy and expense to reuse the metal in a tin can than it takes to produce a new one from ore.

Both wood fiber and the paper produced in our separating tasks would find its way back into the market as new paper similar to the way it is being recycled even now.

Glass has been successfully recycled for decades but could be taken a step further. The main ingredient in glass is silica and this is derived from sand. Glass found unsuitable for normal recycling due to off color, temper etc. could always be simply and mechanically ground back into its raw material, fine granules of sand. If no other purpose is found for it the sand could always be used as excellent road bed material.

The main item which must be dealt with is our necessarily labor intensive sorting process. Where would we get the manpower necessary to do the job and how do we find people willing to handle garbage?

The answers are many and varied. We are now at a point in our history where nearly ten percent of our citizenry is, at any given moment, unemployed, despite what our government is telling us. A certain percentage of these would be willing to take any kind of work. We also have a huge prison population, a labor force greatly underused. The taxpayer is footing the bill for their food, shelter, education and medical care. Why deprive ourselves of a small return on our "investment" in these miscreants? Similarly, our welfare rolls are full of people otherwise fit, but for some reason considered unemployable. (I would rather move them off the rolls, but that is the substance of another chapter.)

Again, the next time a judge sentences a person to a number of hours of community service, what better place to have him spend it? If the work proves too objectionable it might serve as a deterrent to repeating an offense.

During summer vacation our youth, if failing other attempts, might find ready employment here if nowhere else. And what better incentive to go on to college and pursue a *good* job?

Finally you may be surprised to find quite a number of people who actually don't mind picking through garbage. We have but to try.

As an alternative, the sorting task should be turned over to free enterprise. If it could be managed at a profit, and it is my guess that it could, companies would be set up to do the sorting. Their pay would be that they get to keep the products of their sorting. This would be entirely dependent upon the quality of the trash, and the current market value. Remember it would not necessarily be governments goal to turn a profit, but rather to be happy with the reduction of the garbage problem from one of crisis proportion to one which can be managed. All things considered, manpower might prove to be the least of our problems, and not costly at all.

One thing is certain. If we continue in the direction and at the speed that we currently are, solid waste management will be among the most expensive of our utilities. I have offered here a comprehensive plan which is not only workable, but quite cost effective when compared with any ideas proposed by government to date.

THE OZONE LAYER

"Everyone complains about the weather, but no one does anything about it" The old saw goes something like that anyway. Well the same can be said about the hole and/or thinning of the ozone layer.

A number of scientists would have you believe that our problems with this fragile and important layer of the Earth's atmosphere are of catastrophic proportions, while a good number of equally qualified scientists will tell you that there is really nothing to worry about. Who to believe? And does it matter?

There are certain radio talk show hosts of low mentality who would prefer that you panic. "If we're not sure, (regarding ozone depletion) wouldn't it be better to err on the side of safety?" is the rhetorical question they pose. Oddly, the people who I am referring to are also rabidly pro-abortion and would never apply the same rule of "erring on the side of safety" to that issue.

The problem in dealing with the ozone layer by deciding to err on the side of safety is that when you haven't any data, there is no end to the measures you would have to take. In fact, many "ozoneites" actually promote the dismantling of society as we know it to accomplish their goals. No cars, lawnmowers, factories, etc. They would all be taboo according to their desires. There must be a better way, and of course there is. Certainly we should be continuing research to monitor any supposed depletion, ascertaining whether it really exists, and to what extent. Simultaneously, we should be experimenting, searching for the most positive solution to the problem which is of course that we actually attempt to repair the damage.

Fluorocarbons as used in aerosol propellant have been outlawed since 1976. Recently Freon as a refrigerant has been replaced with substitutes, again by law. All seemingly worthy moves. Neither of those however address the bigger issue of restoring things to where they were.

Ozone itself is a molecule comprised of three atoms of oxygen as opposed to the two normally found. If we are to believe what scientists tell us, the ozone layer is comprised of this and the various other gases which have the same basic makeup as does smog. To put it another way, it seems that we have too much air pollution near ground level, and not near enough high up in the atmosphere. The solution to the disappearing ozone layer may be as simple as transporting our earthbound pollution upward.

Some methods which might be investigated are rocket or missile delivery systems, jet fans, or high altitude balloons like the ones used in weather tracking. If we have the technology to succeed at satellite deployment for the purposes of telecommunication, surely we could solve this problem.

There are but two things standing in our way. The first is that we haven't tried yet. We study the problem. We complain about the problem. We try our darnedest to shift the blame. But we haven't tried to fix the problem. Chances are that this is the first time you've seen anyone address it from this direction. Shame on us for our lack of creativity.

The second problem is that those in the "green" movement will try to thwart the effort, preferring instead that we all be forced to return to the Stone Age.

As one who promotes a synergistic lifestyle, I'd like to point out a couple of benefits of my plan, should it prove feasible. Assuming that the idea works, it would actually provide us with a place to dispose of our harmful air pollutants. That which is coming our of a chimney or smokestack today, would be shipped "out of this world" rather than into the air we breath.

The second major advantage is that if the ozone layer can be thusly repaired, the use of refrigerants, fluorocarbons, and related compounds with all their attendant benefits might again be permitted to be used. The third benefit is of course that it is much preferable that we actually restore the ozone layer than to only slow the rate of its demise.

I cannot guarantee that my idea will work, we have but to try. But right now we are both playing chicken little, and sitting on our hands.

THE ENVIRONMENT AND POLLUTION

It will take a sharp knife to cut through the thick smoke and fog that surrounds this issue, but I will do my best to present you with the facts.

During the past twenty years, literally hundreds of groups have sprung up across the U.S.A. identifying themselves under one banner: Environmentalists.

A handful of these groups are on the up and up and do fulfill some needed function. The rest of them exist by one means, and for one purpose alone. They seek to not only alarm America about this "crisis" or that "crisis," but to keep our concern about the natural world around us both misdirected, and forever at a fever pitch.

If not successful in playing up the problems regarding our relationship with nature, two terrible things happen, at least from their way of looking at things. First, funding dries up. Were this prospect not horrifying enough to contemplate, the second is not far behind: It becomes obvious to the public that the group serves no useful purpose.

As you might imagine, this triggers the greatest concern that any group like this is capable of having: their own private ecosystem starts to dissolve, endangering the only specie that they are really concerned about. Their high paid executives, and we're talking at least six figures here, find that the next ecological niche they will occupy is on the unemployment line.

Now I'm not saying that all is perfectly well with the environment, just that the picture is not nearly so bleak as those who have a reason to have you believe so, say that it is.

I'll get into what our problems are and what we can do about them later in this chapter. But first, I'd like to give you some hope.

The good news is that the environment is, as a whole, very good and getting better. I must tell you that this is without any help from, and at times despite the interference from, the very groups I was alluding to in the previous paragraphs.

Some examples to the contrary of what I am about to say can always be found, but overall, we enjoy cleaner water, air and land areas then we did just a few years ago.

The Great Lakes are no longer comprised of various chemicals, these having been largely replaced by genuine water. The air around most cities is breathable again, and if we remain both careful and vigilant, progress will continue to be seen.

During the Arab oil embargo of the late seventies, our nation was put into a bit of a tight spot. Oil which had been both cheap and plentiful, just about dried up overnight, and this had to be substituted for. This country has the good fortune to be sitting on immense coal reserves, the magnitude of which can make an oil shortage barely crimp our style. The down side is that much of this coal is high in sulfur content. The trade off in increased air pollution must be carefully weighed before seeking to use this alternative.

It is to our credit that we were able to avoid using much of this coal at that time. Belt tightening, consolidating auto use, reinsulating buildings and other energy saving measures aided us during that period, and our air was not made to suffer for it.

It was only the government-mandated gas rationing which had a negative impact. The foolishness was rampant. Cars could only be gassed up on alternate days (as determined by license plate number) instead of being allowed to come in whenever needing gas. This resulted in *everyone* waiting on line every day they could get gas, for fear of being caught without. The amount of gasoline one was allowed to purchase at any one time was limited to but a few gallons, compounding the problem and forcing people back on line again who otherwise might have tanked up. To add insult to injury, those which were termed "economy" cars were allowed less gasoline per fill-up than full-sized cars. Imagine that. The very people who by owning smaller cars, were conserving fuel all along, were told that they weren't *entitled* to as much petrol as an old gas guzzler was!

As an interesting aside, I personally knew of more than one person who would pull the old Cadillac up to the pump, fill it, and then return home to siphon it out into their Volkswagen. If Americans are nothing else, we are innovative.

The result of this misapplied "rationing" was that much gas was wasted by people sitting on those long lines when they should not have had to, and of course, an increase in air pollution for the same reason. Let us hope we have learned our lesson on that one, otherwise we are destined to make the same mistake again next time.

Governmental efforts not withstanding, the people have done a fairly good job of cleaning up the environment.

When most people think of New York, they only picture the city. But upstate New York presents such beauty and diversity as to rival that of many other states. The resident deer population stands at upward of one million, and the state is home to several thousand black bear as well. Turkey and pheasant abound and there is talk of reintroducing the wolf and the moose. All of this in a state which is thought of as overdeveloped. Many other states fare even better.

Most U.S. rivers are cleaner than they have been since the beginning of the early 1900s, and work has continued to progress through our efforts.

We have learned a great deal through our experience over the years, and most of us do recognize the concept of "One Earth, don't wear it out."

So that is just a small fraction of the good news, that things are doing much better than is the common perception.

The bad news is that we still have a ways to go.

The environment consists of three basic things. The air, the water, and our land mass. Everything else that concerns us is made up of varying combinations of these three. So the task is simple. We must be prepared to repair any damage, and avoid any future damage to these three areas.

We are most fortunate in that the earth possesses a certain degree of recuperative ability. If we can keep the quantity of pollutants which we pump into our environment below a certain level, the self-cleansing nature of the earth will negate any harmful effects. It is only when we cross that invisible threshold (as we have in the past) that we run into trouble. Due to the fact that the exact point where we have gone too far is so hard to identify, it is in our best interest that we be conservative (isn't that a beautiful word, conservative?), trying as best as is reasonable to reduce the output of pollutants and enjoy the comfort of the earth's built-in cushion that nature has provided us with.

Our air is generally in great shape, although there is still room for improvement. The single most polluting factor for our air which we have any control over is the automobile. Again, there is much good news here.

The cars of the 1990s enjoy the advantage of modern technology, resulting in excellent gasoline mileage. Increased fuel efficiency results in fewer total gallons of fuel consumed. Other things being equal, this translates out to less pollution produced.

Thanks to sophisticated advancements like fuel injection and automatic overdrive, mid-sized cars with peppy six cylinder engines like the Chevy Camaro, now get combined city and highway mileage of around 25 m.p.g. This is approximately what "economy" cars like the Vega, Pinto, and Volkswagen Beetle used to deliver only two decades ago, and these with standard transmissions.

Most full-sized eight cylinder cars hover around the twenty m.p.g. mark, an accomplished goal undreamed of twenty years ago.

The real gem in the struggle for better performance is in today's economy cars. They start at 30 m.p.g. with most of them capable of an impressive 40 m.p.g. It must be mentioned that these cars are quite unlike the Volkswagen Bug of years past, having none of the Spartan qualities which were then the best offering of the day. Today's economy cars boast all the modern amenities of rack and pinion steering, power disc brakes, front wheel drive and so forth. And some, like the diesel Volkswagen and a few of the Japanese gasoline-powered cars actually exceed the 50 m.p.g. mark, an excellent accomplishment by anyone's measure.

Beyond this, we have the advent of the catalytic converter. Although far from perfect, this device makes it possible to more thoroughly burn gases (after the firing process) which were formerly sent out through the exhaust. Most notable is the reduction in unburned hydrocarbons.

Lead has been removed from all grades of gasoline, so this is just one more harmful by-product of the internal combustion engine which we will no longer be pushing out into the air we breath.

Before I move on from the subject of the automobile, I must mention one piece of bad news looming over us. Just over the horizon is coming a big push for the electric car. Already in California, it has been legislated that by 1995, a full five percent of the new cars sold within the state must meet a zero emissions level. This is a typical dirty little way our politicians attempt to speak without resorting to the actual use of the English language. What this really means is that they are mandating the battery-powered car.

You have no farther to look than determining who it is that is pushing the idea of the electric car to know that it is a bad idea. The politicians and the environmentalists have banded together to shove this concept down the throats of the residents of California without giving any study to the possible problems which are likely to crop up. This is not the first time these clowns have done this sort of thing, nor will it be the last.

The electric car is not in itself pollution free. There will, of course, be considerable pollution generated in the manufacture of the necessarily massive batteries. After each couple of years, when these batteries go dead, there will be more pollution produced in their re-smelting, either that or the problem of disposal. This, of course, assumes that we are talking about a lead base. If the final development goes in the direction of the more exotic metals, that only makes matters worse. I am here stating the probability that they will be going with the wet cell, which carries its own undesirable baggage of acid, the production thereof, eventual disposal and the likelihood of spillage whether due to defect or accident. On the subject of accident or spill, has anyone weighed the danger of acid in regards to our valuable human cargo?

This is just one more problem which must be considered before taking this dangerous plunge.

Nor are battery-powered cars truly emission free in themselves. Each and every time a battery is charged, it gives off noxious fumes, most commonly sulpher dioxide. And when the system is charged, that power comes from somewhere. A good portion of the fuel which the car would have burned were it gas-powered, is now burned at the electrical generating plant in order to charge those batteries. No one speaks about this.

I have no desire to beat a dead horse, but this creates yet another problem.

If the number of electric cars on the road becomes high enough, as is the *goal* in California, the power companies will have no choice but to build more power plants. This is something they have been trying to avoid for a variety of reasons.

In many communities across America, local power authorities have engaged in a program of giving away free, expensive but highly efficient light bulbs. They are aware that fully twenty-five percent of all electricity produced, goes to provide lighting. Their best hope to avoid building additional costly power plants is to curb our electric use by providing us with these efficient bulbs, and through other devices. They offer free seminars on energy conservation, off-peak hour rates, etc. All this hard work on their part can be quickly undone by the forced institution of the electric car.

There is still one more thing that these supposed environmentalists and non-thinking politicians have failed to take into account.

The law, as it is written, insists that five percent of the cars sold in the state be zero emissions (battery-powered). What is to happen if the public does not buy them? Will one out of twenty new car buyers be compelled to purchase one of these expensive disasters on wheels? This question has yet to be answered.

We must abandon the effort to produce and force upon the public this fools solution to our air pollution problems.

I offer here three better alternatives.

The first is that we allow our standard gasoline powered cars to continue to evolve. The natural competition within the auto industry will force the continued improvement of gas mileage. The same innovativeness which has produced the stratified charge engine, the crucifix engine, and the Wankel, will someday perfect the external combustion Sterling engine, or perhaps the turbine. Smoother lines will evolve as well, resulting in a reduced drag coefficient.

The second is for the government to get behind the development of the hybrid electric car.

Unlike a battery-powered car, the hybrid electric runs off a smaller battery bank taking its original charge from an electrical source but augments this charge from a small on-board generator powered by a five to fifteen horse power motor. As things stand now, the engine used to run the generator is usually a standard gasoline motor, but expect to see gas turbines, diesel, alcohol, compressed gas, or multi-fuel motors in the future. This small generating system is designed to extend the range on the primary charge held by the battery.

This design is not my own original idea, but rather one which has been around in various forms for a number of years. The ideas which I offer for enhancement to this basic concept, however, are as follows:

The car should have a second gearbox, whereby the engine may be directly engaged to drive the wheels should the battery, electric motor, or other components fail, a loss of charge is experienced, or an extra "kick" is required to either boost speed, or for a difficult hill.

Because it is designed for only intermittent and occasional use, this additional gearbox would spend most of its time not engaged, and add but a few pounds to the overall package.

The exterior of the car should be covered with solar cells (once they are no longer cost prohibitive) as opposed to a painted finish. The network of solar cells will help keep the batteries up to full charge (or return them to that level) anytime the car sits in the sun. Whether at home, parked at the market, or even while rolling down the road, a portion of the charge being used by the batteries will be replenished so long as it is a sunny day. This will extend the range and allow you to rely less on the energy being produced by the generator.

Once our technology allows for it, an overspeed generator can be geared to pick up power from the wheels anytime the car is going faster than it needs to while coasting down long steep hills. It is most probable that an electronic switching device will bring this generator into use when it detects a combination of speed and forward inclination.

The car must also possess a small onboard 110 volt charger so that the battery can be brought up to full charge anywhere there is an outlet.

As I mentioned in my chapter on "our failing auto industry," the government must clear the way for developments like these by suspending the antitrust laws to allow a cooperative effort of the full auto industry.

We should go so far as to even provide financial incentives for meaningful breakthroughs in this technology. The initial cost will be minimal but the rewards great through cleaner air and reduced fuel usage.

The third and last need for auto improvement lies in the realm of body shape, type and style. We must press on in our search for better materials. Aluminum body panels will provide a lightweight, rustproof fuel-saving alternative to steel, as will an all-plastic body once we have developed a composite which is difficult to ignite.

Body shapes have improved enormously and of course, we must continue in this direction.

One area which I do not believe anyone has looked into is a search for an improved body coating to reduce drag. It is a fact that a well-polished car slips through the air easier than one which is dirty, resulting in a slight improvement in reduced fuel consumption. If we are able to develop a coating so slippery that it not only glides through the air easier, but virtually repels dirt (for double efficiency), the fuel saved over the life of each car could be substantial. Multiply this by the number of cars produced each year and you start to get a picture of the potential.

As I have been pointing out throughout this chapter, there is an enormous amount of good news everywhere with regards to the progress we are making.

Detouring slightly within the subject, another bit of good news. The Whirlpool company has just won a major design award for practically reinventing the refrigerator.

The model in questions uses no CFCs and eclipses the efficiency of most all the existing models. Since the average home refrigerator uses more than twenty percent of the total amount of electricity consumed in the home, you can see the impact this could have on lowering energy requirements, resulting in a reduced need to produce this energy at the generating plant. All of this, of course, is reflected in less air, water, and thermal pollution.

Beyond the automobile, the next largest air polluter is American industry. Stringent controls have been imposed here since the mid-sixties, with good results.

In the future, we have but to ensure that any new manufacturing facilities, as well any retrofitting of existing ones, must be done only with state-of-the-art high efficiency generators, smelters, afterburners, heaters, etc. so as to produce as little pollution as is practical. In this way, time itself will see to it that antiquated systems will fall by the wayside as we move forward to greater efficiency and less pollution.

The prospect of cleaner water is the next item I wish us to explore, and here again the news is good and the chances of future improvement are excellent as well.

Over the past few years, the job of the department of conservation (or their equivalent) in most states has been broadened to include investigation and enforcement in the areas of air and water pollution. Originally set up as a group of game wardens, their role has grown to what it is today; a quasi-environmental police force. This is productive in many ways.

Nowhere else in government will you find such a dedicated group of individuals performing a largely thankless job, and for so little compensation.

They have the ability to check pollution at its source, striking a blow for prevention and early detection.

No longer will factories and industrial sites located near waterways be able to discharge waste and by-products into any convenient watercourse, treating it like a sewer. All this is very well and good.

Along with this, however, we need a strengthening and extension of certain laws regarding allowable discharge.

In the mid-seventies, in an attempt to clean up the Hudson River, a clean water bill was passed in New York State. The once beautiful Hudson had become the dumping grounds for everything from P.C.B. laden wastes, to raw sewage. Fact was that the polluting of this river began over one hundred years ago far up river in the Adirondacks with the opening of

The Environment and Pollution

a paper mill. Abuse increased over the years until one had to question whether water or pollutants comprised the greater portion of the river.

When the situation got bad enough, a successful cleanup campaign was mounted, aided by the aforementioned bill.

What the bill did not accomplish however and what most people remained unaware of, was the major polluting by the World Trade Centers' Twin Towers. Technically, the World Trade Center is located at the mouth of the Hudson River and therefore, exempt from any laws pertaining to the river itself. It was never the intent of those who enacted this legislation for the saving of the river that the mouth of the river should be allowed to receive different treatment. What purpose does it serve to clean up a river all along its course, only to have such enormous efforts undone at it's final outflow?

The fact is that this is brackish water for several miles upstream of the mouth, demonstrating tidal movements which push water back upstream twice daily. Any pollution placed at the mouth of the river is thereby sent upstream creating a problem area there as well. As of this writing, this problem may have been corrected (my research has produced conflicting stories from the different agencies involved), but not very long ago, this one office complex discharged into the water three million gallons of raw sewage daily.

It was precisely this type of activity which wiped out New York's once famous oyster beds. Few people are aware today that at one time, the shellfish taken from the waters surrounding Manhattan Island were renown for being among the best in the world. Oysters there were so plentiful that their discarded shells were commonly used as road bed material. Connoisseurs from around the globe prided themselves in being able to identify these seafood delicacies as to exactly where taken, from their taste alone. Typical pollution (sewage, etc.) from an overpopulated N.Y.C. made short work of this thriving shellfishery and it is most doubtful that it will ever be reestablished.

The Twin Towers is also granted another exemption under the law. Being owned by the Port Authority of New York, it is a law unto itself and not subject to the laws of New York State. Again I say, it was never the intent of the founding fathers of this great country which we are quickly losing, that any person, business or agency should hold itself exempt from any law. It is this type of cavalier attitude on the part of some which has led to so many of our modern problems.

So this is what I mean by tightening up our laws. We must go back and reexamine the intent of any of these laws and extend the wording thereof to reflect this intent. People are only bound by the word of the law and so these must be changed to clarify what was desired.

Another great source of water pollution is the runoff of farmlands. This consists primarily of excess fertilizer, pesticides and sludge.

Many farms make good use of sludge, the end product of sewage treatment, but if it finds its way into a water source, all hell breaks loose. If improperly treated, fecal coli bacteria can invade our drinking water, at times in too large a concentration to be successfully treated by chlorination. If the sludge is properly treated and contains no live harmful bacteria, its high nitrogen content can still cause a problem. It is this high nitrogen content which algae thrive on resulting in a pea-green body of water downstream from any such introduction. Again, the concentration of this algae may be too overwhelming for proper water treatment measures. A similar thing happens with fertilizer runoff.

The simple solution to all of this is a buffer zone of vegetation between the fields upon which fertilizer or sludge is used, and any watercourse in the direct vicinity. This buffer zone would be comprised of trees of varying types and size, and mixed undergrowth. The purpose served would be to stop direct runoff from the fields, and to promote absorption through the natural transpiration process.

This is similar to the shelterbelt system instituted in the 1930s to prevent windstorms from destroying croplands. Most of you are aware that millions of tons of topsoil are lost from our farmlands each year through erosion. An added bonus of these buffer zones will be in their reducing of soil erosion.

The buffer zones would vary in width and vegetation type due to such variables as topography, geography, soil type, and natural angle of recline. Guidelines for this should be easily formulated similar to that which has been designed for watershed management, and then provided publicly through the department of agriculture.

Fertilizer application recommendations should be changed also to account for the slope and soil type of a field. Early in the growing season, when the runoff probability is greatest, fertilizer and sludge application should favor the upper parts of a slope to allow for the linear movement of these materials during heavy rainfall.

The only one small trade-off to this system is that a minor amount of tillable land would necessarily be lost to provide for the vegetation belt. The upside is a much reduced pollution of our water sources with even pesticide runoff controlled to a great degree, soil conservation, and a shade belt along each stream.

In the actual cleanup of our larger waterways, we are faced with a bit of a dilemma. Certain heavy metals and long-lived toxins such as P.C.B.s may have been deposited over several decades. Now they lie in the sediment of these rivers and lakes, usually in a deep layer of silt, and they have managed to make their way into the food chain. The longer lived a species of marine life, the higher up the food chain, and the longer the organism lives in this particular environment, the greater the concentration of these chemicals will be found, and thus the less desirable for human consumption.

Crabs and other crustaceans will have large concentrations, as will fish like the sturgeon, which is not only a long-lived specie, but a bottom feeder as well. Much less affected will be species which are migratory in nature, spending little time in these hot spots.

A major problem is born with our attempts at cleanup. P.C.B.-laden silt may continue to do its toxic damage if left in place. But the disturbance of this silt, unavoidable in the dredging process, may do even greater damage over the short term. You are then, of course, forced to consider the question of what to do with this contaminated silt upon removal. If placed where eventual runoff will only put it back from where it was removed, you will have accomplished nothing, and at considerable expense.

The solution is to take each case individually, determining which direction to go in based upon the particular circumstances of each case. There will be occasions where dredging will clearly be the answer, with the removed silt being incinerated or perhaps stockpiled until the day that a reclamation process is devised. On other occasions, it will prove advisable to "leave bad enough alone," letting the offending material remain in place until a workable solution is found.

The least we can do here is to learn a valuable and expensive lesson: if we can avoid polluting in the first place, we won't have to worry so much about the eventual cleanup necessary and its attending cost.

This, of course, brings us back to my original argument for increased investigation and enforcement at the source of pollution by our regulatory agencies.

Properly applied these efforts can be nearly self-supporting. The fines levied at companies who willfully pollute should cover the lion's share of the salaries for the officers who are doing the work.

Networking with the public is also desirable. In a perfect world, we would expect that citizens would report polluters as part of their civic pride, but then in a perfect world, no one would pollute, would they?

Our world being one which is far from perfect, we must search for substitutes to the civic pride we often lack.

Many states, in attempting to properly address this problem, have adopted the T.I.P.P.S. Program, where members of the public are monetarily rewarded for, as the acronym means, *T*urning *I*n *P*oachers and *P*olluter*S*. This serves many purposes. John Q. Public is given a financial incentive to guard the environment, those who would abuse our ecosystems know that they may be observed in their activities, and a greater portion of our conservation officers time can be spent in tracking down meaningful leads. Anyone who knows me is aware that I usually shun any attempts at Big Brotherism, but I don't see this as being anything like that at all. This merely helps to implement a concern on the part of all of the public to serve our own important interests, and the despoilers be damned. The T.I.P.P.S. Program must be extended to every state, and nationally as well.

To continue our discussion on water pollution, we must now travel offshore.

For far too many years, we have treated the ocean as an inexhaustible dumping grounds where we have both legally and illegally deposited untold millions of tons of trash. We thought for decades that we could get away without paying the price for this behavior, and it wasn't until the results of short stopping started washing up on our beaches that we became concerned.

Short stopping is where the operator of a garbage scow dumps the load of trash before reaching the required destination. Instead of the garbage being dumped one hundred or two hundred miles offshore, it may be let loose as little as ten or twenty miles away from the dock. Although this is illegal, it has become common in areas where there has been little attempt at control. The opportunities for a fast buck saved through reduced time and fuel expenditures is hard to resist. Transfer stations tried setting up time clocks to catch those returning to dock prior to what was possible if the complete trip were made.

Like all well-meaning but half-baked ideas, this one did work for a short while.

But soon, those who were short-stopping in the past, continued to do so only modifying their behavior to waiting a distance offshore to kill the allotted time. No longer were they able to save time, but they could still save fuel. Any garbage washed up on shore could be blamed on "freak" or "errant" currents.

Communities that were serious about dealing with the problem resorted to tracking devices to ensure that the vessels went the total distance. This was a step forward, but it couldn't control the possibility of dumping the cargo part way out, then completing the journey and pocketing the fuel savings of having piloted the circuit, for the most part empty.

The main point here can easily be missed, it was the trash washing up on beaches due to short stopping which should have tipped us off that ocean dumping is, in and of itself, a bad idea.

That which did not arrive back on shore is most certainly impacting the area where it is dumped.

If we do not wish the ocean to slowly but certainly follow in the path that New York's oyster beds took, all ocean dumping must be stopped.

Almost as nefarious a garbage scow ocean dumping is another form of dumping which most people are unaware of.

If you take a cruise ship to Mexico, the Bahamas, etc., or a transoceanic crossing, and are on deck early in the morning when most of the rest of the ship sleeps, you might catch the crew dumping the ships garbage in international waters. This dumping is done at the time which it is, so as to avoid offending the sensibilities of the passengers, who will doubtlessly arrive at their destination unaware that all the trash produced during their journey has gone overboard. It is as if the excursion they have been on produced no garbage at all! But all this trash must end up somewhere, and it causes some degree of damage wherever it does.

Because there is no law against this, it might seem that nothing can be done to bring a halt to this practice. But much can.

We can certainly make it the law that ships whose registries fall under U.S. control refrain from this form of polluting as a requirement for licensing. And though the cry may go up of "international waters," we can likewise insist that any nations doing trade with us (whether tourist or shipping) cease ocean dumping in transit as a condition of continued trade. Inspection procedures will be simple and easy to implement, boiling down to: "Did you arrive in port with any refuse on board, and if not, why not?"

Taking things just one step farther, it should be no big thing to come to an accord on this issue, reaching an international consensus between participating shippers.

The last major area I wish to investigate in regards to the environment and pollution is our land. Again, this is one of those areas where people do a lot of complaining, but those same groups which could do something about the problem, limit their efforts to bitching about it, and expecting someone else to deal with it. A little cooperation on their part would accomplish a lot.

As an example, I cite so-called "investigative reporters." Once or twice a year, your local paper probably runs a special report on the illegal littering and dumping in your town or county. Complete with pictures, the journalist documents the location where some slob has backed in a dump truck full of debris, leaving the load on someone's private property, a mess the owner will get stuck having to clean up. The article will go on to decry how this practice has despoiled a woodlot, dirt road, closed factory road or what not. They sound like real champions of justice, don't they?

But as reporters, why is it they can't be bothered to pick through this trash a bit in an attempt to locate its' source? Is it because they are only interested in stirring up controversy, and not in actually solving problems?

Along the same lines, where I come from, local officials will fine the *property owner* when they discover that trash has been illegally dumped. If you are an absentee landowner, you can't possibly have any control over what goes on behind your back. So you get doubly screwed. The very government which cannot seem to look after your interests in preventing this type of vandalism, sticks you with the fine. Talk about punishing the victim. Since the fine is levied at the injured party, there is little incentive for said officials to attempt to track down the culprits who did the dirty deed. And so on it goes. First, you get abused by the slobs who surround you, those who cannot be bothered to drive to the dump, then you get abused a second time by the same government which failed to protect you from the first act.

Something must be done, and it is this: landowners must no longer be held accountable for dumping which occurred on their property (unless, of course, it can be established that they are the perpetrator). Government must thereby lose its favorite scapegoat, the victim, and be forced to investigate each act of clandestine dumping in an attempt to bring the guilty party to justice. Government (the police, inspectors, sheriff's department, department of highway, etc.) must be held accountable for their inability to protect the citizens, the very ones paying taxes for just this purpose.

In concert with this, landfills and transfer stations must be provided to receive debris at reasonable cost, so as not to provide an excuse (legitimate or otherwise) to dump illegally. Market forces are capable of running most things well in America, and if a legal dumping fee is low enough, and the fine for dumping illegally is sufficiently high, much of this problem will take care of itself.

Toxic waste collection days have been set up in many communities throughout the country. On a designated date, private citizens are encouraged to bring in partially used containers of paint thinner, turpentine, cleaning fluid and so on, of which they have no further use. It is supposed that this effort is designed to prevent these same individuals from dumping those products down storm drains, sewers or other convenient places and in doing so, harming the environment.

This, though a good idea, is being gone about in all the wrong way.

Once collected, these various fluids are invariably incinerated. This adds to our air pollution, wastes the material in question, and produces nothing.

If person "A" walks in with a quart of kerosene, person "B" with two quarts of the same, and person "C" with one more quart of kerosene, wouldn't it make sense that person "D" should be able to *go home* with a gallon of kerosene?

There is, for the most part, nothing wrong with the fluids which are being brought in for disposal. Why is it that we can't simply recycle many of them back into society to people who can use them?

Kerosene, benzene, lighter fluid, gasoline, paint thinner, insecticides and waste oil—these are all fluids which are currently being wasted by the programs we have in place.

Liquids of a questionable nature could be stored separately to await the day when advanced technology will allow us to properly deal with them.

Our industrious innovators have always shone through with new designs and processes when presented with a challenge and offered the appropriate financial reward. To go along with the program I envision, we must again tap into the brain power of our inventors to come up with a multifluid distillation or cracking process.

Should they be able to provide us with a device capable of reducing unknown or known mixtures into their various components in similar fashion to the manner in which crude oil is refined into gasoline, motor oil, etc., we would have the answer to our problem of waste and recycling of hazardous liquids.

Should this system prove workable, its use could be extended to the refinement of landfill-produced leachate. If this can be accomplished, we can considerably reduce the negative impact our landfills have on the environment.

Left for incineration would be only that small amount for which no other solution can be found. Yet, here again, there are other ways to handle incineration other than the way it is being done now.

Those by-products of the refining process which must be incinerated should either be stored until the winter heating season to supplement that use in applicable facilities, or should be burned in multifuel cogeneration plants as mentioned in my chapters on solid waste management and energy.

Now is as good a time as any to bring up another lesson in limited mental capacity as exhibited by Mr. Clinton. I know to the overly sensitive reader it may appear that I pick on this man incessantly, but I can only be honest enough to point out major faults where I see them and if they are to be found in a larger degree in him, so be it. If I were of the mind to actually attack this individual, I should never run out of ammunition, most of which he supplies himself. It would fill volumes.

Near the end of his own presidency, George Bush refused to sign a biodiversity treaty with the European community. For this refusal, he took much flak from the liberal press, and none of it was deserved.

Within a few months of taking office, Bill Clinton proceeded to sign this same agreement which Bush rejected, although none of the objectionable material had been removed.

One of the key clauses, which apparently did not bother Mr. Clinton, but should bother the rest of us nonetheless, relates to "shared technology." With the stroke of the pen, the President has signed away the rights of any American company to develop technology related to recycling or pollution control and to expect to keep any discoveries as their own.

Thanks to President Clinton, they will be forced to share any results of their research and development in these areas with all other parties to this accord without compensation. What will be the result of this legislation? Companies which might have created and developed advancements in this field, while secure in the knowledge that their hard-won discoveries will be protected by patents, will stop searching for breakthroughs once they are expected to give away the fruits of their efforts.

From the other direction, smaller countries and poorer countries will also stop experimenting in these areas, expecting instead that the "bigger brother" countries like ourselves, will be forced to hand them the desired technology free of charge. Everybody loses.

What you see in this is a microcosm of the damage that socialism produces. Those who could be the most productive stop doing so when they learn that they will not be allowed to retain the results of their industriousness, and those who were less inclined to produce stop entirely, thinking that all their needs will soon be met by those who are more capable.

It is for reasons like this that the type of people exemplified by Bill Clinton should never be allowed to gain any position where they can wreck such damage on the free enterprise system. Most citizens have no idea what the biodiversity treaty is all about, its name alone leading one to think that it cannot help but be good for the environment. It is only upon closer examination that the truth becomes apparent. In short, you can dress a pig up all you wish, but underneath all the ruffles and frills, you still have a pig. Far from kosher indeed.

Over the past one hundred years or so, certain groups and at times, governmental agencies, have sprung up and in time have proven themselves to be worthy of our trust. As I alluded to earlier, one of them is the Department of Conservation.

In most states, this agency has shown that it can usually be counted on to conduct its business with the express purpose of good stewardship of its assigned task, and to perform its designated function free from the encumbrance of political contamination.

When I implied that treaties on biodiversity and the like are far too important to be entrusted to the hands of Bill Clinton (a politician's politician if there ever was one), these are exactly the kind of groups I had in mind which should be given that sacred charge.

Let us place the future of the environment in the capable hands of those who should hold the reigns, the proven experts, not some individual or group with an axe to grind, only interested in advancing their own agenda.

Our environment, as I stated in the beginning of this chapter, is in excellent shape. The areas in which it does need help are easy and inexpensive to approach if we make the proper and logical choices.

But should we choose instead to listen to the panic mongers, those self-appointed experts like Al Gore, with his fairy tale book "Earth in the Balance," we will not be able to avoid taking the wrong turn and both we and the environment will suffer for it.

Asbestos Removal
(or much ado about nothing)

It was only a hand-full of years ago that asbestos, the fireproof organic substance which served us well for so many years, was discovered to be a carcinogen. In no time at all, the alarmists and media blew its dangers and significance all out of proportion, bringing upon us the mess we are in today.

At enormous expense and hazard, asbestos is being removed from wherever it is found, and removed in a manner reminiscent of the handling of fissionable materials. Decked out in moon suits and respirators those doing the removal shuffle about in plastic lined rooms, passing back and forth through double air lock doors while performing their duties.

The attendant danger of this job boosts the average hourly pay to about the twenty five dollar level, for a type of work which otherwise might command about ten.

There has got to be a better way, and there is.

Only recently was it discovered that it was only through repeated and continued exposure to asbestos particles suspended in the air, that lung cancer was caused. Also that the disease took about thirty years to take hold.

Also discovered was the fact that the removal process more often did more harm than good.

Asbestos Removal

By stirring up otherwise sedentary particles of asbestos dust, or even creating them in the tearing and cutting during the removal process, people in the work place were being exposed to more of the hazards of this substance than they would have been had things been left alone.

The answer to this second problem is encapsulation.

In the overwhelming number of cases where asbestos is found to be undamaged and basically intact, it is far more practical and safe to cover the asbestos with a liquid plastic coating, like spraying on polyurethane, and live with the presence of the substance now rendered, for the most part, harmless.

The first problem, that of actual removal when found necessary, is as easily solved.

Due to the fact that asbestos takes so many years of repeated exposure to cause cancer, the answer is of course to simply have the removal crews composed of very old people.

There are any number of retirees seventy years of age or older just "itching" at a chance for a second career, although perhaps only part time. Not only would this field permit the hiring of seniors, it should insist upon it! The downside is that some of these people might find themselves succumbing to work-related cancer at the age of one hundred or so. Those are the breaks.

With the health risk to the work force no longer a major consideration, the cost might be more properly stabilized in the ten-dollar-per-hour range. And again with the prospect of cancer fading into the background the need for overly protective, and thereby restrictive clothing, disappears. Without the moonsuits, the cost further comes down while efficiently increases. An additional savings.

Most of our seniors are honest, hard working, and dependable people. This would open up a whole new industry for them while saving the taxpayer, business and the consumer a small bundle. All this in addition to preserving the health of the young who currently do this work, and freeing them up for the type of work where their skills would be better utilized.

AIDS

Don't you ever get tired of being lied to?

Those who have a political agenda would have you believe that we are all at equal risk to get this dreaded disease. "It's not a gay disease" they keep repeating. They very much want you to forget that the name was changed from what scientists first called Gay Related Immune Deficiency Syndrome, or Grids. To no longer bring to memory that for the first several years in the spread of this deadly virus infection was almost unheard of in any but gay men. They are quick to remind you that spread is slowest among gay women, as if being a lesbian is some sort of virtue.

Do you remember that after extensive research and meticulous backtracking that doctors and scientists tracked the first case of AIDS in America to one gay man? He was an airline steward so promiscuous that he routinely had sex with more than two hundred and fifty new people yearly. Upon learning that he had the disease he went on to purposely infect as many people as possible. Nearly everyone in the U.S. who has died of or will die of AIDS can thank this one man's irresponsible behavior.

The truth of the matter is that AIDS is a deadly, highly communicable disease that is primarily spread by behavioral patterns. Behavior which is for the most part controllable and a matter of choice.

The number of people infected with AIDS will more than double every ten years. It will continue to grow exponentially until something even worse may happen. If it hasn't already, the AIDS virus will mutate. It may very well change in the way it spreads. Do you wish to see the day where being sneezed on may be fatal? It could easily happen. The well orchestrated conspiracy co-enjoyed by gay rights activists and liberals has done an excellent job of keeping any discussion about AIDS, its spread, and its cure, in the political arena where history shows us that nothing will be done. Our government has consistently lied to us about the rate of and method of spread, and they have denied that it can be spread by casual contact. When someone then claims to have gotten it in just this way, they claim that this isn't possible, since it has never been shown to be spread in this manner. Such circular reasoning will be the death of all of us. Also, there are several books on the subject of AIDS which are decried as fallacious by our government.

But slowly they are letting the truth out and actually agreeing with what is being said in these books. Without proper credit, nor admitting to having misrepresented the truth, they eventually say the same things which were printed in these books two years earlier.

The fact is that in the shedding phase the virus is found in large concentration in tears, sweat, saliva, any and all mucus, urine, feces, blood, tissue, etc. etc. In short, it is found in all body fluids. Further, the AIDS virus is not short lived, but even when placed on a slide and dried remains viable for one of the longest periods of time of any virus. Finally it has been shown that infection and eventual death can come about through the introduction of just one viron!

Possible to get AIDS only by unprotected sex or needle sharing? I think not.

The only way to halt the spread of AIDS is to wrench its future out of the hands of the politicians and see to it that it gets treated like any other communicable and preventable disease.

Routine blood tests must be given whenever sensible. To apply for a marriage license, to get into the military, when beginning college, upon admission to the hospital, to get medical coverage, upon imprisonment, arrest for intravenous drugs and prostitution. In short, blood tests should be given anytime an individual is about to have a major change in his or her lifestyle, one in which the person is more likely to infect others if he harbors the virus.

If tested positive, the individual would by law be compelled to disclose his or her sexual history. Only in this manner could the contacts also be tested and warned about possible exposure.

And while I am not in favor of wholesale quarantine, something more moderate along those lines must be done. A very loose and mild form of monitoring must be instituted. Upon being notified that he or she has tested positive, the individual would fall under the control of a new law. This law would forbid the individual from engaging in any sexual activity with anyone who is not likewise infected. They might carry a medical card or medallion so identifying themselves for "dating" purposes. The only allowable exemption for this would be in the case of informed consent.

The major instance where this exclusion would come into play would be where a person upon finding he is infected, advises his wife (or the other way around) and the spouse chooses to take the risk of future exposure. It would not be society's position to demand that the sex life of a marriage end, but it is hoped that in these few cases that safe sex practices would be followed.

The monitoring system I mentioned would serve to keep track of those infected. If it is found that an HIV positive person is continuing to engage in non-informed sex with those who are uninfected, they would be found in violation of the law. This type of behavior is, when you think about it, deliberately and knowingly life threatening. Attempted murder or attempted manslaughter are existing terms that come to mind.

Punishment for such irresponsible and life endangering behavior would appropriately be life imprisonment. A shorter sentence raises the question of just when would you be able to trust such a person in the future? Lest you think that my view in this matter is too restrictive upon some individuals rights and lifestyles, I would remind you that today over a million people in the U.S. are HIV positive. That's quite a dating base wouldn't you agree?

The other and most important consideration are the rights of those who are not yet infected. Any consideration on the privacy and rights of the HIV positive person must be balanced against other peoples rights. This is the way that it is with anything in our society when there is a conflict. The entire society must not be allowed to die so as to not risk the stigmatizing of a small percentage of the whole. Do I not have rights? Do you not have rights?

If an infected person does not manifest irresponsible behavior he or she would of course be allowed to live out his or her life in normal fashion, unmolested by government intervention. The only addendum I would suggest is that they be required to wear an inconspicuous necklace or bracelet so that in the event of vehicular or similar accident that medical personnel might be advised to take proper precautions.

Of those who must be incarcerated because of their behavior, penal colonies should be formed. AIDS infected people should not be infused into the general prison population. This is for everyone protection. The infected prisoner is protected from possible ill treatment by other, more criminal prisoners, and exposure to their nefarious and often violent ways. The regular prison population is in the same way protected from possible exposure to an always deadly disease via homosexual acts, blood exchange, or others.

While it is understood that you, the reader may not have any particular love or concerns for convicts in general, I would like to point out that the proper punishment for petty theft, drunken driving, etc. is NOT the death penalty.

The third and most important group to benefit from this division of prisons is us, the society at large. Remember that the greatest portion of the prison population is destined to be released some day. It is to our greatest benefit that the smallest number of these as possible return to our society now infected. Protecting them is what eventually protects us.

Nay-sayers to this plan would point out the considerable cost of setting up these penal colonies.

Only a handful of years ago we were told that in the last year of life each AIDS patient costs us, the taxpayer, forty thousand dollars. Today that figure is over one hundred thousand dollars per infected individual in the final year. For each ten people our plan saves from becoming infected we will have saved over one million dollars for such a project. This is in addition to the actual lives saved, and the accompanying misery to their families.

I envision these penal colonies as being quite different from ordinary prisons. Because everyone in there is infected, the central structure quite naturally would be a hospital. The surrounding community would be much like anywhere else. The only difference in all actuality is those who live there would not be allowed to leave. In time even the doctors and nurses who work there would probably themselves come from the infected community. An additional savings.

The monitoring system I had mentioned earlier would not prove difficult nor costly. Most of the implementation would take place through already existing channels, the police, health care providers, our educational institutions etc.

Most of the cost would be met with a small surcharge placed upon health insurance policies of the infected. In this manner the burden of this project would fall squarely on the shoulders of those on whom it belongs, while still allowing them to retain medical insurance. To those who think this is in some way unfair I would remind, that our youth pay disproportionately higher auto insurance premiums because they are considered a bad risk. No one screams about the unfairness of that. With appropriate prodding we could look forward to the approval and eventual assistance of the homosexual community, and the infected in general, of this monitoring plan. It would be viewed as an unfortunate but very necessary intrusion into peoples privacy. I believe that we can look forward to the support of these groups as it serves their best interest. Such a plan as this, once it proves workable, precludes the need for more drastic measures. Showing themselves to be responsible people would also go a long way toward gaining respect of the general public and serve to help slow or stop the rising resentment, hatred, and homophobia evident in society today.

A further part of our plan to halt the spread of AIDS is a necessary change in our immigration policies. It is to say the least, uncaring and irresponsible of us to allowed a known infected person to either leave or enter this country. To those foreign countries who have in some way managed to be successful in stopping the spread of AIDS, who are we to further jeopardize their lives, their society?

Likewise in our attempt to contain and start to win this difficult battle why would we allow additional infected people to enter our shores? Again the rights of the individual must be weighed against the welfare of all the rest of us. I would allude to what I said about immigration. Our damned government has spent a lot of our own money to try to convince us to aim for zero population growth. They have put no lid on spending our tax dollars to get us to believe that we are somehow un-American if we would like to have a large family. But at the same time this same government has thrown open the flood gates of immigration, escalating population growth to the highest rate ever. The population continues to grow unrestricted despite the sacrifices of those who would have preferred to have larger families.

Similarly, what good would it do us to work hard, and spend countless tax dollars to treat AIDS patients and to attempt to slow its spread, only to have all this hard work and the results of this great expense undone by allowing others who are infected to enter the country?

What right does the government have to inflict this added expense and risk on us? None whatsoever. Make no mistake, we are engaged in a race, a war of attrition as it were. There is no question that most if not all of those infected with AIDS today will have died before a cure is found, assuming that a cure is forthcoming at all.

The only question is whether or not they will die off faster than they will be replaced by others who are similarly infected.

People are working on cures. Billions are being spent toward this end. Drugs such as A.Z.T. and others have been found able to extend the life of the AIDS victim (although even this is now in question). Many, notably the Japanese, are putting their efforts into the perfecting of synthetic blood, naturally disease free.

All of these avenues must be vigorously pursued.

The key however is to slow the spread as I have outlined above. At the same time we should work on removing other vectors for this disease.

Prostitution is illegal in nearly the entire United States. Prostitution also flourishes almost unmolested by the law everywhere it is found. Is it any wonder that AIDS is spreading so rapidly in the heterosexual community?

Literally tens of thousands of hookers make such cities as Los Angeles, New York, Chicago, and San Francisco their home and workplace. Some use protection (prophylactics), about half do not. Noteworthy is the failure rate of condoms. The same condoms which the school systems are trying so hard to push to our youth have a failure rate of about five percent.

When one of these "working girls" takes on several men per evening, and works several days a week it isn't long before the percentages go against her. So much for safe sex.

Naturally the risk is increased dramatically for those who forgo the use of any protection at all. These girls are virtual reservoirs for the AIDS virus.

If America is to win the war on AIDS, we are going to have to begin to be serious about applying our existing prostitution laws. On most city streets, both the prostitutes and the police coexist together, and rarely is their presence discouraged.

While it is true that this supposed "oldest business" will always be with us to some degree, far better it would be if most were eliminated and the rest driven underground.

I propose that we not only start to enforce the existing laws, but that we add a surcharge to the punishment as well. This surcharge would be whatever amount of money is necessary to pay to have the girls tested for AIDS. As I've said earlier, the infected would then come under a new law with regards to their behavior if they continue to walk the streets. Their next arrest will be for good. Rather good incentive to get a straight job, isn't it?

Of nearly equal importance and equally challenging is our need to address the media's love affair with sex and titillation.

No longer can you flip on the television or go to the movies without viewing half-naked or totally naked, and always beautiful people, deep in the throws of ecstasy.

What I'm promoting is not censorship, merely a rolling back of the boundaries of moral responsibility to those of a few years ago. Let us adopt some form of community standards. It is very difficult to ask your children or even yourself for that matter to exercise a degree of restraint when everywhere you look you see more examples of the media's attempt to forever push forward the envelope on what is acceptable.

While I may not agree with Dan Quayle that it is the job of Hollywood to promote family values, I do believe that it should not be Hollywood's purpose to work at the destruction of those values.

Porno films are one thing. They will always be there for those who wish to rent them. My objection is to their content spilling over into regular film and television.

The last thing most of us need in this age of AIDS is to have our libidos constantly heated up.

As a side note, I would like to mention that I think our educational institutions give our young people too little credit. While continually hawking their condoms and so called safe sex, they laugh with disdain at any mention of the possibility of abstinence. Their priorities, as usual, are backward.

The most preferred avenue is abstinence. For those who will not or cannot adhere to it, the next most preferred answer is monogamy. The idea of promiscuous sex and condoms should fall far down on our list of preferred behavior.

This brings us to another area that has to be addressed: our educational system. We have simply got to stop this ridiculous "politically correct" movement from trying to convince our youth that it's "OK to be gay." This is being done both at our expense, and against our wishes. I cannot speak for you, but the basic reason I allow the schools to teach my children is that I thought it was more efficient for the school system to teach them how to read, write, spell, add, etc., than for me to take on the task myself. Never has it been my desire that the schools take it upon themselves to teach morals (while throwing out the Bible), a revised historical perspective leaving the contributions of white Europeans largely out of the picture, nor to insist that my children agree with their very leftist and one-sided political agenda. We have no further need for more "sensitivity training," revisionist history or "programs of inclusion." If my children do not choose to become gay, agree with or embrace the gay lifestyle, they shouldn't have to put up with the abuse of being labeled "homophobic" by a group of people whose sexual practices are to say the least, "questionable." School is not the place where they should even be exposed to it.

Most sociologists would agree with me that a great number of our youth are confused and uncertain about their sexuality at around the age of twelve. Hormonal changes and emotional feelings and yearnings in most cases haven't quite made a definitive stand, and quite often it is at this point that their sexuality is still in a stage of flux.

It is at this point in particular that they must not be told that being gay is simply an alternative, and quite acceptable, lifestyle.

To be sure, many of those with homosexual leanings are going to go in that direction anyway. But how many more, in deference to education, peer pressure, and a sense of values will end up being heterosexual?

How many of our youth in our misguided attempts at being "compassionate and understanding" will we doom to death at the hand of AIDS? We don't have any problem telling a small child "no" as he reaches for a hot stove, "That's not good for you."

While teaching our children about being "compassionate and understanding" with regards to the gay lifestyle, our educators cleverly omit exactly what that lifestyle entails.

They have managed to sanitize the entire discussion by purposefully leaving out the details.

The truth is that a majority of the men caught up in said homosexual lifestyle, those who find themselves frequenting the clubs and gay bars, engage in dangerous sex. An average evening of entertainment for them is to routinely pick up several often anonymous partners. Either in the rest room or another room set up for just this purpose, they engage in oral and anal sex, most often without benefit of a condom. "Love and caring" do not even enter the picture, the only thing that counts is the quantity and intensity of the orgasms, often enhanced by drugs. Fisting is also quite popular. Fisting is accomplished by inserting all of one's fingers, and finally the entire fist, all the way into another man's anus, then pushing the fist as far up the colon as possible, sometimes up to the elbow. This is usually done with the assistance of a lubricant such as K-Y Jelly, although in some instances it is done "dry" for those who prefer things rough.

The insertion of dildoes or artificial penises usually of outsized proportions is also enjoyed.

Having neglected to mention these things in reference to this "sexual preference," the educators can also avoid discussion about the attending fecal matter. Common also is the gay man who enjoys pulling a "train." Bending himself over a convenient sink or toilet, he invites any and all the men in the bar or club so interested, to take their turn at having anal intercourse with him. Many homosexual men find no problem accommodating thirty or forty "partners" in an evening's fun.

Less common than the above is the insertion of habitrails or cut down whiffle ball bats up the anus, into which is then trapped a hamster or gerbil. The scratching of the frightened rodent in its attempts to escape, supposedly provides the height of sexual ecstasy for those so inclined.

All of this, not to mention more radical departures from normalcy like the details involved in sadism and masochism. What I will mention, however, are two more facts which you can easily document. The first is that the medical profession has coined a term called G.B.S. or Gay Bowel Syndrome. It refers to what happens to the rectal area of those who use it for other than its intended purpose. The other is that even if we didn't have AIDS to contend with, the sexual practices which gays involve themselves in are anything but healthy. Syphilis, gonorrhea and herpes are just a few of the venereal diseases harbored by the practicing homosexual (outside of monogamy). Most noteworthy is that at some point in their lives, fully seventy five percent of all homosexual males will contract hepatitis.

Please be advised that I pass all the above mentioned information on to the reader as a mere description of what this type of sexual activity is. It is not my purpose to make any personal statement about it, just to bring what the school system would like to withhold from us out into the open.

If you still wish to think of this as an alternate lifestyle, a matter of sexual preference, then by all means do so. It is nonetheless a lifestyle which should cease to be promoted by our school systems.

With regard to gay rights, our nation has lost all sense of balance. On the one hand, we have some people who would promote dragging those who are gay off into the night and killing them. On the other hand, is a group of liberals convinced that the best thing they can do in life is to force the rest of us to acknowledge homosexuality as some supreme virtue, one to be held equal to or possibly superior to heterosexual behavior. They champion this cause and will not rest until they have forced their opinion into the church, the home, and into every other pocket of resistance that believes people have a right to their own opinions.

The proper perspective, of course, is that both of these extremes are far off base.

There is considerable evidence to support the contention that homosexuality is in the majority of cases, a genetic predisposition, and thus the tendency itself is beyond the control of the individual so affected. What is, however, within the control of the individual is what he or she chooses to do about these desires.

We all have desires. That in itself does not make us either bad or good people. How we act on these urgings is the defining point of just what kind of people we are.

Additionally, how we go about the followings of these urgings continues to define us.

I would prefer that no one was homosexual. Too late. Fact is, many are. Taking that as a given, I would next prefer that those people restrain their desires. Many will not.

Since I will not win on either of these two alternatives, I would only wish people to keep their wants, needs, and desires in this area to themselves.

What any people do behind closed doors is none of my business, and I wish it to remain just so. Let people do as they want, but keep it to themselves.

Despite the fact that what these people do may be beyond my comprehension, I have no desire to ferret them out, and drive them into the open. Quite the contrary.

If you are gay, and feel that you must be a teacher, keep your sexuality to yourself.

If you're gay and in the military please don't disrupt the majority of those around you, etc., etc.

Remember, you get what you pay for.

Hazardous Waste Sites

A few years ago, our federal government created (with your tax dollars) what they termed "the superfund." Billions of dollars were put aside for the express purpose of the proper handling of hazardous waste sites. These were not to be confused with places which were merely normal landfills, although many of those are being improperly labeled as such.

The presence of large quantities of toxic substances, poisons, by-products of manufacturing or refining, and heavy metals properly define a hazardous waste site.

But as is typical of government-funded projects, much of the money has been improperly directed and the fund is dwindling while showing few positive results.

I'm sure you are all familiar with New York's famous "Love Canal." Although that particular toxic dump caused one of the most costly cleanups ever, it was one which was handled properly. So successful was that problem dealt with that people have since moved back into that area, which was once thought never again to be inhabitable. Rarely are these things handled this well.

Hazardous waste sites came into existence by one of two basic means.

Sometimes, items of this nature were dumped there on purpose and within the scope of the law prior to the time that it was fully understood how bad the results might be for the environment. But just as often, they came about when unscrupulous people knowing full well the harm that could be caused, clandestinely disposed of these items illegally, either for lack of legal alternatives or to save the required and hefty fees associated with their lawful disposal.

Ways must be found to stop the repetition of this type of behavior.

Some have irresponsibly suggested that we "tax it at the source." By this, they mean to levy fines on all companies who produce hazardous waste. They are not referred to as fines, of course, but as surcharges or user fees. This equally punishes all involved manufacturers, the ninety-eight percent who are responsible companies, as well as the two percent who cause the problem. There is neither justice nor logic in this move. Our society, our government, must never be allowed to degenerate to the point where people are fined before the fact, and based on what they might do, in a catchall attempt to solve the problem. Removed will be the incentive to continue being a good citizen. If you are being fined anyway, lumped in with all the irresponsible, why bother to comply with difficult and costly regulations?

Our approach to this matter must be just the opposite. We must clear the way for the easy and inexpensive disposition of hazardous waste as the best mechanism to curtail illegal dumping.

Modern technology has given us many tools for this that we never had in the past: chemical and catalytic leaching of compounds, ionization and other methods where waste materials may be reduced to their less harmful components. We must put our efforts into seeking other ways to process these waste materials as an alternative to disposal.

Of those wastes where reclamation is either not possible or not feasible at this time, they should be stored in non-reactive containers awaiting the day when processing methods become available.

The facilities that should house these wastes must be located away from populated areas and in no proximity to water courses or aquifers. This service should then be provided at cost to those who produce such wastes.

At the same time, fines and penalties should be steeply increased on illegal dumping, so as to make proper disposal too attractive to pass up.

As for existing hazardous waste sites, they can be classified as to their degree of danger, according to three variables:

1. Toxicity level
2. Relation with respect to human exposure
3. Potential threat to underlying water sources

Each site should be dealt with in accordance to the threat it poses.

On a scale of one to ten, a level one—low toxicity, long distance from human encroachment, and no reasonable danger to water sources, can be virtually ignored. You may wish to put a rain-excluding barrier over the top to contain the waste and post signs to preclude accidental disturbance, but that's about it. No big expense. No reason to panic.

Worst case scenario is level ten—high toxicity or longevity, in close proximity to areas of high population density and either endangering a stream through runoff or an aquifer by percolation.

These are the ones which must be pounced upon due to the high level threat they pose.

At times, the most cost-effective solution will be to remove the people from the hazard, rather than the other way around. Costs of the properties to be compensated for must be taken into account. This was the first stage at "Love Canal," as it was the only practical direction to go in.

Other sites may call for total containment or actual removal. Containment is the best option when disturbing the toxic matter might do more harm than good. It can best be accomplished with the addition of a waterproof covering of several inches or more of heavy clay with a butyl-rubber liner as a top layer.

Sites which require excavation are those located over aquifiers or underground streams.

Less sensitive sites can get by with a covering of several feet of clean fill dirt. These can be reclaimed by the planting of trees. Some of the hazardous waste sites of today can become the park lands of tomorrow.

There are cases where not much can be done topside, but leachate is presenting a major problem. The simplest solution to a problem of this nature is the installation of low level sumps, whereby the leachate is pumped out on an ongoing basis, short-circuiting the substance before it reaches groundwater.

The most important thing to remember is that we must prioritize our response.

By taking a pro-active role in reducing future hazardous waste sites, reclamation and containment, dealing with this problem need not be an ongoing and expensive crisis.

If we do it right.

Section III:
THAT WHICH STEALS OUR SOUL

THE GOVERNMENT ITSELF
(A Matter Of Attitude)

Your perception of what the government *should* be is probably pretty close to my own.

Do we want a government that tries to be the be all to end all, no matter what the monetary cost and the invasion of our personal lives? Or is the function of government as we envision it to simply take care of things that would be impractical for us to attempt ourselves?

Few would argue that one of our governments proper function should be road maintenance. The alternative, if you can picture it, would be for each of us to get up an hour or so earlier each morning and start patching potholes, and resurfacing whatever amount of road outside our driveway is deemed to be our responsibility.

Far more convenient and efficient to pool our resources, in the form of tax dollars, and have the town, or state, or federal government take care of that.

Similarly our educational system evolved out of a need to address the question of efficiency in regards to schooling each of our children ourselves. It was felt by most that the hiring of professional educators to work with our children in a controlled environment was preferable to each of us taking that task upon ourselves. It must be mentioned here that recently that trend seems to be reversing as more parents find public education to be far less than adequate, and have returned to either private, or home schooling.

On the other extreme, this consolidation of effort and the shifting of responsibility to government can certainly go too far.

If shelling out tax dollars were never any problem and a "sky's the limit" attitude prevailed, we could certainly go so far as to have government employees show up each Christmas to relieve us of the burden of trimming the tree and wrapping presents for us.

There has to be a happy medium.

If we can forgo mud slinging and name calling for just a moment I'd like to discuss a couple of definitions.

A conservative is one who desires that government stay out of his life to the greatest degree practical and possible.

A liberal on the other hand is one who wishes government to involve itself in the individuals life to the greatest extreme. The further the better.

Taken to the farthest illogical conclusion the conservative finds he and all his fellow men totally fending for themselves, each on his private island.

Likewise the liberal in the extreme, creates a government where his every movement is decided by the governing body even so far as choosing the right toilet tissue color for him.

It shouldn't be too difficult for these opposite ideologies to come to a meaningful compromise.

Ah, but it is.

The unfortunate fly in the ointment is the government itself.

Once wound up and set off to work, the government, by its nature, tries every trick in the book to grow itself.

No longer does it find itself capable of listening to input from both of these warring factors (the liberals and conservatives) one screaming "shrink!" the other, "grow"! Because it feeds on its own growth coupled with an over estimation of its worth, government finds itself more often than not siding with the liberals who think that further government control is the answer to most anything.

Additionally, once it has built up steam in its quest for self growth (and self justification) it becomes very difficult to turn back the clock and return to a place of moderation.

So long as it is two against one, the government itself and liberals on the one hand, with conservatives on the other, there is no hope for a meeting in the middle.

To make matters worse, the laws of economics come to the aid of the liberal persuasion.

When they vote to spend more money for any given program, they don't just vote to spend their money, but yours as well. In addition this spending of your money at their behest further weakens you economically, leaving you less capable of fighting back. Raise my school taxes for instance to pay for yet another pie in the sky program and I have but two choices. Work more hours to cover the additional expense, or lose my house. Both are disgusting alternatives. If I lose my house I am nowhere. But if I put in the additional hours required to raise the money, where will I find the time and energy to fight this unfair system? A conspiracy of natural progression. There is one last bit of poison which has been placed in our well.

Each time that the implementation of "more government" fails, far too many people swallow the faulty logic that it was because "we didn't go far enough"

Gun control is just one example. There was a time in our history when virtually anyone who was so inclined could own a gun with no restrictions.

Everything went along smashingly for a while until some bad people who had guns, shot some good ones who did not.

"We've got to do something" non gun owners said.

Allowing the logic that criminals are criminals to escape them, this group managed to get some restrictive gun laws passed.

Quite naturally honest citizens obeyed these laws, and just as naturally, criminals did not.

As one might expect, crime figures remained the same and so the logical answer was to pass more restrictive laws.

For some reason those of a criminal bent continued to ignore the law, but those who created the laws still didn't get the message.

Increased fees, fines and penalties were inflicted on the law abiding citizenry who owned firearms, and then something interesting began to happen.

Mr. Honest gun owner began to decide that it just wasn't worth the hassle and expense, and gave up gun ownership.

Never having obeyed any of these laws, Mr. Criminal quite predictably continued to keep his illegal firearms and prey on society, but with a twist.

He now sensed that the armed citizen was no longer the threat to his illicit livelihood that he had been in the past. The criminal began to broaden his activities, and act more boldly, secure in the knowledge that there was little likelihood that future victims would posses the means and ability to resist.

Of course the crime rate soared. This despite, or we might more properly say *because of* ever more restrictive gun laws.

This same ridiculous battle continues to rage on today.

Those who push for more government control still "don't get it"

This has been but one example. As with most things in regards to government, overly restrictive control only seems to create the need for more control.

As this country moves further toward socialism, an idea whose time has *passed*, the resulting pain and suffering it causes only seemed to bring cries for more of the same. "We simply didn't go far enough" they say.

Yes we need control all right. We need to learn how to control the government not the other way around!

But I'm afraid that things are destined to get much worse before they get better. It is only when those who are in favor of big government have a change of heart that things may get turned around.

I only hope that by then it won't be too late.

Government Mandates

The large group of tax protesters has gathered around the podium. From its elevated position speaks the county executive. In whining tones he explains to them why nothing can be done to reduce yet another whopping increase in their taxes.

"You've got to understand," he pleads, "seventy-five percent of all these programs are mandated by the state. There isn't a thing we can do about them." As usual, he is lying.

Only one of two possible things get in the way of his ability to get around these burdensome mandates. Either his lack of creativity and imagination, or the fact that he really has no desire to. Passing the bill on to the suckers gathered around him has always been easy enough anyway.

Politicians have a way of making a term like "mandates" sound as if it were some form of unbreakable natural law such as gravity, or having Wednesday always follow Tuesday, but it simply isn't so.

The way it usually works is this. The state legislature passes a law, and we foolish sheep just go along with it as if we had no alternative. Ah, but we have.

What would happen, for example, if the state were to pass an edict that all counties must remove all stop signs, and replace them with very expensive traffic lights? Although the cost to a county could easily run into many tens of millions of dollars, the state would expect them to comply, and with naught but a whimper, they traditionally would.

Let's examine now what would happen if, for instance, one of those countries would refuse to go along.

Not being able to allow a challenge to its power to stand, the state would come down quite hard on such a county. First it would threaten, and then it would make good the threat to cut off *all* state funding. That's right, the state would deny the counties the very funds it drained from them in the first place. Quite a plot, isn't it!

Now think what you could do if you were able to organize all the counties to stand up to the state as if one, and say "No! We will no longer stand for your bullying, no longer obey your every whim."

What sort of sanctions could the state place upon all of its counties? Call out the national guard and have every taxpayer shot? I don't think so. Cut off state funding to each and every county? Hardly. The counties could just stop sending their monies up to begin with, thus giving the state a taste of its own medicine. It is only when we act together as a unit that we are able to overcome the divide and conquer tradition which has helped the state keep the counties under their thumb all along.

Implemented like this, the new power exhibited by the counties would prove to be a force which the state would have no alternative but to address.

The result? Fewer imposed mandates, and the encouragement of county input into such matters in the future. Lower taxes, and a freer society as well.

The same principal could be extended elsewhere through all levels of government. All it takes is a little creativity. Something your county executive knows nothing about.

THE ELECTORAL COLLEGE
(And The Need For Runoff Elections)

One of the greatest frauds ever perpetrated against the American voting public is the electoral college. Many misunderstand, and so downplay the impact of this system. I cannot tell you how many people have said to me that since the choice of this body is most usually in agreement with that of the popular vote that there is little harm in its existence.

These people never stop to consider that in reality the electoral college picks every president, and the popular vote either agrees, or it does not.

In effect we have no vote. On those occasions where it would appear that the popular vote has chosen the leader, that is because the result is the same as that which the college wanted anyway. If the potential even exists whereby the popular vote can be overridden (as it has been), your desires become irrelevant. Your vote is a waste of time under this system, and you are being treated like little children. Foolish children in fact, for most of us still believe that we do the electing.

Nearly as bad is the fact that the electoral college allows the news media to present us with a slanted view of events. As interesting example of this is what occurred in the 1992 presidential election.

The Electoral College

Bill Clinton was elected president by forty-three percent of the popular vote. He was declared the winner despite having received less than half of the votes cast, and this due to an unusual three way split in the election. But all the papers, all the news programs reported to the American people and to the world that he had won by a landslide. Where was this landslide? In the electoral college, of course. This alone should point out how out of touch they are with the American people, as is the news media.

The electoral college serves no good purpose, and like all useless and obsolete institutions, it must be done away with.

The Presidential election of 1992 should have taught us a good lesson if we had paid attention and were willing to learn. For the first time in recent American history a third party candidate, Mr. Ross Perot, garnered a substantial portion of the popular vote. The one in five voters who supported him caused the man with the most votes, Clinton, to win the election with less than a majority of the votes as I've noted above.

What will happen in the next election? Will we have four viable candidates? Five? Six? With six serious contenders it becomes quite possible for the country to be run by a man who less than twenty percent of the electorate voted for.

In the future we must change the way we hold presidential elections. Not only must we eliminate the electoral college, but we must institute runoff elections anytime that no candidate receives more than fifty percent of the popular vote. Only in this manner can we ensure that despite our differences and political desires we will have a government headed by a person that at least half the people wanted.

A runoff election under these circumstances will involve only the two candidates who received the most votes. It would more properly reflect the wishes of the people and make it easier to galvanize the people as a whole behind the chosen leader. It will otherwise be difficult at best to muster support for a man who most people did not vote for.

These two moves I have shown in this chapter were designed to instill in the voting public a renewed sense of hope. Hope that we can return to a day when Mister Average Man felt that he was more a part of the process, where he exerted more influence over those who purport to serve him. The new found confidence this could bring to the citizens of this country should not be discounted.

As I have stated many times before, anything that works toward the proper empowerment of the people as a whole can't be a bad thing.

The Homeless

Again, we have been fed a big lie. Lord, they must chuckle each time they put this one over on us.

Whenever the subject of homelessness comes up, the first and last thing out of their mouths is "low income housing." What is wrong with Mr. Politician Man? We are not talking about people living near the poverty line. These are not people with minimum wage jobs. These are people who are destitute, without jobs, or the skills needed to get and keep a good job. Low income housing doesn't help them at all. These people would truly require no-income housing.

Typical of our politicians, you tell them you need a fish, they hand you a smokescreen.

The most important thing these people need is meaningful employment.

The government has proven itself incapable of producing jobs except a the taxpayer's expense, nor should it even be in that business. If the government should get involved in this at all, its role should be to gently nudge private industry toward that end. The emphasis is on "gently."

Financial incentives in the form of tax breaks should be afforded businesses who take on additional employees. By giving such businesses solid reasons to hire, everyone benefits. A slight temporary reduction in reserves will quickly be offset by the income and FICA taxes paid by these new employees. Taxpayers are added to the rolls, down the line sales tax is paid, the economy is further strengthened by their purchases as well as the production of their new jobs.

By providing jobs to them, those who we now refer to as homeless would soon be taking care of their own problems.

Until we are able to accomplish this task, temporary housing will have to be provided. Once again, our government has gone about this all the wrong way.

Most of us live in houses. Usually quite nice houses. The homeless by definition live out on the street. Their abode may vary from a park bench, subway terminal, alleyway, or the doorway of a storefront which has been closed for the night.

As a temporary solution, shelters had been set up. On too many occasions these shelters were soon closed down due to not meeting certain standards with regards to sanitation, etc.

A curious thing, isn't it? Taking someone from what you or I may consider substandard conditions, and quite logically throwing them out into the street?

What may not be the perfect abode for you and I may very well do quite nicely for someone who has no other alternative. In any event, shouldn't that decision be made by the victims in this scenario, the homeless themselves, as opposed to some fat-cat bureaucrat? While an overcrowded, somewhat unsanitary place may not be the best of all possible worlds, it could be the best of the available choices. Please don't forget that what we are talking about here are temporary quarters.

Additional temporary housing might be provided by a sweat equity program where the skilled among the homeless could restore the many vacant city buildings that today lie boarded up and useless. This would probably have a wonderful snowball effect. Those with the carpentry and other skills would be doing the renovating, while training those under them to be their eventual replacements. Having proven themselves competent, and depending on the economic climate the job market would become more rapidly accessible to those who were so recently unemployable.

A number of these buildings would be candidates for total renovation, and become salable once again when finished. Some of the apartments could be retained for superintendent quarters as in buildings of old, when the super got his apartment and a small salary in exchange for performing basic maintenance on the other apartments. The city, the formerly homeless individual, the taxpayer, and the suppliers of building products all benefit under such a plan.

But what is to become of all the homeless who possess no skills?

Many years ago it was common in towns across the U.S. as well as the rest of the world to have a town square. This quaint place was a gathering spot, meeting place, a spot to exchange gossip and post a bulletin board with items of public interest. It also served an excellent public function. For those needing work it was the place they hung out looking for it. For farmers, masons, carpenters, and nearly any enterprise in need of laborers, it was the place to pick up workers. By a loose but effective arrangement, those seeking employment would show up at a certain hour, usually staying until shortly before noon. Anyone needing to hire workers on a seasonal, part time, or casual basis would come in and offer employment. The numbers did not always match up, but to the degree that they did everyone benefited.

This is a system we should return to. Although most of the available work offered would by nature be raw labor at low wages, it would be employment, and employment is what these people are in immediate need of. The important thing is that this system would recycle the homeless back into society. It would be the first and most important step to returning them to the goal of self-sufficiency.

The last but perhaps most important thing we can do to stop homelessness is to address one of the main root causes: overtaxation.

If people who rent and are living close to the bottom line could recoup twenty percent of their earnings, money the government now steals from them (yes, steal is a term we use when someone takes something without permission), it would go a long way to insuring that their lives would not be pitched into the abyss.

If people who own their own home were no longer permitted to have it confiscated from them for non payment of property taxes, we would avoid another type of travesty.

Speaking strictly on a moral basis, how can we raise a citizenry expected to make their living by the sweat of their brow, pay taxes on a portion of their income, provide goods and services to the community, pay sales tax on purchases, utility and fuel tax, and then when for whatever reason they fall on hard times and can't pay the yearly tax imposed on a house that they own, steal it from them, and then throw them out into the street? Is this the society we wish to be?

This must be the cruelest form of homelessness there is; that which we have created through our unfair tax system.

At the same time that we reach out to those who are now homeless, with the programs that I have outlined above, we must do something to alleviate these unnecessary and burdensome taxes. Only in this manner can we stop adding new people to our homeless problem to replace those who we are successful in helping.

Racism

There are a great number of things which mankind can do better than nature. I am aware that among the lunatic fringe who refer to themselves as "environmentalists" that this statement will be regarded as heresy and considered just cause for lynching me, but I stand by it nonetheless.

Take for instance the manner in which "mother" nature deals with her trees. Few species of trees are what arborists refer to as self-pruning. In the natural world, it is normal for a tree to grow from the top, and with the passage of time, fill out. This filling out causes a natural progression of reduced sunlight reaching the lower branches which in most cases then die, no longer earning their keep as it were, and capturing enough sunlight to properly benefit the tree.

After these branches wither and die, they are eventually sloughed off by the tree. This leaves a branch stub which will finally rot off, allowing the bole of the tree to heal at that point, and leaving a scar. Please note that the operative words here are "finally" and "eventually." For in the world, time is seldom a determining factor for change, but it may be a considerable component for cause and effect.

While the tree seems in no hurry for the branch stub to begin the healing process, insects and disease waste no time in taking advantage of the opportunity to enter a tree thus wounded.

What you end up with is a race wherein the tree attempts to heal before unhealthy factors enter in to jeopardize its life, while the insects or disease (primarily fungus) attempt to gain entry through the branch stub wound before healing is completed, and the window of opportunity is closed.

The tree often loses.

When a forest technician on a regular maintenance schedule prunes off dead or dying branches close to the trunk of the tree, he is going nature one better. That is from the standpoint of the tree.

Properly pruned, the place from which the branch was removed will heal over correctly years before it might have if nature had its way. The result is a stand of trees possessing a much improved overall health and vigor, generally free from disease and accompanying insects. Score one point for mankind.

Now step back from the aforementioned stand of trees for a while until you can see a bit more of the forest.

Again, in the natural world, many forested areas occur in pure stands due to any of a number of natural factors. Erosion down to mineral soil, the overshadowing of a climax forest, forest fires and bottomland flooding by beavers are just a few of these. Any of these factors may result in one dominant species taking over an entire area.

When man comes along, he usually aims for a more diverse forest structure in both age spread and species represented. This he achieves either through planting or by various silvicultural practices. These diverse forests will be less susceptible to suffering total loss through major insect infestation, disease, or even wildfires.

The natural forest on the other hand, where pure stands of only one specie often occur, may suffer total loss when an opportunistic and parasitic insect like the Sawfly, or a fungus such as Dutch Elm disease, comes into play. Man hedges his bet, as it were, by having several species occupy the same tract of land. Many of these species will not succumb to the same problems. Rack up another point for mankind.

Now let's delve into a little anthropology, shall we?

Primatologists are now telling us that we have long labored under an immense weight of false information with regard to chimpanzees, man's closest relative. Nearly everything we have thought about them, and indeed would prefer to think about them is inaccurate.

Wild chimps, in organized groups, and with malice aforethought, hunt, kill, and eat several species of monkeys. Not content to leave us only thus disturbed, they do, on occasion, resort to cannibalism. This usually takes the form of their ripping an infant chimp away from the breast of its horrified mother, killing it, tearing it limb from limb, and devouring it while Mom looks on helplessly.

Mating season seems to be accomplished in any manner save monogamy, with most of the males of the group taking their turn with any female who is in season.

A hierarchy is established by the dominant male first subjugating, through intimidation and violence, all the females in a group, and then each of the other males in turn. By this means a pecking order is formed with the best suited male as top dog. This whole sordid process starts over as destiny produces the chimp next in line to become dominant male, and so on it goes.

On occasion, and generally as adolescent experimentation, both chimps and their distant cousin the baboon interact sexually. This might be considered a form of bestiality in itself, for it is in fact trans-species coupling and incapable of producing offspring.

Chimps kick and scratch and bite and steal. They kill and cheat and in general, to put it in the words of those who are far more polite than myself, they treat each other and their fellow animals with a great deal of disrespect. Not exactly the picture you'd expect of cute and cuddly animals. They sound a lot like us, don't they?

But herein lies the major difference: unlike any other animal, and to the greatest degree, only man is capable of exercising conscious choice.

Inside the best of us but in differing amounts, is contained the desire to treat our fellow man in the worst ways imaginable. This concept may frighten us when at first we recognize those seeds of hatred and desire within us, but they do exist and are part of our basic makeup nonetheless.

The point in which we rise above the other animals is that also within us is a desire to suppress that part of us which would seek to kill and spoil and destroy. This compulsion is not nearly as natural as the first, and as evidence I submit to you that it is one which must be exercised. It is with *effort* that we apply the desire to do right and suppress the desire to do wrong. Wrong I define here as that which brings about pain, suffering, and destruction.

Pure and good thoughts are difficult to measure against themselves. They are more easily seen when contrasted to the actions they suppress.

You find a wallet whose contents would certainly better your position. A part of you causes you to return it anyway. You have an opportunity to kick an adversary when he is down. For the sake of peace and at possible future disadvantage to yourself, you do not take advantage.

Indeed, it is only that component within us, while at times with great effort, suppressing the desire to do evil, which makes it possible for us to have what we refer to as civilization.

As bad as this world may seem, and in fact may very well be at times, can you picture what it might be like if we all gave in to our lowest desires, indulging our most evil impulses? Picture this happening not just occasionally but as a matter of course.

Imagine a Bosnia, or wartime Vietnam the world over, and without even an attempt at or a desire for peace. A world of constant and widespread war orchestrated by the efforts of thousands of Hitlers.

But the world is not like this. Peace is the rule, not just a rare exception. I emphasize that it is not that we are better people than this, but simply because we make the conscious effort to get along with those whom we might not. Score yet one more point for mankind.

Now let me tie this in with our chapter title. It is my contention that racism is a natural, albeit undesirable phenomena. Sometimes people are taught to hate, but for the most part it comes naturally. To a degree this explains why it has persisted generation after generation. Even those people who are my ideological opposites still talk in terms of ignorance as being the main contributing factor. And what is ignorance other than nature not being interfered with by the learning process?

Hate, fear, prejudice and in fact all that is negative comes as natural to the human animal as they do to our tree dwelling counterparts.

This hypothesis alone can answer the question as to why government has failed so miserably in its attempts to stop or even reduce the effects of racism, anti-semitism, sexism, etc.

When you try to do something which is not your job, and that which you are no good at, you are of course destined to fail. Every attempt the government has made to end racism has resulted in the additional fanning of the flames of hatred and intolerance. Studies bear this out, the government is aware of it, and yet they persist in acting only in this one direction. One who is of a cynical nature might even come to the conclusion that they *want* to perpetuate racism. Could this be possible?

Affirmative action was instituted. It originally was meant as an attempt to right past wrongs by giving a slight edge to minorities in hiring practices. At first it was designed to work in the following manner: if the two top applicants scored the same on an entry exam, the benefit of doubt was given to the minority applicant. Unfortunately, the effect of this legislation was that for the small gain of a few minority jobs, a greater number of racists were created as whites rightly wondered why they were no longer hired on a performance basis alone. The non-minority losing the job opportunity wonders why his skin color was allowed to be used as a liability against him, and in fact why it was allowed to be used as an excuse not to hire him.

To those groups who had originally been repressed, this shift might seem to be a form of justice, where those who had been on top are given a taste of their own bitter medicine, that which the minority had to suffer with for decades. But from the view of those now displaced, those who had in the past succeeded in the job market, it seemed that they were being asked to accept the premise that the proper way to pay Peter *is* to rob Paul, or that two wrongs somehow do make a right after all.

You'll notice that the same liberals who we constantly hear screaming for more minority representation in every area of the workplace, would balk at the suggestion that perhaps they should just step aside and give their jobs over to "the oppressed" in order to accomplish that goal.

But that is exactly what they expect and oftimes demand be done to others than themselves, and all in the name of "equality." Note that everyone wants equality, but without exception, at the other guy's expense.

As if affirmative action were not damaging enough to both sides in the equation, the next move was to broaden its scope. Its definition was changed to give additional points to minorities on civil service exams, while at the same time going so far as to actually remove points from non-minority applicants' test scores. This of course made a farce out of the exam process itself while again accomplishing the purpose of propagating more racism.

The ramifications of such actions continue to spread like ripples on a pond as additional damage is done, all resulting from this one wrong move.

The taxpayers are, as usual, betrayed once again by their government, in no longer getting the very best people for their money, but rather a work force which was chosen on a curve, and specifically not for its talents, but rather to accomplish and advance a particular leftist political agenda.

Even the minorities which are supposedly to be helped by affirmative action are damaged instead.

That black man, Hispanic, woman, or handicapped individual who truly excelled and obtained his or her position based solely on performance will forever be tainted by the existence of affirmative action.

Those who work around this individual will always hold his presence as suspect if there was even the slightest chance that the person in question got to where he did as the result of some "program." Thus is every minority member stigmatized by being lumped in with those who have succeeded through dubious means.

As is too often the case, the government has in this manner created a system which does an enormous disservice to everyone. But of course it gets worse. Affirmative action even when broadened in definition just didn't take things far enough as far as our beloved government was concerned. With total disregard for the constitution, it was decided that we should go even further in the direction of reverse discrimination. This was done by two basic means, those being the quota hiring system, and racial or minority set asides.

In the case of quotas, the scam works thus: if an area is for instance twenty percent black, then blacks must comprise at least twenty percent of the work force. Any firm not having as its racial breakdown of employees a minimum of twenty percent blacks will be considered prima facie racist. It need not matter that when these jobs were originally created the neighborhood was at that time only five percent black. It also need not matter that few or possibly no blacks applied for the positions when offered. Tragically, it also is to be given no consideration at all the possibility that among the minorities who may have applied for any such position, that few if any were qualified. To those people who are in favor of this type of social engineering, it is of no relevance that a job which requires certain qualifications which we might expect to need the level of a post graduate degree to achieve, cannot be filled, cannot be handled by those who possess not so much as a high school diploma.

I am by no means advocating discriminatory hiring practices in the case where the applicants *do* meet educational or skill requirements. I make no excuse where this is the case. I am merely stating that it is wrong to place the burden of proof on the shoulders of the employer.

Jobs are one of the most important components of just what business is all about, and those jobs are precisely what businesses provide to a community, in addition to a stronger tax base. Government does not supply jobs. Government is not capable of creating so much as one single job, without taking the money for that job, again, from the pocket of the taxpayer. So just why is it that the government can't seem to let business get on with its job without having to put up with false charges of racism being leveled at them? Since government is of little value and in itself produces nothing but bills, is it possible that the motivation we see here is jealousy?

To take things to the next level, are you aware that the quota bill as usual exempts Congress from compliance? This is the sort of thing I mean when I refer to a "do as I say, not as I do" Congress. Why would they wish to hold themselves exempt from this or any other legislation? I'll tell you why.

They are an arrogant group which believes that the same restrictions, the same burdens, which it forces upon the general society, are too obstructive, too burdensome, for them to have to deal with or work under. But their conscience has no problem with imposing their will upon you and I. Under such a system, the natural result will be that with time, all burdens and restrictions placed upon the public will become greater, more painful and more objectionable since those who legislate will never suffer with the results of any of their defective thinking. In the preface of this book, when I mentioned that the poison which was killing the patient comes in the form of racism in the name of the removal of racism, this was just what I was writing about.

Racism is abhorrent, but it is not, nor should it be the government's job to try to put a stop to it. If, as they say, the proof of the pudding is in the eating, then the proof of what I am saying lies in the fact that government has so dismally failed in the attempt. And not just failed as you or I or any fallible human might fail at something, but rather, failed to the extent that all of its foolish programs have managed to bring about the exact opposite results of their stated purpose.

A Historical Perspective

Our public school system, which most of us have no alternative to in the education of our youth, has of late pursued the furtherance of a political agenda. While there can be little excuse offered for the past practice of enslavement of Africans, this is certainly no reason to allow for the deliberate misrepresentation of historical facts. The revisionist history taught in today's classrooms purposely leaves out many of the basic truths of that time. These truths, when exposed, paint a somewhat different picture of what had occurred at that point of our history.

In today's schools, you will rarely hear it alluded to that those who were enslaved were captured by neighboring tribes, by their own brothers and cousins, and sold to the slave traders for mere money or goods. It is not politically correct to remind students, or any of us for that matter, that a required component for this filthy business to succeed was the cooperation of other Africans.

These are the same classrooms which will not tell you that long before blacks were enslaved, and for a much longer period, whites were the subject of slavery. This happened not in America, of course, but rather in parts of Europe and throughout the Middle East. It is not my purpose here to play the game of "who was the biggest victim," but simply to try to bring all this information out into the open.

According to history, it wasn't until the supply of white slaves ran thin that the trade turned its eyes toward Africa. I cannot say if this was due to the necessarily higher costs, the language barrier, or if Africans were believed to produce inferior workers. Perhaps this was even an indication of some racism at the time, and that slave owners preferred not to have black people around. We'll probably never know answers to these questions, as modern educators seem willing to deny the whole affair.

In recent times, those in America who call themselves black leaders further distort history. It is interesting that they call *themselves* black leaders since they were neither elected nor appointed to the position. The black community was never polled to see if they are in agreement with these charlatans, and indeed there is much reason to believe that their thoughts on any given subject do not truly reflect those of the black community as a whole. If this is true, unfortunately it is not for white society to remove them from their self-proclaimed positions. But rather it is the duty of blacks to band together as one, to stand up for their rights to proper representation, and tell these troublemakers "shut up and sit down, you do not represent our views." Only time will tell if they possess the fortitude to do so.

These so-called leaders continually inflate the numbers in regard to how many Africans were enslaved. I am not here saying that it was right and proper for any number of people to have been so treated, but it is important to be truthful especially in history for a number of reasons. First of all, it is in and of itself, the right thing to do. Secondly, exaggeration and lies reduce the effects of that which is the truth. For example, if we say that there were one hundred million slaves, an obvious lie, some people will begin to doubt that there were any at all. How has that served the cause? Once you misrepresent the truth, many people will find it necessary to question just when you can be counted on to tell the truth.

I have heard black leaders make statements that there were as many as one hundred million blacks taken as slaves from Africa. A little research and some arithmetic will show you that this is a physical impossibility. At no time until recently in the history of the African continent did the total population even remotely approach this number.

The actual figure is probably closer to four million over a period of two hundred years. Again, I emphasize that were the correct number so few as one, that it could be by no means excusable, but that the barbarity of the system is just one more reason that we should stick to the facts.

You will also hear these supposed leaders state that fully one third of those who were brought to America on slave ships died during the voyage due to the poor quality of treatment they received in transit.

I have no statistics to back up what I am about to say, but I ask you to apply some simple logic to the charge.

Once a person has been reduced to the status of a mere possession, he becomes nothing more in the eyes of his owner than a commodity. A commodity, a possession which nonetheless has cost his owner a considerable amount of money. How do you treat your property? This was an investment. It is possible, but extremely unlikely that once you have purchased slaves that you would allow fully one-third of your investment to perish because you are either too lazy or too stupid to properly care for them during shipping.

On that subject, it must be mentioned that the shipping alone was done at considerable expense, and that it did behoove the shipper to see that as many slaves as possible made it to their destination both alive and healthy. Perhaps I just don't have a handle on this, but let me ask you, was there ever a market for either ill or dead slaves? I'm not saying that deaths did not occur, but that anyone with a bit of business sense would agree that the numbers are much exaggerated. I can only imagine that some would have us believe that *all* slaves perished on the way over.

Because I would like you to see just how far revisionist history has taken us, I must ask the question "What about Abraham Lincoln?"

While it is obvious today that certain black leaders have attained near worship status, it must be pointed out that if there was ever one man who deserved deification by blacks, it was a white man. Abraham Lincoln was a man who, despite not having any vested interest in the future of the black race, made sacrifices all out of proportion to those of any black leader.

He knew full well that his signing of the Emancipation Proclamation would start a war which would pit white brother against white brother, divide a nation, and cause untold bloodshed. And he undoubtedly knew the probability that it would cause his assassination, as indeed it did.

Revisionist bullshit aside, he did this basically for no other reason than it was the right thing to do. He was aware, and so stated, that it was intolerable that one man should own another. Against enormous pressure to do otherwise, he took up the cause of freedom on behalf of a race not his own, and paid for it with his life.

I can think of only two other historical figures who sacrificed greater. The second being Anwar Sadat who fully knowing that it would result in his death, did what no one had done up to that point. It was through his efforts alone that Egypt made peace with Israel. Egypt, Israel, and the world reaped the benefit of this peace pact, and Sadat alone paid the price. The president of his country, a man having everything, shot down in the prime of his life by his own people because of his selfless overtures for peace. May his soul forever reside in heaven.

The greatest example I see along these lines is, of course, the historical Jesus. I say the historical Jesus because I am not interested in debating on these pages, the deity of the Christ. That is for another book, another time, and not the purpose of this one.

In any event, he was the one person who willingly died, offering himself up to pay for the sins of others, not his own. Like these other great men of history, President Lincoln had it all, yet gave it all up for strangers, people he had never met and personally owed nothing to, when he could have most easily just walked way from the situation, it having nothing to do with himself.

Why is it that he is not the number one hero of black Americans? Could it be because it is simply not politically correct?

If we can be allowed to ignore the obvious personal sacrifice and contribution of Mr. Lincoln, then we can of course continue to ignore the actual historical significance of slavery and its attending results for modern African Americans.

This was a short and shameful period in our history, but it is our past. The pain and suffering of that era should not be allowed to be carried on into our future. The descendants of slave owners, and whites who have arrived on these shores after abolition have nothing to be ashamed of. They were never part of the problem, and should not allow a guilt trip to be laid on them.

Were I a very distant relation of past slave owners (which I am not), I would have no more reason to feel guilty than does a black man whose third cousin twice removed, who he has neither met nor heard of, has robbed a liquor store.

It's time we put that nonsense to rest.

The benefit to the descendants of slaves is never accounted for. There are on occasion examples where an evil perpetrated may lead to much good. The advantages of modern American life as they apply to the descendants of those who were once enslaved cannot possibly be compared to those enjoyed in any African country. In Africa, what percentage of the population own automobiles? Go on to higher education? Own their own businesses? Air conditioning, health care, the list goes on forever in the advantages that the average black person can find here and here alone.

If this is not true, then why is it that we do not see boatloads of blacks heading back to their homeland? Perhaps it is because, like their white counterpart here in America, that they have come to realize that this country, with all its faults, represents a considerable step up from the countries from which our roots originate. The same reason why no component of American society can be seen making a mass exodus back to the land of their birth.

Yes, the black man may have been brought over in chains, but he is in chains no longer. There is little reason that any black person today cannot be part of the American dream. The only chains which hold him down are the chains on his mind. These are most often placed there by the Sharptons, the Jesse Jacksons, and others who insist that he maintains his victim status, as it fulfills their political desires. After all, if you know that you are already free, how can any activist lead you on to a freedom which you already possess? Could it be that certain rabble-rousers would find themselves out of their jobs if their people caught on to a vision of their own true potential, and a realization of their actual position?

Oprah Winfrey, General Colin Powell, Bill Cosby and countless others must be embarrassments to the black leaders, for they stand as constant reminders to their people that a black person not only can make it in America, but make it to a level that anyone, black or white, would rightly envy.

It was reported, for example, that Oprah made sixty-three million one year. I wonder what her potential earnings would be in Africa? The black activists do not want you to think of that, nor the fact that her audience is predominantly white. Whose purposes do the black activists then serve? Certainly not those of the black community. It gives you something to think about.

The revisionists, the white liberals, and the black activists do not seek peace, but rather wish to heap more guilt on the heads of the white race *en toto*.

They work hard to see that you forget that not all American whites owned slaves or even sanctioned ownership.

Slaves were in fact owned by an exceedingly small minority of landowners, primarily in southern states. Even throughout the south it was rare to find someone who had both the land and the monetary resources to own slaves even if that was his inclination. The behavior of a handful of long deceased whites is being allowed to reflect unjustly on all members of the race. Is this not of itself the actual definition of racism? And yet it is our educators who either by their lies or by their silence allow the continuation of this. This is the very reason that America, all of America, white, black, and otherwise, is allowed to be held hostage by the improper and unending application of guilt which is not their own.

These same "educators" and revisionists don't want you to know that the antislavery movement was started by (white) Quakers in 1671, and spread to America by 1696. They would keep it from you that as early as 1652 Rhode Island passed laws seeking to limit slavery in terms and transfer. In 1807 the United States outlawed the further importation of slaves, although the ownership of existing slaves did continue for another sixty years.

Don't rely on a perverse educational system to supply you with the facts. For that matter, don't rely on me either. Research them for yourself. They are there for you to find if you are willing to dig, but don't just be sold a bill of goods by the revisionists.

In America today, the white race is reaping the bitter harvest of things they had no control over. The flames of hatred against them are often fanned by those I have mentioned as having an interest in seeing that racism doesn't ever die.

Everyone ignores the fact that there is not one white today, living in this country who has ever owned slaves.

Equally ignored is the fact that likewise, there is not one black alive who has himself ever been a slave.

Until minorities can see the wisdom in the necessity to forgive and forget the past, there will be little hope for their future. If blacks were not constantly reminded that their ancestors were once enslaved, they would be able to get on with their lives unencumbered by the past.

There are today in fact few descendants of those whites who were involved in the original problem. My ancestors for instance came over from "the old country" around the turn of the century. This is not the exception, but rather the rule. Most of American white society today is comprised of second or third generation progeny from recent immigrants.

I hope by now you agree with me about the stupidity of blaming a person for what race he happens to belong to. Again, I emphasize that the arguments which I have presented here are those that the revisionists and activists would not like you to consider.

Another weapon in the arsenal of those who would attempt to divide blacks and whites is the constant reference to supposed cultural differences. This is an enormous fraud and one of the greatest injustices perpetrated on the black race by those pretending to represent their best interests. You'll notice that these people continually refer to the term, but always refuse to define it. What cultural differences?

Blacks, whites, and others have been parts of the American cultural makeup for centuries. As a result, the culture which we all share has roots and components common to all. Of course as one might expect, the European influence is greater due to their much larger numbers. It is not we Americans who have produced this culture, but rather the other way around. It is the culture we have been born into and grown up in which has shaped and produced us!

Within the context of this American society, there are very few real cultural differences between black and white. Do we not subscribe to the same basic philosophy of law? If a black man were to rob a drug store, would either he or the community be justified in citing "cultural differences" as his defense? Of course not. The reality is that it is our common commitment to society which binds together our approach to that society without regard to the color of our skin. It is also that very sameness that tends to make us fairly good neighbors to one another, if left to our own devices, and not agitated by people of ill will. Next time someone brings up the myth of cultural differences, do not ask, but rather demand that they define the term.

Only by being responsible, employing logic as opposed to rhetoric or inflamed emotionalism may we band together to defeat the real racists in our society. And who are they?

For the most part, the most dangerous racists in this society, by which the worst efforts of the K.K.K. or the Black Panthers pale by comparison, are white liberals.

I beg your indulgence and patience at this point. I will be returning to the statement I just made, explaining it in full, dear reader, at the end of this chapter. For now, trust me when I tell you that white liberals are the largest enemy of all that is good about this country, as their vision of America is one which would necessarily destroy our Constitution, that sterling document which our forefathers had so painstakingly and lovingly crafted.

Not A Racist Country

You couldn't possibly believe what I have to say on this subject if your mind has been steeped in that dank and fetid tea we call "the network news."

It appears that racism and the attending destruction is going on about us at a crescendo level each day, if you can believe the news reports.

The other possibility is that the news takes enormous pains to ferret out what few racially inflammatory incidents do exist each day in our society (just as they do all about the globe) and by drama, commentary, and the free use of the instant replay button, make these incidents appear to be the norm.

I am in no way condoning the barbaric behavior with which on occasion we treat each other. Nor do I condone a suppression of the reporting of the news as it occurs in some vain attempt to keep the peace.

What I am condemning however is the laziness of the news promoters who find it to their advantage to report the incidents in such a manner as to keep racial tensions running high, keep inflamed the hatred we might feel for one another. Their carefully crafted phrases, skillful use of adjectives and penchant for gruesome and graphic detail serve to bring others into the fray who might otherwise have remained on the sidelines. When further fighting or even rioting breaks out as a result of their efforts, well of course, they get to cover that story too. That is what I mean about their being lazy. No longer are they satisfied with finding and covering a story. They have found it more expedient to create the news!

Let's have a look at the real America, the one we all live in each day, not the one falsely portrayed on the TV screen.

Do minorities have a chance in society today?

With the exception of cities like New York, which seem intent on driving out all business so that no one has a chance, the answer is a resounding yes!

In every county of each state, at every level of the workplace you will see minorities of every race and creed achieving the American dream. Admittedly, this may not be in the same proportions as with the predominantly white population, but these discrepancies are changing at a reasonable rate.

This change comes not overnight, but if you would indulge me for a moment, I would like to show you why it is in our best interest that the change be more gradual.

Most change, that is to say most change for the better, must come about somewhat slowly if it is to have lasting effect. The concrete which dries the hardest is that which has dried more slowly than it might. There is a sort of curing process to which speed is the enemy of quality. Any mason could tell you this, and steps are often taken to physically slow down the process so as to produce a superior result.

Now in terms of racial diversity in the workplace, I would say this. When non-minority workers are rapidly or even forcibly replaced by minorities, it gives understandable rise to enormous resentment. Exactly what do you say to placate the third generation fireman for example, who although he did well on the exam will NOT be allowed to follow in the footsteps of his father and share in that proud heritage?

It is easy to understand the feelings of animosity held by those who have actually been replaced but that is by no means as far as it goes. What happens to those who do not yet lose their jobs, but by virtue of what they see going on round about them, hold justified fears of what may very well happen down the line? They also are forced to become enemies of such change. Only when change comes about slowly, and through the devices of such things as attrition replacement, for instance, hiring a minority applicant to replace someone who has retired or moved, will resentment and fears have a chance of being exchanged for acceptance. After all, is that not the eventual goal in the quest for racial harmony? Acceptance in the work force, rather than mere placement in a job? It is only fair to point out that if you are willing to settle for the latter, that it will be this very thing which stands in your way of ever attaining the former.

The only problem from the standpoint of those who are waiting to benefit from this aforementioned change is that by this system it will necessarily take another generation or two. The one consolation I can offer them is this: it *is* happening.

If we were to plot a graph from the beginning of this century through to the present, we would see dramatic increases in minority representation in the work place. This graph, if projected for another generation or two, would show a society fully integrated to all reasonable extent.

Government mandates notwithstanding, I would point out that it is this type of true equality which is being achieved through the efforts of the people of our nation. Whereas there are and will always be small pockets of resistance, I must point out that the American people and business as a whole are trying to do what is right.

As you will see elsewhere in this book, I do not subscribe to that foolish half-full, half-empty allegory on optimism versus pessimism. Nonetheless, I would like to give you a fresh approach for looking at things in a different manner. While the media's purpose is to continually point out to you just how much farther we need to go to secure equality, it is I who choose to remind you how far we have come.

They wish to keep your focus on the mountain still before you which we have yet to cross, while I seek to remind you of the several mountain ranges we have already traveled over. I do this not to lull the reader into a false sense that all is well, but rather to inspire you with the knowledge that past accomplishments should give rise to future hopes. This is where your focus should be. The media, however, is not content unless you are made to be continually unhappy with any progress you may have made.

At times these people would point out to you that while unemployment in certain areas is at the six percent level, in that same area minority unemployment approaches nearly twice that, standing at eleven percent. I would bring to your attention that it would never suit the media's purposes for you to think in terms of the minorities in this area as being eighty-nine percent employed. They dwell instead on the disparities, but to what purpose? Could it be that they wish to heighten racial tension, that they wish people to be continually unhappy? It's certainly something to ponder.

A realistic prognosis for minority success in America? Good and getting better all the time.

I have up till now only pointed out the gains made by the average person of minority status, in average America. My purpose in doing so is that average America, that is to say the middle class, is where most of us live, and where advances made have had the greatest impact.

I would now like to direct your attention to that which is less important, but still worth mentioning. The Superstars. Bill Cosby, Michael Jordan, Geraldo Rivera, General Colin Powell, Janet Jackson, Connie Chung: dozens or possibly hundreds of mayors and other high ranking officials, Sally Jesse Rafael, Whitney Houston, several presidential administrative appointees, Supreme Court justices, entrepreneurs, etc, etc, etc. The list seems endless. Make your own list if you don't like mine.

There remain few areas which we in middle class America consider to be the top, that do not possess considerable minority representation. This of course includes Hispanics, women, blacks, Jews, and any other group that our media elite would have you believe do not stand a chance at success in our "oppressive" society.

And the areas of this super success cover nearly all the bases as I have pointed out. The military, politics, sports, entertainment, business, and so forth. If there exists a gold ring to be plucked by those of us riding the carousel of

American life, all of us are open to the potential of being the one who may someday grasp that ring.

Those who I have mentioned as well as those who you may wish to add to this list have two things in common. The first is that they owe a huge measure of their success to undeniable talent, hard work, drive, and ambition. A willingness to strive to achieve, and damn the consequences if their best efforts are met only with failure.

The second and at least equally important component of this success is without question the overwhelming non-minority support.

As clever as Bill Cosby may be, I would point out to the reader that if he didn't enjoy considerable acceptance from predominantly white audiences, that his success would have been severely limited. If white people did not attend basketball games in large numbers, stars like Michael Jordan would have heard the sound of the basketball they are dribbling, rather than the enthusiastic roar of the crowd as they run down the court. Were it not for white voters, no minority candidate for office would stand a chance supported only by the votes of those of his or her own race.

It is with the overwhelming support of a white majority that the types of superstars which I have mentioned have attained the pinnacle of the profession which they have chosen. Where else in the world will you find such opportunity, and the fulfillment thereof?

I do not at all say that we do not have some distance to go on our journey, but America as a racist country? Not at all.

Before I move on, I wish to make just one further point in this area. France. Since the beginning of this century, France has been known to particularly embrace blacks when it comes to artistic expression such as song and dance. It was our touring American black performers who returned to us from

France touted as divas due to the obvious acceptance they enjoyed while over there.

This type of acceptance in France is often alluded to by those who would have you believe that America is by comparison living in the Stone Age.

I'd like you to notice that despite the commercial success enjoyed by some in this, the land of art and wine, that other than in the realm of the stage, acceptance is extremely limited. How many blacks have made it anywhere in French politics? How many rank high in the French corporate structure? Where else other than in the performing arts do we see any minority representation? Nowhere. It would do us well not to compare ourselves with France.

As a last evidence that we are not a racist country I offer you the following: the nature of the anti-racism movement itself.

The very fact that we of this nation both hear and encourage an anti-racist voice is proof of the good intentions of most of our citizenry. Were we by and large racists, we would never stand for advancements in the area of race. It was the large white population who fought the civil war. It was the white population who supported the civil rights movement, who supported Judge Clarence Thomas, who are outraged into action when they see racial injustice. And it is the white majority who should be given credit when any measure of success is achieved by groups such as the N.A.A.C.P. I hate to burst their bubble, but regardless of their enormous efforts, the key to their success lies in the agreement which they have found within the white community.

The Real Racists

As I promised earlier, I will now explain why I claim that liberal whites are far more dangerous to future race relations than any other group in America.

In the last segment of this chapter, I alluded to the irresponsibility of the media in its biased reporting. When we turn on the news, are we not desirous of gaining a non-slanted reporting of the facts regarding what has occurred on any given day? Do we want news which brings forth historical and factual content, or would we actually prefer to be titillated with some individual's personal slant on things?

The very purpose of broadcast news was to be of an informative nature. By the clever manipulation of and at times the outright misuse of words, those who are supposed to report to us the happenings of the day, can easily succeed in shaping our perception of what they would have us believe are facts. And the news is for the most part run by the very liberal whites to whom I have been referring. While they may try to convince you that their political ideology is never permitted to get in the way of good, clean, honest reporting, I assure you that quite the opposite is true.

About ninety percent of all news reporters are liberals according to their own admission. Though they would deny that this has any reflection on how they present their news, I point out to you, dear reader, that their leftist leaning heavily flavors anything they might have to say.

Although I was never any great fan of Ronald Reagan, I ask you, when the last time was that you heard a news report linking anything favorable with him? Surely some good accompanied him?

On the flip side, please consider the administration of Jimmy Carter. Most everyone agrees that he was at best, a well-meaning but inept leader. Here was a Democrat who oversaw a likewise Democratic Congress, and still experienced the same governmental gridlock that we viewed with George Bush. During Carter's one term we saw high unemployment, record high interest rates, and twenty percent inflation.

His was a presidency so lame that it made the mediocre one of George Bush look like excellence incarnate by comparison. Still you would be hard pressed to find any news articles written on President Carter either then, or especially now, which report accurately the dismal quality of leadership he provided. The press seemed to cut this court jester every break. Why?

When was the last time you saw a news segment on gun control which did not present the foregone conclusion that we need a great deal more of it, and that anyone with opposing views were either idiots, or Nazis? Why?

Let me show you how similar biased reporting pertains to issues of race. While those from the leftist media would have you believe otherwise, conservatives want nothing more than to see minorities come on board. The melting pot as we used to refer to America was a vision of our nation which suited us well.

It was considered desirable both from the viewpoint of those on the outside and those on the inside, that as different races and ethnic groups join us, that they do to a large degree assimilate. Sharing their culture and values, art and idiosyncrasies with us, and us with them. We then move on as one to share a somewhat modified culture, and a future conducive to all our needs.

A thorough examination of the evidence will lead to the conclusion that the blame for our racial problems cannot rightly be placed on conservatives.

Then what about the minorities?

In their case (and here I am primarily referring to blacks), you can hardly blame them, either. They only want what most people want; the rights, privileges, and representation which they perceive to be their due. Well, perhaps a bit more when you add to it that which white liberals, at all cost, try to convince them that they have coming to them.

The blame for misrepresentation, exaggeration, oft times outright lies, and so forth belongs no other place than in the hands of the white liberals of whom I have been referring. And why? The reality is that they hate minorities, especially blacks. Think about the following for a while. When the unfortunate Rodney King nearly met his end at the hands (and feet, and clubs) of L.A.'s "finest" gone berserk, and the verdict pertaining to these officers did not go the way that mob mentality demanded, we had a riot on our hands. Several, in fact. I in no way condone what happened to Mr. King, but his treatment is not what I am bringing into question here, neither is the probable miscarriage of justice on which the riots have been erroneously blamed. I'm talking about the fact that during and after the ensuing riots, the news media continuously said, "You have to understand their rage."

I, for one, do not understand their rage. But I'll get into that in just a minute.

That statement about understanding their rage tells us one very important thing, and that is that the leftists of the news media do not think that blacks should be held to the same high standards to which we hold whites. And this is because those on the left, those "loving liberals" actually think of blacks as being just a bit subhuman. They would never voice this openly, but their behavior towards them bears this out. If all the details in this terrible incident (of Mr. King) were precisely reversed, would we have seen thousands of whites rioting? And in the unlikely event that they did, can you possibly imagine this irresponsible news media echo that same tired refrain, "You have to understand their rage"? Not on your life.

Why this major difference? As I said earlier, the reason is that those of the news media really have no respect for blacks. They do not wish them to be held to the same high level of accountability that whites are held to, because the reality is that underneath their thin veneer of "love" for their fellow man, they really do think that blacks are inferior.

You won't find this type of coddling coming from those on the conservative right.

It is only the liberal leftist whites who treat blacks as inferiors when it comes to accountability for their behavior. To further illustrate this point, let's look at what I mean when I say that I did not understand or condone the so-called "rage" which is in reality what led to the riots.

No liberal will ever be honest enough to say what I am about to.

After Mr. King was beaten, and the criminal justice system had let him down, if we had seen the relatives or even the friends of Rodney King, drag off, and beat to a pulp those police officers in question then perhaps I could have understood *their* rage. Mind you, I did not say I would agree with that behavior, but to a large degree I would understand what would have motivated it.

But that is exactly NOT what happened. And again, the liberals would never tell you this either.

What did happen was the following:

After the verdict came in, both blacks and others, nearly none of whom even knew Mr. King, rioted not against the police officers in question, nor against the judge or jury in the case, but rather against their neighbors, innocent shopkeepers, and other citizens. They burned and otherwise vandalized the properties of those who had nothing whatsoever to do with the problem. They looted neighborhood stores for no other reason than to steal, this act having nothing to do with any perverse concept of "their rage."

Of the more than fifty people who died for nothing in the rioting, not so much as one had anything to do with the damage to Rodney King. As a final twist of the knife, it is most likely that those who were killed were also outraged by the verdict. So what really happened here? People who neither knew, nor had anything to do with Mr. Rodney King took it upon themselves to burn, destroy, steal, and finally to kill people who they well knew had nothing to do with either King or the verdict.

Did anyone in the news media ever put things in that way?

Is not the picture I have just painted you an accurate representation of what happened?

Again, I submit to you that the liberal news media neither respects nor loves the very blacks who their words are so quick to venerate. The fact is that they despise them.

I want to tell you about just one more unfortunate incident in relation to the deliberate misuse of words, a misuse which causes much trouble.

In Brooklyn a rabbi returning from a cemetery visit accidentally ran over and killed a seven-year-old black child. This of course was tragic, as all accidents of this nature are. The reaction of the black community was to riot. Three days of rioting followed which again served no purpose except to hurt the persons and properties of those who were in no way a cause of the accident. A visiting Jew, Yankel Rosenbaum, was viciously murdered for no reason other than his race.

When reporting on this incident, the liberal news media again chose its words carefully. In their attempt to justify the rioting and murder, they said that Yankel Rosenbaum was killed "as retribution" for the earlier accident which took the life of the seven-year-old black child.

All of which raises one question. Since when would you properly apply the term "retribution" as a response to that which was an accident? Some reporters even used the term "retaliation." Again I ask, when do you retaliate for an accident?

Yet no one questioned this as I am questioning it right now.

Does not the misuse of terms like this seem to justify uncivilized and barbaric behavior?

Does this irresponsible reporting not serve to increase racism on both sides, rather than to abate it?

What is the true purpose for this kind of lack of journalistic integrity?

Some people in this huge industry, the media, want nothing more than to further foment racial problems. They are quite clever at shifting the blame over to those who hold conservative viewpoints.

Others are of a more insidious nature. They will stop at nothing in their efforts to not only report the news, but rather to create it, while again somehow blaming the conservatives.

If you are beginning to catch on to what I am saying here, I hope you can find it in your heart not to forgive these people. They know exactly what they are doing. They are the type of people who will gladly cause blood to be shed if it means an opportunity to cover another story.

The Answers

I thank you for your patience in reading all that has preceded in getting to this point. However, I felt that it was most important to precisely show both what is, and what is not the problem before I offer solutions.

The most important thing we can all do is to insist that the government get out of the business of trying to eliminate racism. It is no good at it; it fails miserably at the attempt, creating more of what it claims it wishes to eliminate, and it does not properly belong there.

The area in which government does belong, and where it would be best advised to direct its efforts is that of race relations. This is what my next chapter is about, and I promise that I will be keeping that chapter much shorter.

The second and equally important thing we can all do, which goes hand in hand with the first, is to take the responsibility of the reduction of racism upon ourselves. The questions which this raises are twofold, and ones which only you, the reader, can answer, for they are personal.

First, what can you do to change inside, and hold less animosity for your fellow man? Work hard on the answer to this one and the second as well, for they are of a deeply spiritual nature, and by that very nature not to be found within a government sponsored program, or any book you are likely to find inside a classroom.

And the second is like the first. What can you do to change inside, to help alter your fellow man's perception of you?

As I attempted to show you way back at the beginning of this chapter, I firmly believe that racism is a natural tendency and component of our makeup. That it is only through deliberate and purposeful effort that we can overcome that which naturally springs up within us, and grow on to be better people than we otherwise might, if we only follow our inclinations.

Again, I am not at all saying that growing up in a racist home will not make things worse, it certainly will. Nor am I saying that we are all innately rabid racists. No, rather that the component, that potential for hatred, exists in each of us to a very large or perhaps very minute and nearly invisible extent.

The next step is to properly identify society's biggest enemy in the war on racism, other than the government. That group, as I have said, are the liberals. The K.K.K. is not the biggest enemy. We know where they stand, and they make no secret of either their feelings or their agenda. I would rather have an adversary whom I can identify, standing in front of me face to face, than to have one at my side whom I had mistaken for a friend. In that case you find out too late, as the knife is plunged into your back.

The white liberals profess to be the only true friend to the blacks and other minorities, while in reality creating the root cause of mutual hatred and simultaneously pointing the finger of accusation toward the conservatives.

By no means the last thing we can do, yet the last thing I will list here, is to demand (not ask for, but demand) responsibility and accountability from the media.

Again, I say that it is the oft times purposely twisted stories they present which succeed in the mission of further abrading the wounds of racism.

We must demand of them fair and accurate reporting. And the proper use of words, not for some alternate purpose. A reporting of the facts as opposed to an attempt to sway opinion, and actually influence or create the news. We must demand of them the full disclosure of the facts, not a logic crippling selective reporting.

Oh yes, there is one other piece of information they would like you to remain unaware of.

Abraham Lincoln was a Republican.

Race Relations

As I wrapped up the last chapter I made the highly controversial statement that government has no business attempting to address the problem of racism. I will now say something which is more easily digested. It is in the area of race relations where governments efforts would best be employed, and in that area is precisely where government belongs. What is the difference?

Any approach toward attempting to end racism is a ridiculously foolish effort to tell people what to think, to demand of them how they must feel about each other. If racism is a natural, albeit negative inclination, as I have proposed that it is, any and all coercive attempts in this area are predestined to failure.

Furthering race relations however, is simply promoting the concept that in a free and just society it would behoove us all to learn how to get along, and this despite any hatred or prejudice we may have for our fellow man.

The government tries to change how you feel about one another while I merely attempt to improve how we behave toward one another. Whose plan do you think has the best chance of success? As a little aside I must warn you that in order for you to buy into the governments idea, you must first be prepared to swallow a great number of lies, which are racist in themselves, while the way I approach anything is to simply tell you the truth. And this is irrespective of whether you wish to hear it or not. It is more important to me that you hear the truth than it is that you feel comfortable about it.

I'll give you just one example of a necessary government lie which they have worked so hard to perpetrate on us.

They would tell you that any and all hatred which blacks may feel for whites is justified and only a response to hatred directed at them. Then they try to apply their version of logic and demand that you believe that any fear or hatred which whites hold for blacks is totally unjustified, a result of a foolish phobia held by an ignorant people.

Why do they wish to convince you that anything for good or bad can possibly be born and grow in a vacuum?

Unless the government starts becoming truthful about the causes of our problems it can't possibly be honest in its search for cures.

Worse than Don Quixote it will find itself not only tilting at windmills, but even tilting with the wrong windmills and moreover, losing. This is the natural result of not only deluding itself but outright lying to itself as well.

The manners in which we can improve race relations are many, varied and simple. Some will be difficult to implement but their essence is simple just the same.

First we must replace all of public educations failed attempts to control racism with an equal effort to foster good race relations. The multi-cultural nonsense's whole purpose it is to play up our differences, and it should be made to fall by the wayside as we seek instead to educate our diverse children to their overwhelming similarities.

We have an opportunity to get it through those not-yet-thick skulls that any race which they may hold a dislike for is not simply going to go away. Also that, like it or not, we are all forced to share this world with one another and the sooner

Race Relations

we get used to this idea the better. You'll notice that this reasoning is not rooted in any warm gushy feelings toward one another, but rather only in fact.

Much of the trouble in the middle East is not due to the hatred which Arabs hold for Jews. It is caused by the fact that the Arabs still think there is a chance that they can, to put it in their words, "Push Israel into the sea."

Were they to come to the conclusion that this just never is going to happen, they might instead direct their efforts to seeking a mutual, although probably uneasy, peace.

If we could convince ourselves starting with school children, that it is a foregone conclusion that we will all have to work, learn, travel, and live together, the choice between peace and constant friction becomes easier.

It is here that I would also enlist the aid of our churches and other religious institutions. To the degree that they are willing to do so, this same message should be going out from the pulpit. Not only could this reinforce what would be heard in school, but it would provide a degree of consistency.

I would even bring the church into the schools on occasion, but not in any way that would violate the separation of church and state, the crux of which forbids any imposition of a particular religion by the government.

Their purpose on visiting the schools would be to reiterate that those who already subscribe to various creeds have bound themselves to certain concepts and premises regarding their obligation of how they must treat their fellow man.

Additionally, those who speak eloquently from the pulpit could use their talents to read in classrooms those Scriptures which have none other than secular connotations with regards to this subject. In this way no ones religious rights would be violated.

Now I must again evoke that dreaded term "The media." For this is another group which we must bring on board if we are to further the cause of good race relations. We must see that they are held to a higher standard than currently is the case. The news must be presented in such a manner that it merely represents a factual retelling of occurrence. Sensationalism and editorial have little place in modern society. Because of the direction we have for too long been going in, the similarity between our daily papers and the supermarket tabloids is uncanny.

At this rate it won't be long before we seek our facts through the *National Enquirer*, and titillation from the main stream press.

I would be the last one to step on anyone's first amendment rights. Holding the purveyors of television, newspaper and radio newscasts accountable for accuracy and truthfulness in no way abrogates these rights.

Not every attack by blacks upon whites or whites upon blacks is racist in nature, and it should not be the purpose of the news to make it appear so. This is not to say that when prejudice is the motivating force that the truth should be stifled. All I am calling for here is a clear and proper representation of the facts. Uniting the media, schools, religious institutions and others will properly reflect and guide the direction that society would prefer to go in this area of race relations, and will accomplish more to bring about true justice than ever was dreamed possible.

Prostitution

There is, perhaps, nothing more demeaning from the standpoint of human degradation than the selling of, for sexual use, one's body for money.

In polite conversation, it is usually referred to as "the world's oldest profession," as if the antiquity of the practice must necessarily lend it some measure of legitimacy. Since Cain killed Abel near the beginning of time, I imagine that same line of reasoning makes murder desirable as well.

Those on the outside of the problem of prostitution quite often glorify the system and the activity, as does Hollywood in general. Yet for those who are living the hellish nightmare of human bondage, the experience is anything other than glitter and gold.

Recent films, *Pretty Woman* in particular, bend the truth, stretching it to the point of painful breaking in order to present an illusion quite disconnected from reality.

The heroine of this film is a good-natured hooker who uses no drugs, carries no diseases and of course, finishes off this great charade by marrying the movie's version of Prince Charming.

The movie was a box office hit, received very favorable reviews and drew few, if any, negative comments.

Those of us who are of a more conservative leaning tip our hats to the ex-wife of comedian Steve Martin. She was the only one I recall having the gumption to decry this film's attempt to sanitize and glorify the sordid lifestyle of prostitution.

Emotions aside, what are the facts? With the exception of most of Nevada, prostitution is illegal in the United States and for very good reason. Accordingly, statistics which can be relied on for accuracy are sadly lacking. Due to the nature of the "profession," many statistics are also skewed as to their genuine meaning. This leaves us in the unfortunate position of only being able to speak on the subject in somewhat broader terms than we would like.

For example, while there is no question as to a strong link existing between those who sell sex and illicit drug consumption, the exact percentage of that use is difficult to nail down.

In the larger cities of the U.S., the majority of prostitutes are habitual drug users. It is anyone's guess what percentage of these girls were driven by their drug habit into a life of working the streets, and what portion were pushed into drugs having first fallen into prostitution.

Since the use of crack has spread throughout our cities, an enormous number of young girls have been turned into hookers in a very short period. So desperate do they become for the next hit that the going rate for their services is ten dollars, just enough to purchase another brief high. This is a far cry from the lifestyle depicted in *Pretty Woman*. Obviously, anyone who will sell herself so cheaply is not going to "waste" a half dollar on a condom. Perhaps this explains why this new breed of streetwalker evidences such a high rate of venereal disease, including AIDS.

AIDS is the disease which has rocked the foundations of the world. Always fatal, it is spread primarily through sexual contact and intravenous drug use. For the prostitute who is addicted to heroin, morphine, methadone or other injectables, there is a double whammy. The percentages are working against her from two different directions, as they are for her clients as well.

The organizations which purport to keep track of such things give statistics varying from fifty to seventy five percent for AIDS-infected prostitutes living in New York City and the San Francisco area. My guess is that this figure is somewhat high due to the likelihood that most prostitutes who come forward for testing do so because of suspicious health indications. Yet, it is possible that the number given is actually conservative, since only those girls who are disposed to take any care of themselves at all will submit to testing. As I've said, hard statistics are difficult to come by and the exact truth is elusive.

Were it not for the presence of AIDS, could prostitution be cast in a more favorable light? Not really. There exists a plethora of both exotic and rather ordinary sexually transmitted diseases out there, just waiting to be spread by people engaging in this activity.

Chlamydia, genital warts, herpes (the gift that keeps on giving), hepatitis, the list goes on and on of the S.T.D.s that prostitutes can and often do spread routinely.

I will detail just a couple

The gonococcus bacteria causes gonorrhea, which attacks the mucous membranes of the body, primarily those of the sex organs.

Once contracted, it may appear to clear up all by itself, only to reappear later. It often attacks the eyes, resulting in blindness. In women, the disease may wreck havoc with the reproductive organs and should be of particular concern to pregnant women. At the time of birth, gonorrhea can be spread to the child and is the reason for the application of silver nitrate to the newborn's eyes.

Syphilis is a common venereal disease which, since the arrival of AIDS, seems almost innocuous by comparison. But left untreated, it can produce horrifying results and eventually death.

Treponema Pallidum is the interesting little spirochete which opportunistically invades the body through mucous membranes and breaches in the dermis during sex with an infected person.

As with many venereal diseases, syphilis does not manifest itself dramatically during the first stages, but this is when it is most contagious. Sores may or may not be evident where the disease first entered the body, but most of the serious damage is done in later stages if the illness is not properly treated.

The second stage of this disease is a period of apparent dormancy. Little, if any, outside symptoms are showing, but the illness progresses unseen, setting the victim up for the third and often deadly phase. The brain and central nervous system is most often attacked, commonly leading to insanity and, in many cases, paralysis. At times, the heart or blood vessels are targeted with the expected results.

Were S.T.D.s in themselves not a major problem, there would still be a lot to be said about prostitution, and all of it bad.

Many of the girls in addition to being hookers, are also garden variety criminals, engaging in everything from picking pockets to extortion to subsidize their incomes. The activity itself is often used to swell the coffers of both organized crime and non-organized crime alike. That man driving the pimpmobile—do you think running a string of girls is the only illegal activity he is involved in? Not by a long shot.

Blackmail, murder, kidnaping, drug sales, loansharking, assault—these are just a few of his sidelines.

Pimps guard their territories jealously and perpetrate violence against their girls, the johns, and other pimps on a regular basis.

A working girl without a pimp finds herself at the mercy of the streets. These girls are abused by their customers, other prostitutes, and pimps trying to recruit them. If they yield to the pressure to go with a pimp, they will get protection from most of the violence, the exception being the abuse they will suffer from the pimp himself.

The type of men who make their living by turning women into sex slaves to be rented out to any stranger with a few spare dollars, are never kind by nature. Regularly beating the girls keeps them in line, and besides, how else would they make the girls remember that they care?

Heaven help the prostitute whose pimp thinks she is holding back money from him. If she is not dealt with swiftly and painfully, the pimp will lose face with his entire stable. This will result in the other girls also seeing how much they can get away with. Forever the good businessman, most pimps will seek to reduce their losses by "cutting loose" the disrespectful employee. Her body will probably turn up somewhere, an appropriate warning to the rest of the girls that it just doesn't pay to mess with their old man.

Does any of this really remind you of *Pretty Woman*?

If we are at all going to have a measure of control of prostitution, we are going to have to start with a public education program.

The average citizen must be made aware of what the lifestyle for a "working girl" really entails. We must not allow the realities of drug abuse, physical and mental abuse, venereal disease, personal degradation and death at a young age to be glossed over by a Hollywood version bearing little resemblance to the truth.

Any idiotic notions that legalization of this trade will clean it up must be dismissed. Legalization can have but a marginally positive effect, as the drugs, violence and sexually transmitted diseases will, for the most part, remain. Also remaining will be that which is more difficult to measure. The emotional and physiological wounds run deep, so deep that some will never heal. With few exceptions, most girls will find it extremely difficult to recover any degree of self-esteem after submitting time and time again to performing oral or anal sex for anyone with a handful of dollars. Those dollars get spent, but the bad memories persist.

Once we establish a consensus that this is neither good for society nor for the women engaged in this activity (would you wish *your* daughter to be so employed?), we can go forward with a program which, although it will not eliminate prostitution, will reduce it meaningfully. I do not labor under the delusion that we can put an end to all prostitution, but we can rid our streets of a great portion of it and drive most of the remainder underground. When I speak in terms of elimination, in this case, what I mean by it is an impressive reduction, something along the lines of seventy to ninety percent.

Only when we decide to take the wholesale reduction of this business seriously can things start happening.

There are just two things which need to be done. Both are difficult, both are necessary, and nothing else will do.

The first is that this move for elimination must be a grass roots effort. Those in the political arena have failed us too often and so we must do an end run around them. Although most will admit that morality and ethics have declined considerably in modern America, more than half of our people still attend church or synagogue on a regular basis. Both mainstream Judaism and mainstream Christianity hold strong prohibitions on prostitution and their memberships should be easy to rally for this purpose. The best way to approach and inspire the members is to form a coalition comprised of recognized leaders from each faction and denomination. Church leaders like Billy Graham, members of the Archdiocese, and esteemed Rebbes across America must be enlisted for this coalition. These are the core people capable of motivating literally millions of Jews and Christians to stand up and do what is right. Those inert representatives in government will, of course, hate to address such a wide-based coalition and will attempt to denounce them under the old separation of church and state ploy. But religion, in this instance, will be the only practical impetus for this movement, for it is unquestionably a morals issue we are dealing with here.

Once formed, this group has but one purpose. It must remain steadfast and single-minded, not allowing outside agitators to infiltrate its ranks and cause its original goal to evolve into something else.

I mentioned that a second thing must be done. It is imperative that this group go on the offensive and demand accountability. Hookers are allowed to walk the streets with impunity for only one reason: the police look the other way. In most cases, they have been told to do so by their superiors. The patrolmen must be forced to make those arrests which fall within legal boundaries of existing law and for which they are being paid, or explain why not. In this manner, either things will start getting done or more likely, the buck will get passed up to reveal edicts which were passed down through the chain of command. Fine. Along each step of the way, accountability must be demanded until answers are arrived at and final action is taken.

As this process goes forward, laws must also progress to a point which is more reasonable. Currently, in many places, those convicted of prostitution pay fines from fifteen to fifty dollars, or after spending the night in lockup, are sentenced to time served. How ridiculous. We must insist that the punishment for this crime be more appropriate. Unless fines or incarceration are significant enough to take the profit out of the system, the same girls will continue to ply their trade immediately after release. This must be changed.

A jail term of thirty days is not out of line for the first offense, and may cause those so detained to give some thought before returning to business so quickly. A penalty this stiff might be enough to dissuade some from entering into this work to begin with. This period of time will also permit many of those addicted to drugs a chance to dry out, along with an opportunity to reflect on whether they wish to resume this destructive cycle.

As stated in my chapter on the Criminal Justice System, judges who refuse to pass heavy enough sentences must be removed. If appointed, they should lose their appointment; if elected, come under review; if on the Supreme Court, be impeached. However a judgeship is attained, there usually exists a mechanism by which it can be removed. No longer should the citizenry put up with judges who are soft on crime. They do no one a proper service, including the criminal. No longer should the police be justified in throwing up their arms, despairing over the fact that while they may do their job, the courts will not, thereby defeating their best efforts.

I also remind you of something else I touched upon in another chapter. On the subject of AIDS, I said that those who know they are infected with the virus yet continue to engage in sex with individuals who are not likewise infected, should be put away for the sake of the community. It may seem a drastic step, but when it comes to this disease, for which there is no cure, we should long ago have been treating in an appropriate fashion those who do not mind spreading it to others. Each infected prostitute can make countless victims out of her clientele before she expires from the disease herself. Further complicating matters, the johns who visit her will also be taking the deadly virus home to their loved ones. You can see how this problem has the potential to perpetuate itself, and exponentially so.

I am sure that by now, you have observed that many of my subjects, many of the chapters in this book, were meant to work together as part of a cohesive plan. I am well aware that nothing can have a long-lasting, meaningful effect on the problem of prostitution unless we address the subject of drug abuse, as I've outlined it in that chapter. Less girls on drugs, less girls working the street.

Before closing out this chapter, there is one more thing I must say about those girls involved.

I do not wish us to overlook the human component in all of this. Although I in no way condone illegal behavior, we must remember that the girls themselves are also victims in this seedy enterprise. With rare exception, the women who fall prey to this life do so in response to a combination of life-destroying circumstances. Broken homes, drug addiction, physical, mental, and sexual abuse, incest, poverty. This is just the short list of motivating forces which may result in anyone succumbing to the lure of the trade.

Our desire for them should be to restore their lives. This will not always be possible and will often prove most difficult, but the attempt must be made.

There is one organization which has been specializing in this effort with admirable success. The Mary Magdalene Project of Commerce, California, is a nonprofit charitable program that enjoys a success rate of over ninety percent. By selflessly providing these girls with a viable alternative to prostitution, there is no doubt that many lives have been saved. In order for a woman to qualify for the program, she must be at least eighteen years of age, have at least ninety days of sobriety, and be willing to participate in psychological services and screening by the project director, among other things.

Those who qualify and are prepared to work with the program are given food, clothing and household needs, medical care, individual psychotherapy, career counseling and job training, follow-up services and much more. All of this is provided in a safe and secure environment centered around a family setting.

Each woman selected for this program agrees to stay in the home for a minimum of six months, although it is common for them to remain for eighteen to twenty-four months. They are welcome to do this and all at no cost to the participants

The only thing I can see lacking in a program like this is that we do not have one in every city of every state. Completely privately-funded by charitable individuals, this program has managed to accomplish what our government never has: a high measure of positive results.

Due to the poor record every level of government has shown us, I do not wish them to attempt anything in this area other than to step aside while encouraging programs of this sort. People taking care of people. Nothing else, but nothing less.

Concurrent with our addressing the problem of prostitution as it now exists, we must also do what we can to stop the influx of new girls into the profession.

Recruitment comes in many forms. Runaways often see no alternative. To avoid that, we must reshape America to reduce the incidents where this happens. This I have alluded to in different themes throughout this book and mention in the postscript "The Renaissance of America" as well.

A misperception of precisely what the lifestyle entails is another component of recruitment. I have pointed this out in the beginning of this chapter with reference to the movie *Pretty Woman*. The irresponsibility of Hollywood in this matter must not go unchallenged. The pimp is, of course, the worst and most repugnant faction in continuing recruitment, and is the part of the equation most easily dealt with. Upon arrest and conviction, those who make a living at the destruction of another person's being, must be made to pay the proper penalty. I leave it to the readership to speculate on what this punishment should be. As with most other crimes, if we make the profit too low and the penalty too high, the problem tends to shrink out of sight.

If we take a stern and solid approach to the problem of prostitution, first getting serious about the need for solutions ourselves and then demanding that our government do the same, we can get a grasp on the situation.

No, prostitution will never go away entirely. There will always be some address that men will learn about when spoken of in hushed tones, and there is little that can be done about that, as long as the level of activity is low enough to avoid attracting attention. We can, however, look forward to the time when it is no longer prevalent on each city street in the "in your face" manner that it is today.

If we can reduce the problem to this degree, for all intents and purposes we can consider it solved.

Drug Abuse

Americas problem with drug abuse is multileveled and must be handled and attacked from several directions at once.

Quite frankly of all our problems this is the one we have the least chance for success in dealing with.

The key, and at the same time the main obstacle lies with you, the reader.

Drug abuse in America is so widespread that too high a percentage of our people either use or have used drugs in the past. This is so deeply ingrained in our society that there is too great a chance that even you, my conservative minded reader, might be counted in that number. With this as a starting point how much of a chance do we have?

You are usually prepared to hear me bitching about our inability to get Congress and their ilk off their collective asses, but what can be done if the stumbling block is the majority of the people themselves?

You, the American people, could very well be the only insurmountable obstacle.

So our plan has no alternative but to go forward while hoping to convince you to come on board.

Other than this the other obstacles are as follows

1) Addiction
2) Failed treatment programs
3) The obscene profit potential of the trade
4) Our inefficiency in the war on drugs
5) Proper punishment
6) Law enforcement and corruption
7) Drug producing countries
8) Interception
9) Our lack of participation in the war
10) Our committedness

Let us dissect these one at a time.

Addictions cure begins prior to addiction setting in. Money and effort wisely spent on preventative measures can yield far more than any cleaning up of the mess after the fact. Proper education is that important first step in fighting drug use and addiction, but it must be gone about in the right manner.

The damages and effects of each individual drug must be honestly put forth so as to present an accurate picture.

When I was in high school, fear tactics were employed and due to their inaccuracy and dishonesty they backfired. Marijuana, the least noxious drug, was portrayed as being much worse than it actually is. The result was that once a youthful experimenter crossed over that threshold and tried smoking pot he realized he had been lied to as to its effects and hazards.

He then erroneously concluded that since the establishment lied to him with regards to one drug, they must also be lying about the others as well. This in part explains the rapid transition through the gamut of "recreational drugs" up through the "hard drugs" which this generation experienced.

I am not herein condoning the use of marijuana or any other drug, but merely pointing out that we must be truthful in our educational attempts if we do not wish to do worse than fail.

We must also stop foolishly lumping alcohol and tobacco products into the same category as illegal drugs if we are to be taken seriously. Other than also being harmful and having addictive properties there can be little comparison here. I do not promote their use but wish them to remain a separate issue due to their dissimilarity to most illicit drugs.

In the education process we must use to fullest advantage the mountain of statistical information which has become available since the acceleration of the drug crisis in the mid-nineteen sixties. It should be no difficult task for the government to produce charts and graphs showing percentage of addiction, physical and mental damage, death, etc. as produced by any particular drug under study.

Through this means we could properly educate our youth as to the exact danger of drugs rather than that weak and hazy admonition to "just say no."

For those already addicted (at any age) we must provide treatment. As is proposed by that fine organization, Alcoholics Anonymous, "you can't help the addict until he is ready to help himself." This is certainly true. But for those who do recognize that they have a problem and have come to the point where they are ready and willing to take action we must provide the necessary programs and support.

We must provide drug treatment programs at no cost to the user. Voluntary contributions from the subject would always be welcome but lack of funds should never be the barrier to treatment for the user who wishes to become clean.

The return on this investment will be reduced crime, prostitution, urban street violence, disease spread, high insurance rates and taxes and will overall improve the quality of life for all of us.

But there are too many bogus programs out there. Eighty percent of all drug treatment programs have a success rate of only twenty percent. The remaining twenty percent conversely have a success rate of eighty percent. We must learn to jettison that which does not work. The successful programs must be identified and used as blueprints from which to reform others. Those programs which have little or no positive effect must be dismantled, then carefully rebuilt in the image of those which have been proven to work. To destroy the profit potential for drug dealers we must beat them at their own game. We must be aggressive in our attacks and no longer settle for putting a crimp in their style, we must destroy them.

Many of my compatriots even within conservative circles favor the legalization of drugs, an approach they believe will pull the rug out from under the illicit trade. Most notable among them is Mr. William F. Buckley Jr. I have only the highest regard for Mr. Buckley, even bordering on admiration. I agree with him on so many things, but on this we part company.

Whether by statement or by inference, if we legalize drugs we send the dangerous message "go ahead, it's OK we condone your actions." Speaking as a parent, the government-sanctioned legal availability of drugs frightens me. I do not wish it to be misunderstood by my children or others, legality versus morality. We run the very real risk that our objections to drugs (should they be legalized) comes from a puritanical background. We may be perceived as old fuddy duddies, out to spoil their fun when it can rightly be said: "After all, it is legal isn't it?"

All the free drug treatment programs in the world will not make up for those addictions created by sending the wrong signal through legalization. Rather than have my "cured" children have to endure possibly life-time cravings I would prefer they stay clean from the beginning. Both government and parenting must continue to form the bond, reinforcing each other in promoting the message "danger, do not touch."

I have my own solution to taking the profit potential out of the drug trade, but I want to warn you up front that of all the things I've said in this book, this will be the most controversial. It will not sit well with most of you.

Drugs which are intercepted from dealers should not be destroyed. They should be sold to known addicts who demonstrate that they have no interest in entering a treatment program.

By providing addicts with drugs they would have purchased anyway we do twice as much damage to the dealers. Not only do we deprive them of a months profit when we intercept a large shipment, but we can remove the income from the following months shipment as well, by stealing from them their customers!

I admit that of all my proposals this will be the most difficult to implement. If it proves to be totally unmanageable the idea could be abandoned but it is worth the attempt. Everything else that has been tried has a proven fruitless.

We will need a sophisticated lab to test the drugs for strength and impurities. Then a base of users would have to be established. We would have to create a trustworthy group to operate the dispensing clinic.

If we can make this program work, nothing will do more to destroy the profit of the business. Monies brought in through the clinics would be put toward further drug interception attempts. We'd be fighting drug dealers with their own money. Think how ironic it will be to the dealer who after losing one shipment to drug enforcement personnel finds that the very revenues produced from this are directly responsible for the loss of his next shipment as well!

An equal component in destroying the profit potential is meaningful punishment.

If you have read my chapter on capital punishment and find yourself in basic agreement with it you will understand why I'd like to extend the use of it to drug dealers.

If you have any recriminations about executing those who deal in drugs I'll thank you to remember that they deal in death everywhere they go. The users who die from overdose or AIDS, the police who die in performance of their duties, and the citizens who are murdered during drug related robberies are every bit as dead as if the dealer shot them himself.

Even as I sit here typing this, an event of this sort has really hit close to home. A young man in my locality was murdered for his Jeep. The human monster who did this was to receive a mere two hundred dollars for said vehicle—such is the value of human life. One has to believe that drugs were the motivating force, for it is hard to imagine that this crime was committed for beer money. This could just as easily have been my son who died so needlessly. It could have been yours. Who is ultimately to blame? You, if you use drugs and never question where they come from and how they are obtained. Again you, if you purchase stolen property without thinking that it has cost someone far more than you have saved. In this case it cost a fine young man his life. It will cost his grieving parents and friends for the rest of their lives. As for the dealers, these people have been the purveyors of death for years. It is only proper and just that this punishment be made to fit the crime. Murder wears many faces and the purposeful enslavement of another human being into a life of suffering and addiction, prostitution and theft, from which death is a prayed for release is certainly one of them.

There are two levels of drug dealers on whom I would impose the death penalty for starters.

The first is the high level drug supplier or smuggler who is himself not an addict. We must understand that the addict may be compelled to sell in order to support his habit. This does not excuse the act but recognizes that while a stiff prison term will be in order, the death penalty may not be warranted.

Let us also go after the money men.

Many individuals support the drug trade by supplying the great sums of cash necessary to make large wholesale purchases. Those who we can tie in with knowingly fronting the money for such purchases are also worthy of death.

When one hires a murderer to off somebody, he is as guilty as the person who is paid to pull the trigger, perhaps more so. Does not the same relationship exist between the dealer and the one who bankrolls him?

I am not of course talking about someone whose funds are used for drugs without their knowledge or approval.

As I said this is where we start. Death for the top dealers with mandatory lengthy prison terms for street dealers.

As time goes by we should then shift those brackets downward, imposing harsher penalties at lower levels till we squeeze the trade to death.

We must take the profit out of the system. If it can be shown that the chances of enjoying any ill gotten gains are slim indeed, the business will be far less attractive.

Too many people are being lured to the drug trade with visions of piles of money, two gorgeous women on each arm, and a Lamborghini for every day of the week. How many would still be interested for half the cash, one rather plain girlfriend who bitches all the time, and a three-year-old Ford Escort? Add to that a high probability of a waiting gas chamber and now who are the takers?

Another weak spot in our defenses is in law enforcement. As I try to make people aware, there is a natural order of things. If profits are too high for otherwise decent people to resist temptation, then corruption will occur. The solution is to rotate our officers in and out of drug enforcement. We must balance the time required to make an impact, with the point where too much exposure gives opportunity for personal failure.

A study must begin to find what the ideal time period for this rotation will be. My offhand guess is that it should be about two years. By making drug enforcement only a temporary duty assignment rather than a career for some officers, we can reduce to a great extent the number of occasions where police switch sides. With too many corrupt cops we have again lost the ball game.

There still remains a lot of work to be done with the political relationships we have with drug producing countries. Money is the bottom line and always has been. We must cut off the supply at its source at the same time that we look for ways to reduce the demand.

Countries which have major drug production within their borders must be cut off from free trade with us. If serious reform efforts get underway within the country, trade will be restored.

The potential loss of markets for their products, goods, services, and agricultural commodities should be enough to sway their decision to take seriously the major problem they are exporting to us.

Increased interception of drug shipments must be pursued. We must spend the funds necessary to beef up our Coast Guard in those regions of drug traffic, and Customs at our airports and seaports, these by a factor of two if needed. We must also give these services the latest in technological weaponry; radar, satellite tracking, drug sniffing dogs and possibly drug detecting machinery if it is developed.

There are also sociological changes we can make to reduce the demand. Many people turn to drugs to dull their pain because they are not happy with their lives. We must do what we can to reshape our society to be a more friendly place. What I am not advocating here is anything to do with socialism but really quite the opposite. Drug and alcohol use was at a record high in Russia just prior to its collapse. It is the oppressiveness within a society which leads to the frustrations from which we crave escape. We must reach for the renaissance of America I try to paint in my postscript. It is this large combination of factors which can be striven for which will cause people to pursue the joys of life rather than the temporary euphoria of drugs. And we must not fall into the trap of viewing any drugs as "recreational" or we will lose the battle.

Coming back full circle to the beginning, we need to build an organized citizenry. One that wishes to take this task seriously. The most important and yet one of the easiest things we can create are citizen driven neighborhood networks. The best communities are those which are so tightly knit that little if anything ever happens without swift knowledge of every member of the community. We must be more family oriented with the rest of our neighbors considered part of our extended family. When a member of our family starts to develop a drug problem it is up to us, all of us, to see that the person gets help as soon as possible.

When someone aspires to set up a drug dealing operation let us respond immediately and crush the attempt, showing no mercy. If we can foster this attitude and make it as pervasive as drug use currently is we will not only end the drug problem as we know it but will improve extensively the relationship we have with our fellow Americans. This can be an incredible side benefit to this approach.

We will never eliminate drug abuse entirely but by using the hard line attack I have outlined here we can reduce it by seventy-five to ninety percent. Anywhere near this figure can be considered a victory.

But it all starts with your willingness to get involved.

Let us truly make this a war on drugs. We must be willing to commit ourselves to this task as fully as we would any military conflict. Unlike Vietnam, Korea, or the Gulf, this war is being fought (and being lost at this time) on our own soil, on our own streets. Winning will be difficult but the cost of defeat is too steep a price to pay.

ABORTION

When two opposing ideologies are involved, there can be no just compromise.

On one side, there is a group purporting that it is a definite constitutional right for any woman to obtain an abortion strictly based on her desire to do so.

Those opposing, maintain that it most certainly is not a right, constitutional or otherwise, to take the life of the unborn, which is to them the center of this controversy.

Is there any possibility for a middle ground? In order to properly answer this question, we must first examine these two different views in greater depth.

In order for the pro-abortion or right to choose faction to allow themselves to feel the way they do, they must necessarily believe that the item they wish to abort is not a human being at all, but rather just a grouping of cells as they so often put it. You will notice that even the most militant within that group would never say that what they wish to terminate is actually human life, for to do so would be to willingly advocate murder.

Since in their minds, the question boils down to a simple removal of nonviable tissue, they believe it is within their rights to terminate a pregnancy should they choose to do so, and no one's business but their own. Moreover, they contend that since the outcome of Roe versus Wade, the Supreme Court has upheld it as a constitutional right. Indeed, should this be the case, being a constitutional matter puts it beyond debate and public decision since local laws by their nature may not be permitted to supersede constitution.

Also, by their nature, those who take this as a constitutional issue guard their territory vehemently. This partly explains why they are unwilling to compromise on the questions of a reasonable waiting period or parental consent. Their concern is that concessions in any area may lead to peripheral erosion eventually threatening the core principle. I am not supporting this as fact, only that it is their heartfelt and understandable perception.

Those who would restrict the practice of abortion are most often exemplified by those of the "Right to Life" movement. This group is concerned to the utmost degree with the life of the yet to be born fetus, and it is their contention that at any stage beyond conception what we are dealing with is indeed human life, and that no one (and quite often under no circumstances) has the right to end that life. They also illuminate constitutional concerns, primarily the rights to life, liberty, and the pursuit of happiness, and that these rights shall not be denied except through due process.

I mentioned that it is usually their desire that abortion be permitted under no circumstances because the key question is the life of the unborn as far as they are concerned.

When someone attempts to confuse the argument by raising the question of rape or incest, those on this side of the issue who are savvy enough, remind us that none of this negates the principle of the right of the child, a child who is to be held blameless, considered innocent without regards to how it was conceived. And that whereas it will be unfortunate for the woman who is so impregnated to have to carry this child to full term, that even these circumstances do not justify the elimination of the unborn's life in order to solve the dilemma.

It might be argued from this standpoint that anyone discussing the problem has already been born. They are enjoying an unfair advantage in that their decision on this matter cannot impact them in the same manner in which it will affect the unborn.

So do the right to life people say that abortion should be prohibited in any and all situations? They do not. If the life of the mother is clearly in jeopardy, then the decision to abort must be made. This long held view is rooted in the well established Judeo-Christian concept that existing life takes precedence over life which might or might not be. For many right to lifers, this is the sole exception for allowable abortion.

The case is also made for the right to life position that the purpose for allowing abortions; "every child a wanted child, every child a loved child," has simply not come to pass. Since Roe vs. Wade, there have been over twenty million legal abortions and yet it is clear that children are no more wanted nor better treated today than they were before. In fact, it would appear that quite the opposite is true. How can this be? Is it just possible that a society which views the termination of human life from the womb as acceptable, becomes insensitive to the sanctity of all life? And that by legalizing abortion, the precise opposite of what was intended happens?

When a society considers any innocent life (the unborn, the indigent, the aged, physically or mentally handicapped) as disposable, perhaps it lessens the respect for all life.

Although I am sure we have all come to our own conclusions as to whether or not abortion should be legal and why, I am not in these pages going to answer that question for you. What I do wish to do is to examine the law as it stands now, how the decision came about, what should be done about it and to what degree.

Everyone has, of course, heard of Roe vs. Wade, but few can tell you what it specifically means and on what grounds the decision was arrived at.

In 1970, Jane Roe (name fictitious), a pregnant unmarried woman residing in Texas, instituted a federal action against Dallas County. She claimed that Texas statutes prohibiting abortion were unconstitutionally vague with the restriction on abortion. Texas law allowed for the performance of abortion only in those cases where it could be shown that taking the pregnancy to full term would endanger the life of the prospective mother.

What Ms. Roe was seeking on behalf of herself and other women was relief from the law so that the way might be cleared for abortion on demand. Sited by her were many amendments to the constitution with particular emphasis on the fourteenth and it's allusion to rights of privacy.

On January 2, 1973, Supreme Court Justice Blackmun delivered the opinion of the court. The Texas statutes regulating abortion were struck down in a split decision of the court which determined that the fourteenth amendments right to privacy did extend so far as a woman's right to have an abortion. In actuality, the court recognized that the constitution does not anywhere explicitly mention any right to privacy, but that it is implied and may be interpreted broadly enough to encompass a woman's decision whether or not to terminate her pregnancy.

During the course of reaching its determination, the Hippocratic Oath was also examined with its admonition to doctors that they "will give no deadly medicine to anyone if asked, nor suggest any such counsel; and in like manner—will not give to a woman a pessary to produce abortion."

This was a sticking point for a while, but it was the courts' opinion that the Hippocratic Oath itself was only one point of view at the time it was written, and therefore not an unbreachable philosophy.

It was also believed by Justice Blackmun (and others) that the American prohibition on abortion was born out of concern for the health and life of the woman at a time when the procedure was quite dangerous to both. And that with the modernization of medical techniques and the advance of medicine specifically involving the role of antibiotics, this need no longer be a major concern.

And so for better or for worse, Roe v Wade was decided in favor of what has become known as the woman's right to choose.

Justice White voiced the dissenting opinion saying:

> "I find nothing in the language or history of the Constitution to support the Court's judgment. The Court simply fashions and announces a new constitutional right for pregnant mothers and, with scarcely any reason or authority for its action, invests that right with sufficient substance to override most existing state abortion statutes. The upshot is that the people and the legislatures of the fifty States are constitutionally disentitled to weigh the relative importance of the continued existence and development of the fetus on the one hand, against a spectrum of possible impacts on the mother on the other hand. As an exercise of raw judicial power, the Court perhaps has authority to do what it does today; but in my view its judgment is an improvident and extravagant exercise of the power of judicial review which the Constitution extends to this Court."

And furthermore:

"This issue, for the most part, should be left with the people and to the political processes the people have devised to govern their affairs."

Justice Renquist also dissented, saying:

"In deciding such a hypothetical lawsuit the Court departs from the long-standing admonition that it should never 'formulate a rule of constitutional law broader than is required by the precise facts to which it is to be applied.'...I have difficulty in concluding, as the Court does, that the right of 'privacy' is involved in this case...A transaction resulting in an operation such as this is not 'private' in the ordinary usage of that word. Nor is the 'privacy' which the Court finds here even a distant relative of the freedom from searches and seizures protected by the Fourth Amendment to the Constitution which the Court has referred to as embodying a right to privacy...I agree with the statement of Mr. Justice Stewart in his concurring opinion that the 'liberty,' against deprivation of which without due process the Fourteenth Amendment protects, embraces more than the rights found in the Bill of Rights. But that liberty is not guaranteed absolutely against deprivation, but only against deprivation without due process of law...The conscious weighing of competing factors which the Court's opinion apparently substitutes for the established test is far more appropriate to a legislative judgment than to a judicial one...

But the Court adds a new wrinkle to this test by transposing it from the legal considerations associated with the Equal Protection Clause of the Fourteenth Amendment to this case arising under the Due Process Clause of the Fourteenth Amendment. Unless I misapprehend the consequences of this transplanting of the 'compelling state interest test,' the Court's opinion will accomplish the seemingly impossible feat of leaving this area of the law more confused than it found it...

Even today, when society's views on abortion are changing, the very existence of the debate is evidence that the 'right' to an abortion is not so universally accepted as the appellants would have us believe.

To reach its result the Court necessarily has had to find within the scope of the Fourteenth Amendment a right that was apparently completely unknown to the drafters of the Amendment...By the time of the adoption of the Fourteenth Amendment in 1868, there were at least thirty-six laws enacted by state or territorial legislatures limiting abortion."

Summing it up, he admonishes us:

"The only conclusion possible from this history is that the drafters did not intend to have the Fourteenth Amendment withdraw from the States the power to legislate with respect to this matter.

Even if one were to agree that the case which the Court decides were here, and that the enunciation of the substantive constitutional law in the Court's opinion were proper, the actual disposition of the case by the Court is still difficult to justify. My understanding of past practice is that a statute found to be invalid as applied to a particular plaintiff, but not unconstitutional as a whole, is not simply 'struck down' but is instead declared unconstitutional as applied to the fact situation before the Court."

This brief overview, I hope, will illuminate how Roe was arrived at, what it states and what the courts objections to it were as well.

Having said that, what does the future hold? Roe v Wade will be overturned by a future court, as it must, for it is bad law.

There simply *is* no basis found within either the wording or the intent of the constitution, its arguments are flawed and as much has been admitted so by its original proponents on the court. It will not be overturned by the present Supreme Court, especially with the situation ethics mentality of Ms. Ginsberg. It may not even be overturned by the next change in membership but eventually it will be.

The overturning of Roe v Wade will not end abortions, legal or otherwise. To end legal abortions requires the court to outlaw them by finding and reinforcing decisions based on the right to "life, liberty, and the pursuit of happiness" clause or others, and this isn't likely to occur.

To end illegal abortions, it will be necessary to end the perceived need for them as man (or woman in this case) is generally predisposed to do for himself what he believes is necessary.

With Roe overturned, the only thing that changes is recognition that access to abortions is not a constitutionally guaranteed right. Most states recognize it as a right and this will still stand. Then, as Justice White alludes to, it would fall to the responsibility of the individual states to decide whether or not to retain that right, or if nonexistent, whether to legislate it in the future.

Since the ability to get an abortion is clearly not a matter of constitution (Roe notwithstanding), the question would be left to the states to decide, and hopefully with a revitalized due process, the question would be placed before the public.

States whose voters hold a greater respect for life may vote to ban the practice while those which hold the woman's right to choose as imperial can opt for abortion.

Those readers who are rabidly pro-abortion have probably ceased listening to me long ago, but for those still with me, let me calm your fears on a few items.

Women who reside in states which do not permit abortion will still be free to travel to neighboring states for the performance of the procedure if they so desire. Some will protest the burden there placed on these women. Realistically, in today's society, how great a burden is a days journey by bus or hours by automobile as compared to any perceived burden that raising a child to maturity would be?

A similar protest has been launched on behalf of women on welfare. Roe v Wade provides them and all other women with the legal right to obtain abortion, but abortion proponents claim that implied is the provision that this be provided at the expense of the public (read taxpayer).

Opponents to this say that while the law does allow legal access to abortion, it was never intended in Roe or elsewhere that access meant "free" or in other words, taxpayer provided. The point is quite like your legal right to a luxury automobile if you so choose, which does not at all mean that one will be provided for you, without cost or obligation.

A major fear raised by the pro-abortion crowd is that a huge amount of women will start dying from back-alley abortions gone awry. This simply will not happen for two reasons. First, society tends to lean toward the direction in which they are guided by laws. Were abortion to become once again illegal, women will not take so lightly their responsibility in the question of contraception versus pregnancy. I offer as evidence that prior to Roe, there were under five hundred thousand abortions performed yearly. After the procedure became legal that figure more than tripled.

Secondly, unlike in the distant past, there are now tens of thousands of doctors trained specifically in performing abortions. They will not merely fade away if abortion again becomes illegal. Women seeking abortions will never again deal with poorly trained individuals who will endanger their lives with unsanitary conditions. Abortions will be performed by the same doctors who do them today, only the performance thereof will be more discreet if no longer sanctioned by the state.

What I have stated above does not even enter into consideration in the absence of Roe v Wade, but rather only if all abortions are banned.

Until the day arrives (if ever) that the Supreme Court actually renders abortion itself unconstitutional, the two opposing sides (pro-life and pro-choice) should come together on one very important decision.

They should agree that legal or not, abortion should be considered undesirable. It demeans us as a people. It speaks ill of us as a concerned nation. If both sides can agree that legal or not, and personal desires aside, abortion is not a *good* thing, we do have some small but important common ground to work with.

Let us agree that even if legal, we should be striving to have as few abortions as possible by reducing the need for them. If we can agree on that basic principle, we should band together putting our efforts into the following:

Sex education, as taught in today's schools, must also include an emphasis on morals. It is ethically bankrupt to teach children the "how to" and leave out the "why to not." All guidance on moral issues tragically disappeared, coincidentally, with the abolition of prayer in schools. In our society's zeal to separate religion from government (and education), we have mistakenly deleted any reference to morals. Let us correct that error.

Let us recognize the positive aspects of peer pressure. Once there was a stigma attached to teen pregnancy and any pregnancy out of wedlock. We must reverse the direction we have been going in. While we never wish to see people ostracized for making poor choices or mistakes, we should neither hold single motherhood as an ideal to be admired as with childbearing within marriage. Within certain populations in New York City, the illegitimacy rate is sixty-three percent. Nearly two out of three children are born sans the benefit of their parents being married. To the degree that we are capable, let us enlist positive peer pressure to reinforce this as undesirable behavior in both the male and female portions of this equation.

Condom distribution in schools should be halted. Without exception, the pregnancy rate has been shown to *increase* coincidental with these programs. Why? We send the wrong message, handing out condoms instead of moral values. Put aside my opinions for the moment. Abandon this idea for no other reason than the fact that it doesn't work. While not all will practice abstinence, those officials who scoff at it as unworkable have never given it a chance. Our young people deserve more credit than we have been giving them, for they are *not* all on the level of animals in heat as some suppose. Most are capable and even desirous of responsible behavior, if encouraged in that direction. Those who are not, of course, know where condoms can be gotten if they choose to use them. We must walk a fine line between allowing contraceptive availability and actual promotion. A generation ago, there were no condom distribution programs, yet even in the "free love" sixties, the unwanted pregnancy rate was *much* lower, more than mere coincidence. We must stop giving our young people condoms with a wink and a nod and then wonder why they behave irresponsibly.

Oh yes, and let us never again have a Surgeon General who prefers to hand out leaky condoms rather than none at all.

When a woman comes into a clinic seeking an abortion, let us make certain she gets all the information. Feminists bristled at what was referred to as the gag order, when abortion could not be promoted at government-sponsored clinics. A similar gag rule exists today in the opposite direction. Because abortion clinics make their profits by performing abortions, much information is not shared with the pregnant woman. They are not told of the risk to future desired pregnancies that abortion creates. Nor the dramatically increased chance of getting breast cancer. Not informed about post-abortion depression which may set in up to two years later. Never shown what an aborted fetus looks like, so she can judge for herself if it is really just a grouping of cells or an unviable tissue mass.

If we are for choice, let us insure that the choice is made after all the details and alternatives are examined. When any other choice is made in life, it is done thusly, not with a "close your eyes and pick" mentality. The termination of a pregnancy is too important a subject to trivialize by the purposeful withholding of pertinent information.

Next, we must get government to willingly embrace certain religious institutions. Without infringing on the separation of church and state, we must be willing to give credit where it is due. The area of adoption and child placement is one where the church has exceeded all efforts by government. Let he who does the superior job both handle it, and teach procedure to the other. Every adopted child is one less that will be aborted. If women know that good homes are waiting as an alternative, less will opt for abortion, as most do not wish for the innocent to pay for their mistakes.

At this time, there are more couples looking to adopt than there are children available. With a streamlining of the process and the government following the successes of religious establishments, both of these needs could be satisfied.

Lastly, although I abhor censorship, let Hollywood recognize the role it has played both in the lowering of our values and its desire to titillate. If casual sex without responsibility is all we see on the tube or at the theatre, and either overtly or implied is the notion that "everyone is doing it," can we not see how this reflects on us as to our respect for one another in sexual matters? If the likes of Janet Reno can request that television tone down its glorification of violence, should the same not hold true for sexual promiscuity?

The ideas I offer here are not the ultimate solution, but they are a beginning.

In closing, I must say that however it goes with Roe v Wade, and whichever way it goes with state legislation is of less importance than how we as individuals deal with the issue. Making abortion a less desirable choice, along with reducing unwanted pregnancies to begin with, should be the goal of both of the opposing ideologies in this debate.

Herein lies the more important battle, for it is a battle of our hearts.

THE CRIMINAL JUSTICE SYSTEM

You would never get the impression to look at it, but there is actually supposed to be a purpose to the criminal justice system.

What had long ago started out as a system designed to see that proper trials determine the guilt or innocence of a defendant, with proper punishment or exoneration following that determination, has degenerated into what we have today: very little justice, and much that is criminal about the system.

Some judges are so renown for releasing the guilty that they have thoroughly demoralized much of our police force. You have often heard it stated by police officers that they have little interest in their jobs because "the criminal will be back on the street before I finish the paperwork, so why bother?" Of course, this is no legitimate reason for shirking one's duty, but the feeling and its resultant slackness is pervasive nonetheless.

Let us examine what the major faults are and where they lie, what has undermined justice, and what to do about it.

In any criminal court, we have:
> the judge
> the jury
> attorneys for the defense

    attorneys for the prosecution
    the defendant
    witnesses and experts
    and the police.

Who is concerned with justice?

The defendant is usually concerned with justice only if he is innocent. If not, justice is the last thing he wants.

The prosecutor is not at all concerned with justice. His purpose is to get a conviction, and if he has high political ambitions, that much more so. To boost their conviction rate, prosecutors will withhold evidence, distort statements and even allow the climate of the times to steer their approach to a case. Winning isn't everything, its the only thing.

Least interested with seeing justice served is the defense attorney. His notoriety, present and future earnings, will all be determined by the reputation he builds for himself case by case. Of primary importance to him is his ability to either get his clients off entirely, guilty or not, or to see to it that the accused is punished to the least degree, in the event that he is found guilty. He accomplishes this by instilling in the jury that sense of doubt and fear that they may unjustly punish an innocent man.

Through the artful manipulation of words, a craft mastered by all successful defense attorneys, he plays upon a degree of faulty logic, frail emotions, and whatever other chinks in the armor he may discover in the willing and receptive jury. Since all he need produce is a "reasonable doubt" in the minds of the jurors, he is given the advantage of considerable weight placed on his side of the balance scales of justice.

But this is as it should be. Being that U.S. Justice is based upon presumed innocence until guilt is demonstrated, these tactics by the defense must be permitted.

If we are to have true justice where a beguiling defense attorney is not able to pull the wool over the eyes of a gullible jury, we will require two things. The prosecution must present ironclad cases, and juries must become more sophisticated

What do I mean, and how do we get there? Let's examine the problem of the jury. A properly deductive jury is able to cut through the smoke and mirrors presented by a clever defense, sorting out that which is, and that which is not substantial enough to constitute reasonable doubt. Cold logic is called for to penetrate beyond the flood of emotional appeal with which they will be bombarded. This door, of course, was meant to swing both ways. Lately, you hear a lot about "the seriousness of the charges" in regards to certain crimes. Only a logical mind will see that the degree of "seriousness" is of no relevance if the charges themselves are baseless.

The fact that a rape or murder was carried out in a particularly gruesome fashion must not be allowed to reflect on whether or not the person before you is indeed the guilty party or not! Nor should the jury find anyone guilty because they fear reprisals either against themselves or society from any group that disagrees with the outcome of the trial. That type of coercion makes a sham of the whole process. In that case, why not dispense with the trial entirely, just hang the suspect and not even pretend to be interested in due process?

Juries must be above such behavior. But how can we create a better jury?

The law says that you are entitled to a "jury of your peers." This means you must be judged by people who are in many ways similar to yourself. This was designed to preclude the deck being stacked against you. Who, if charged with bank robbery, would not be upset to find that the jury contains twelve bank presidents? Similarly, the poor would prefer not to be judged by members of the aristocracy.

But how far was this concept intended to be taken? Would a retarded person expect to be tried by a jury of similarly retarded persons? Should a plumber be tried only by plumbers?

Of course this is not what "a jury of his peers" means. If you agree with me so far, you shouldn't have a problem with what I am about to say.

During the selection process, the defense attorney tries to weed out prospective jurors who may hold certain prejudices toward the accused. On a charge of rape, he certainly would like to avoid having jurors who have themselves been raped. It's a question of objectivity. Jurors who, by their words or manner, appear to be racially motivated, are dismissed if race is a question.

Meanwhile, the prosecution attempts to remove from the jury pool those, who in his estimation, might unduly side with the accused whether because of race, emotion or political agenda. On the issue of emotion, he might ask a prospective juror, "Will you have any problem reaching a conclusion to convict, given that the accused may be sentenced to death?" If the answer comes back "yes," he sees that this juror is excused.

Clearly, testing the prospective members in this manner goes a long way toward producing a fair-minded jury, but the process must be taken one step farther. Under my system, a jury must be capable of passing a test showing they are able of expressing objectivity over emotion. This will require a jury of somewhat higher I.Q. than the average we now see, but this step is very important. We need juries who are able to suppress their emotions while not being devoid of them, and they must highly value the application of logic. Only logic and objectivity will allow them to see beyond the ploys advanced by both the prosecution and defense, so that they may render a just conclusion. Their decision must be based solely upon the facts in the case rather than some lawyers preferred interpretation and presentation of those facts.

Producing juries of this high level will necessitate starting with a much larger pool than we do now, and will prove a bit more difficult. However, it will result in more criminals being convicted and fewer innocent people being locked up in error, and that is our goal.

Starting with this larger pool of potential jurors, we will begin the elimination process by means of a standardized test designed to determine logic and objectivity *before* they are scrutinized by the attorneys. This will bring the quality of the jury system up to a higher plateau without needless time delays or added expense.

Now onto the other more difficult part of this formula.

Something strange happens in the great matrix of the criminal justice system when it comes to prosecutory personnel. Your district attorney is not picked on the only two criterion which should be considered meaningful: excellence and integrity. Excellence is the measure of his ability to carry out his duties productively, a good case success ratio, while integrity is shown in bringing about convictions while neither fabricating nor suppressing evidence.

Routinely, weak cases have been advanced in the past in which the D.A., in his zeal, promotes manipulation over substance. You read about such courtroom shenanigans every day. Less frequently, you will also read about some bold prosecutor who freely admits having put away persons who he *knew* to be innocent but "that's just the way the game is played." How sickening.

Forcing our prosecutors to be honest reaps a severalfold reward. In time, the conviction rate will improve when cases must be built upon concrete evidence or not go forward at all. Faith in the prosecutor will be restored and jury members will no longer have just reason to suspect questionable motives on the part of that office.

But to accomplish this change in the way the D.A.'s office is run, we must first remove this function of government from the current sewage of standard politics.

District attorneys are normally elected to their positions, a process which has generally deteriorated into a popularity contest. He who looks the best, spends the most on his campaign, talks smoothest to the public and has strong political support will likely emerge the winner in this horse race.

Instead, the District Attorney should be a position which is reached by a series of performance ratings. Everywhere else in America, it is preferred that one achieve the pinnacle of his or her chosen profession by some form of merit system. This usually includes such indicators as the accomplishment of job-enhancing education, record review, stepped aptitude tests for promotion, etc., and it is not at all unreasonable that the individuals up for this high post should also pass through an ethical review board.

In this manner, we can provide ourselves with a district attorney who is not only beyond questionable motives at the moment of inception, but who down the line will not fall prey to political pressure or find himself "owing" someone a favor.

Then we have the problem of our peace officers. Our police must be beyond reproach. But there is too much graft, corruption, and abuse of power in today's police departments. Like a cancer, the bad seeds among them make life more than difficult for those officers who are honest and only wish to conduct their affairs in the proper way.

The police must be held to a higher standard than the general public. When we break a law, there is a penalty. When those who have been entrusted to uphold the law break it, they should pay triple the penalty.

When we formulate a legal system and create the police force to back it up, we as citizens make certain concessions which should be trade-offs. In order to make the system work, we assign to them the right to place us under arrest. In effect, we hand them considerable power over our freedom, and we arm them as well. The trade-off should be that in return for that trust we have every right to expect that their behavior should be exemplary. Impropriety should be close to unheard of.

As I pen this, a commission is meeting in New York City, to discuss police corruption. They are hearing testimony from former officers who were convicted of the most heinous crimes. But the key was repetition. These were not fallen cops who had once been angels but stumbled along the way, as any of us might. Crime for them had become a way of life. And they were hired to look after our well-being? Frankly, the hours of testimony provided, detailing the manner in which they went about their "business" would sicken you.

But through all of this came very little that was constructive. Police Commissioner Raymond Kelly mentioned that it is very difficult for officers to blow the whistle on bad cops. Shame on you Kelly. Nowhere did you make an impassioned plea for them to turn the miscreants in, at no point did you draw a line and challenge the good officers to step over it and help you clean up the system from within. Then you wonder why the people cry for an all-civilian review board!

The system must be cleaned up. To do so requires us to impose stiffer penalties on cops gone bad, and reward those who do their jobs well.

It is the complacency of good or neutral officers which allows corruption in those who wish to go in that direction. Not everything bad officers do can go undetected by those who they work with.

Dates must be set, time frames adhered to, where officers who are privy to, or witness to improper or illegal behavior on the part of their fellow officers are granted amnesty (provided they had no part in the acts) and protected with a suitable umbrella for whistle blowers. Beyond the allotted time, all officers would be considered responsible for first-hand knowledge and stonewalling.

Early in their training, officers must hear it from on top that neither corruption nor looking the other way will be tolerated. That it is not a stool pigeon or a snitch who reports illegal police acts, but rather one who is loyal to the ideals of the profession and who will not stand to see the image tarnished.

Given time, this system will be successful, corruption will be for the largest part exorcised and an enormous amount of money will be saved on every imaginable level.

Shopkeepers no longer will be shaken down, drug dealers not given a free pass, and the taxpayers will not be throwing their money away, because police will be doing their jobs instead of lining their pockets. Crime will go down as will insurance premiums.

And with this money saved, a portion should be put aside to reward forthright officers upon their retirement.

By polishing up our men in blue, the average citizen can feel more confident in the trust he has placed with those in the law enforcement profession, an important central goal.

Next in our cleanup act should come the judges.

In most areas of life, we look for advancement of our positions. The carpenter's helper wants to become a carpenter, who in turn wishes to become a cabinet maker, etc. This is all well and good. What is not well and good, however, is that the same ambition should apply to judgeships. Rather than a stepping stone to carry one on to greater heights, a justice position should be viewed as final achievement. It works in this way with the Supreme Court where the job is for life, and few have any political aspirations beyond it.

But there are a couple of things wrong with the Supreme Court. It is a political appointment, done not for the benefit of our country, but rather to further promote the political philosophy of whoever happens to be president at the time of the appointment. Because of this perversion, the very purpose of the justices has degenerated into one of advocacy (i.e. changing the constitution) as opposed to rendering the proper interpretation thereof.

Nonetheless, if we were to take the principles of such a court system and transfer them elsewhere throughout the criminal justice system, considerable gains could be enjoyed. Instead of being appointed, however, the criminal court judge would be assigned a position by a governing board. That board must be comprised of past judges who have met certain guidelines of jurisprudence and themselves shown the most admirable performance in the courtroom. The other faction of this board are to be ordinary citizens who care about the welfare of our society and the cause of justice.

Any judge selected by this board will come under review every so often to insure that he has continued to render verdicts and orchestrate his courtroom in an impartial manner. In addition, a review of his action could take place at any time, triggered by citizen complaint.

By effectively weeding out the corrupt, the inept and those who intend to use their office for greater personnel gain or political or social grandstanding, we can once again give society what it deserves, courtrooms in which true justice is metered out.

Now I'm going to say something which will alienate me to most judges. GOOD.

We must start this process now, applying it to existing judges, using these guidelines to remove *fully half* the current judges from the bench. Some we must fire, while others we will force into early retirement. These vacated positions we will then fill with candidates willing to be held to a higher standard than we have settled for in the past.

By having fair but exacting judges, educated juries, District Attorneys and police worthy of our highest respect, the public, the victims of crime, and the criminal himself, will all approach the court system knowing that it will now be a place where the cause of justice, and none other, is served.

Poverty

The circumstances which set the stage for poverty are: lack of ability, lack of education, lack of desire, lack of opportunity, and just plain bad luck.

It would be impossible for us as a society to do anything about an individual's bad luck. At times, circumstances seem to conspire against someone where, no matter how dedicated that person may be, things just don't go his way.

However, on the other four points, how we apply our potential as a society can and will have an effect to varying degrees.

Ability or talent is something a person is either born with or not. Is that as far as it goes? Not by a long shot. We are each born with and without certain potentials in a multitude of areas. Athletic or cerebral, poetic or political, most of us have undeveloped talents which permit us to shine brightly in a niche or two, if a way is found to develop and exploit those talents.

Opportunity is required to knock twice on the door of those talents (or in some cases to be chased after). In the first instance, to see that the abilities do not lay dormant and wither on the vine; in the second, to ensure that once brought up to their potential, these talents have a channel to flow through, a manner in which to be exploited, again lest they come to naught.

Should a person suffer the misfortune of being born defective in mental capacity and have no intrinsic abilities capable of development, there is little that society can do for him, for his options, potential, and choices have been considerably limited by nature. Before you jump all over me, I am not at all saying that this person is useless or worthless, just that he or she will never be an astrophysicist. The recognition of this reduced potential is not a character judgment, just a statement of fact.

Education is one of the main keys and, in fact, one of the easiest to be supplied by any society in bringing out most everyone's God-given talent. Tragically, it is also one of the areas in which we have failed our citizens miserably.

What had started out as a grand dream, to provide a government mandated taxpayer-funded basic education for all, has degenerated into what we have today. You are familiar with it I am sure, and the particulars of this failed program can be found in this book's chapter on the education system. A restored education system could go a long way toward meeting the needs of developing our basic talents to insure that they will not go to waste, but it is only the beginning.

I know that a lot of people will fault me for what they perceive as my constant harping on the benefits of the free enterprise system, but yes, here I go again.

When set free of the shackles of socialist ideals, such as the redistribution of wealth, forced mediocrity in the name of "fairness," and government impositions on every level, our free enterprise system is capable of supplying both the advanced training necessary to enhance the value of the individual's contribution, and the opportunity to put that value and ability to profitable use.

For too long, government has both foolishly and jealously attempted to supplant the job of business to supply those two important components, and has failed on both fronts. Government training programs are costly and largely ineffective. Government-created jobs are wasteful of individual talents, curtail individual achievement, and are provided at the taxpayers' expense. And rather than adding to the tax base as does private industry, they detract from it, for a double loss.

It should only be the government's interest to promote the expansion of business, the blossoming of free enterprise to allow it to fulfill its roles of talent enhancement and the providing of opportunity. This it can do largely, as I have said elsewhere, by getting out of the way. Government must be taught to pull in its claws and stop attempting to introduce itself into as many facets of our lives as possible, as it currently does. It must gain a new respect for business and acknowledge the success which business has shown in the past, returning to those salient words as penned in the Constitution; "*promoting* the general welfare." You'll notice it does not say "to *provide for* the general welfare," and there is good reason for this.

Good government will exercise more control over itself than it ever does over its citizens. It must always govern with restraint, preferably self-imposed, or if need be, imposed by those people who it has ceased to serve.

If the government can control itself to the appropriate point where it is once again lending a hand instead of seeking to totally run the show, there is one more area in which it can be of some help. Desire, or the lack thereof, is the responsibility of the individual for the most part. All the natural talent, all the lucky breaks, education and opportunity are of no value whatsoever if a person refuses to take advantage of these things because he would prefer either to be a sluggard or because he'd rather live on handouts.

But the government can help a great deal by providing the climate where the individual feels inspired by his potential rather than being overshadowed by the feeling of despair that all his best efforts will gain him nothing.

Again, I say this calls for the removal of the socialist policies we see growing about us daily. Oppressive taxes and those of a progressive nature do nothing to inspire a person to perform, when he knows that he will experience diminishing returns. Achievement must be rewarded, not punished. Only when a person can see that his efforts will have a good chance of lifting him out of his present circumstance can a desire be instilled to take that chance and work toward positive change. We must provide that light at the end of the tunnel and return to our capitalist roots. Along this line, please refer to Rabbi David Eidensohn's idea of universal capitalism in my chapter on the economy.

We must also remove the financial incentives to remain on welfare and unemployment. These programs of monetary assistance are far too attractive when compared to many of the jobs which will *ever* be available. It is a fact that many people drop off welfare when they are required to perform any sort of work for their check. These people are primarily those who do have jobs already, off the books. They have been cheating the system and cannot afford to leave a good job in order to continue collecting their welfare check. Others have no job, but when faced with the prospect of having to work for the small amount of money which welfare provides, they go out and find a real job in short order. I am not herein promoting "workfare," but merely pointing out that it is the free ride which keeps people from seeking gainful employment.

Unemployment is a more touchy subject. You wouldn't wish to force these people to perform any service for their check, for that will distract them from their primary task which should be a full-time search for a paying job. Nor should you wish to shorten the benefit period. Too many people will stay out as many weeks as are provided for them in order to "get what's coming to them" before making a sincere effort to find work. This, however, does not justify the seemingly endless extensions granted of late. Again, they are counterproductive.

The best answer here is to provide quality job opportunities so that the time out on unemployment will be kept as short as possible. This is done, as I alluded to earlier, by setting free the entrepreneurial spirit which has been repressed in our now stifled business community.

Just how effective can business be if set loose to perform its proper function?

It is the normal working of the free enterprise system which has lifted us up from the position the common man held one hundred years ago, to where we find ourselves today. In the 1890s, the mode of transportation was the horse, and less than half of the population owned one (cowboy movies are *not* historical documents). Today, we have the automobile which is owned by nearly every American of driving age, and indeed many own more than one.

The coal oil lamp has given way to full interior lighting and exterior lighting at the flick of a switch, and over sixty percent of American homes have microwave ovens.

I could easily go on with this comparison for many pages, but I'm sure you get the point. Business has not only created those labor-saving, and, at times, luxurious items, which most of us take for granted today, but it has also put most of these within reach of the average man. Today's middle class largely experiences a lifestyle only enjoyed by those who were among the wealthy in the last century. Our wealthy live in circumstances undreamed of by their predecessors. And even those living at the poverty level cannot be compared with those who experienced poverty decades ago. Poverty today usually means a lifestyle with none of the amenities enjoyed by the middle class, but nonetheless, even our impoverished usually have access to indoor plumbing, electricity, potable water, taxpayer-sponsored health care, etc.

How much more farther along could we now be had not the last fifty years seen an escalation of taxes on business and ever-increasing government control?

Where can we go from here if we are successful in relegating government to its proper job and function?

Something both simple and wonderful would most certainly happen here.

Excess taxes and restrictions must be removed from business, and by firm law, leave no question or doubt in the business community that enterprise will be free to expand without fear of having the rug pulled out from under it again.

No longer fearful of the antagonistic governmental and media-driven attitude toward free enterprise, business will again flourish, reversing the massive layoffs we are witness to today.

More people will be employed at every level and our society will enjoy the benefit of a natural snowball effect. As more people escalate in the job market, disposable income goes up, resulting in increased personal spending, more consumer goods purchased, leading to more firm production contracts, resulting in more hiring. We would soon experience an upward spiral in our economy brought about by the same economic conditions whose absence has caused our present downward spiral.

Even government would benefit. A lower tax rate paid on a much larger base will increase revenues, much unlike today's wild chasing after every shrinking and fast-disappearing dollar.

Eventually, this type of growth, which is self-sustaining and self-promoting, extends to the point where it revitalizes the export trade reaching out into new and unexplored markets. This is like a shifting of gears, and the whole process of expansion takes off again.

This type of advanced growth in prosperity even takes on a spiritual dimension, as those who are part of the process see their efforts benefiting their fellow man in every respect. Who, involved in the manufacture of well drilling equipment, for instance, does not delight in the fact that, as less expensive and more efficient systems become available, people in impoverished nations will soon have their first opportunity for nearby clean, plentiful water?

Prosperity for the nation as a whole cannot help but to positively affect those living in poverty today.

Let us examine the other side of the coin and see what damage further government intrusion into business will do.

More pressure in the direction we are going in will necessarily crush the entrepreneurial spirit. It is a fact of life that when the profit motive is entirely removed from an enterprise, even those with the staunchest constitutions eventually throw in the towel and give in to the economic pressures which have been set up to work against them.

A perfect example of this is Russia and what was until so very recently known as the Soviet Union.

Russia has been suffering under socialism for enough decades that a fair retrospective may be provided.

For the several generations which have labored under this system, the key element in one's life is that the value of the individual is only recognized in the manner in which he serves society as a whole. The crux of communistic philosophy is that concern for one's own being as an ideal to be pursued, is selfish, decadent, and counterproductive to society.

One reason for the failure of this system is the natural spirit-destroying effect, the result of seeing that one's life's work as having no positive effect on that society you had held so dear. With no spirit, no incentive, the individual produces mediocre work resulting in mediocre products, as is the case with everyone around him. We were never designed, never meant to be totally selfless creatures. Exports suffer for they are forced to compete in a world market against that which was produced with pride, items skillfully crafted to compete in, and win market shares. The inferior exports return limited wealth to the homeland, for they sell for only what little they are worth.

The human spirit is further squashed as the people are forced to self-consume most of their own inferior production, little of it having met import standards elsewhere. Most of you readers know how depressing it is when you are occasionally forced to work with junk, either produced that way or as items which have been kept in service beyond their useful life. Now imagine most items you work with being of that quality, how much more-so your lack of hope? Receiving and using poor quality products doesn't exactly inspire one to produce superior products yourself, and so a vicious cycle is created.

As if the poor quality of available goods were not upsetting enough, most goods are commonly in short supply. Rationing is usually instituted with the resultant long lines.

There is an old joke about two Russians who had been waiting for hours on a particularly long line. One turns to the other and says "Vladimir, I cannot take it anymore with these stupid lines. I'm going to get a gun and shoot the Premier!" Surprised by his friend's sudden outburst, all Vladimir could say was "Good luck." After only a short while, however, he appeared back on the line looking more dejected than even. "What are you doing back here so soon?" asked Vladimir. "I thought you were going to shoot the Premier." "I was," his friend responded, "but the line for that was even longer."

As is evident, even dark humor is not born in a vacuum.

The result of the Soviet system is that nearly all of the average people, those not protected by government privilege, are largely impoverished.

Cold water flats, group home dwellings where one apartment may be shared by several families, no genuine quality possessions, and almost all family members working at unproductive, uninspiring jobs. These are common reflections of life for most Soviet citizens.

Now that this entire system has become nothing more than a pitiful shambles, it should be evident to all what will most assuredly happen to our way of life if we follow in their footsteps, as we seem bent upon doing.

The free enterprise system as expressed through capitalist methodology has but one fault, and this one fault is not insurmountable. It has a tendency to treat those who are less successful as disposable items. Excellence is rewarded (as it should always be) by allowing an individual to continue climbing onto greater achievements as far as his self-induced momentum is able to carry him.

Those who are on the bottom, however, are destined to stay there unless they make certain logical moves. Everything boils down to what the individual has to offer. There is very little wealth to be accrued if the highest job a person is capable of performing is digging ditches. Compound this picture of economic misery when some up and coming star invents the backhoe. Now that ditch digging individual has not only one of the lowest paying, most labor-intensive jobs imaginable, but he finds himself about to become unemployed from even that!

As I said, it is natural that this type of system must discard those who have little or nothing to offer but raw, untalented labor. The solution, if there is to be any at all, must lie not in the hands of yet another insipid and wasteful government program or mandate, but rather within the individual himself.

He who is willing to make the necessary change and meet the challenge will survive.

When that spanking new backhoe arrives to steal his job, he can either fight this unstoppable progress (and lose) or he can respond. If he wishes to be victorious in this particular battle, he will either move on to more promising employment elsewhere, or perhaps even learn to operate that very same backhoe himself.

Those options are in his own hands and with him resides the responsibility to take the needed actions in seeing after his own marketability and survival.

This brings us full circle back to the question of our educational system. It would be best to infuse in the individual at a young age that he must prepare himself to be a survivor. The "one job training for life" concept of the past is no longer applicable in today's more demanding world. Our next generation should not be made to repeat the mistakes of this one.

The young person entering tomorrow's job market might well possess skills in welding, computers, and in nursing, all at the same time. Whichever way the wind blows in America's future economic storms, this sort of individual will be prepared to take advantage of whatever portion of the employment spectrum is most profitable to him at any given time.

The job market in America is in a constant state of flux and it will remain so for the foreseeable future. Any person who wishes to succeed must be prepared to bob and weave like a football player attempting to avoid being tackled. The traditional job market of the past is gone. It is no longer the reliable rock steady anchoring point that it once was, nor is it likely that it will ever be that way again.

The other thing that our educational system can do for us is to pursue the program of universal capitalism as I've detailed in the chapter on the economy. By unveiling and promoting the option for each individual to go into business for himself, many doors will be opened which otherwise would not. While it is true that the majority will not take advantage of such an offer, most of those who decline are better off working for someone else anyway.

Poverty is a reflection of two things. What a society has to offer its total people, and whether or not devices exist to help those who are interested, to take part in that potential.

A nation which is itself impoverished, cannot offer anything to its populous. The natural result is that most of its citizens *must* live in poverty. At this moment, this is not the problem with America, although we are fast moving in that direction. We are still a nation of abundance, but we have not provided those devices I speak about for bringing most people on board of the American dream. We have instead tried to go the socialist route, and have of course suffered as a result. If we are to survive, and in fact, prosper, we must go with my program.

Government incursions must be removed from business so that it may thrive, and then we must do what we can to encourage all to partake of that system to the utmost degree.

If we follow these principles, poverty will be diminished to the point of being negligible, and the only have-nots left will be those few pitiful individuals who actually prefer to live that way.

Section IV:
AND THE REST

The Public Education Disaster

"The problems with current educational conditions do not reflect evil intentions on the part of American educators. Rather, these difficulties and shortcomings stem from structures and policies which, whatever their original objectives, have become destructive of educational quality, injurious to American students, unfaithful to family expectations and finally harmful to American society as a whole."

I didn't say that, I only wish I had. The above quotation was from professor Quentin L. Quade, the director of the Blum Center for parental freedom in education at Marquette University.

What is wrong with American public education as things stand today? I'd like to turn that question around. Can you possibly tell me what is *not* wrong with this failed system?

The cost per pupil is more expensive than most private schooling, the quality of education much lower, schools themselves are not the safe haven they have in the past been portrayed as. In New York City it has been proposed by David Dinkins (the now former Mayor) that each school should have its own police officer, so out of hand has the situation gotten.

Overall the needs of the community are being ill served by the system which purports to have its best interests at heart.

Currently this is where we stand: at an average cost of seven to eleven thousand dollars per pupil per year (depending on what area of the country you are focusing on) our children receive an education which is substandard. It is substandard when compared to Europe and Japan, substandard when compared to private education, and even substandard to its own performance of only a few years ago.

For enormous quantities of our money we get back children who are not only poorly educated but indoctrinated by unneeded sociologists to resent their parents. The same socialism which was correctly predicted to meet its downfall in the Soviet Union is being pushed by the majority of liberal educators as the best thing that could happen to America. And all this against the direct wishes of the parents. What went wrong?

Around the turn of the last century education in some form became compulsory. This was undoubtedly a good thing. The level to which our entire society had risen was brought about to a great degree by mandatory education for all. No longer were the poor to be kept forever in that state, as access to the fundamentals of those still important basics, reading, writing, and arithmetic, opened doors of opportunity for advancement.

Quite naturally the well to do could afford to send their children to the best of private schools available, as they always had, but for the first time basic education was opened to all, and all benefited.

Those on the bottom of the economic heap could more easily move up the job ladder. Those already well off who owned businesses could now get employees who were far more valuable than they had been.

The lowest employee in a dry goods facility for instance, could only sweep the floor and stock shelves. Now with a basic education he could take and ship orders, inventory merchandise, ring up sales, and interact with customers.

But the problem with even some of the best things on Earth is that they may tend to evolve to the point where they no longer perform their original intent. As with most government projects when that which was wonderful has gone bad, it is almost impossible to get rid of. Yes, despite the fact that a system no longer works properly, once it has been carved out as "their territory" it is jealously guarded.

Teachers unions have often placed a stranglehold on community interests and school taxes, but they aren't the biggest factor to blame. It is the lethargy of the average citizen, you and I, which has allowed them to gain total control.

Somewhere along the line an exceedingly irresponsible move was allowed to happen. Teachers began serving on school boards and the purpose of these boards was forever altered. Originally the purpose of the school board was to serve the interests of the taxpaying community and often in a necessarily adversarial position to the educational establishment. The systems wants, needs, desires, and vision for the future was tempered by the board with those of the parents and non parents of the taxpaying community. A certain balance was achieved although the board always did lean toward the concerns of the educational system, as it was always difficult to separate the true meaning of the words "more" and "better."

All concepts of balance were thrown out the window when teachers, both retired and active, started winning elections to positions on the school board. No watchdog came forward to suggest that it was an ethical violation to allow someone to hold a position of responsibility in this area who would be voting on teacher contracts, power and autonomy, and indeed even board structure, purpose, and function. In reality this gave the teachers not only a peek at the other fellows hand, but control of all the cards.

In this way school boards have become a virtual rubber stamp of approval for the requests of the educational community.

The taxpayer and parent have been told that it is none of their business what the teachers and administrators decide will be taught to their children. It is also to be none of their concern how or at what grade level sex education will be taught. That if condom distribution and pro-homosexual curricula is adopted (all in the name of "tolerance") the input of concerned parents is neither asked for nor desired.

Bilingual education, Afrocentrism, multiculturalism, the politically correct movement, animorphism, situation ethics, existentialism, politico-scientific theory as fact, socialism, atheism, feminism and fascism have all been embraced by modern educators with no tolerance for the validity of opposing views.

In fact the National Education Association would bristle at the suggestion that they should be constrained to operate under control of the public.

Gone is the concept that they are a public trust. Gone also the idea that the parents should formulate with what, and how our children should be educated and that the teachers as skilled technicians should then do their best to carry out the project of education, adhering within the bounds of the will of the public.

There is only one thing left we do get. The bill. Their desire is that we also have no control over that. School budgets are approved in the overwhelming majority of the cases, this despite the dizzying heights to which they have risen. Were it within their power I have no doubt that most educators would prefer that we have no voice in the matter, no voice in future school budgets.

In the Northeast many school districts have top teacher salary levels of eighty thousand dollars with the average teacher making close to sixty thousand. This does not take into account benefits, perks, retirement, sick days, sabbaticals, and overtime. Not bad for one hundred and eighty days work per year.

The school administrators make even more of course. In some areas, particularly in the Northeast and the West Coast the ratio of those administrators has reached the point of being between one in seven and one in three, compared to teachers. The cost of education in these areas is not only high, it is top heavy to the extent where fully sixty percent of a school budget is for teachers and administrators. Is it any wonder that there is little money left for books and school supplies?

In a growing number of communities throughout America taxpayer groups are finally saying "enough!" and for the first time voting down proposed budgets.

Not to be outmaneuvered, the school officials pull out several of their favorite weapons. They threaten to cut out all sports and extracurricular activities, and then brand the opposition as a group that "doesn't care about the children's future."

With very few changes they put the budget up for a vote again and again hoping to wear down resistance, and with this they have been quite successful.

In order to further trounce their opponents at the next vote they mobilize the forces of the P.T.A. They start telephone campaigns where only parents of school age children are called and encouraged to get out the vote and pass the budget "for the children."

They point out that you can't put a price on a good education. What they wish to ignore is the fact that any education, good or otherwise, comes with a price tag. It is a rather high one which must be paid in full with hard cold dollars, not with witty sayings or in foggy terms.

Because the cost of the educational system is paid by and linked solidly to your property taxes you are faced with making one of two dreadful choices, if they can be called choices at all. Pay whatever you are told to, or lose your house.

So much for a free and just society.

Here is a system which costs so much yet delivers so little. Only those who are in the upper income brackets can even partially opt out of this system. With enough money you can send your children to a private school, one which comes closer to upholding your ideals, is more in tune with your desires, and more capable of providing what you require: excellence in education.

But these people do not get off easy. In addition to paying a stiff bill for their children's education they must also continue to pay their "fair share" in the way of school tax. This is despite their willingly removing from the system their portion of the costs associated with educating their children.

Because the system as it has evolved today, no longer properly serves the purpose for which it was originally set up; a substantive education for all our citizens at a reasonable cost, it must be dismantled and forced to properly compete with private education.

The voucher system must be implemented throughout the nation by law.

This would recognize how much money is going toward the annual education of each student, and allow the individual parents to transfer the use of that money to any school they wish their children to attend.

If for instance the community is currently spending seven thousand dollars per student per year, that is the amount the parents would be awarded to spend on their children's education either elsewhere or within the public schools if they so desire.

The public school system if it wishes to survive at all will be forced to clean up its act and actually work at attracting people back to its ranks. If it can show that it is capable of supplying a superior education for an acceptable fee, few people will choose to leave. If not it will fail, as fail it should. Where else do we put up with mediocrity being delivered at a premium price?

Parents who choose to school their children elsewhere can either then spend that seven thousand dollars in a private school of equal cost, or put it toward an even more expensive education as a partial payment with the remainder to come out of their own pockets.

To avoid the possibility that some ill meaning parents will try to profit by sending their children to substandard institutions and pocketing the rest, excess funds will be returned to the taxpayer. This is why the funds will be provided by means of a voucher rather than in monetary form.

Parents would thus be encouraged to seek out the best education affordable for the available dollars, and competition for these dollars will set in. Each school (and the public schools as well) will set out to get its share by attempting to provide the best educational value it can. As in any other legitimate business where monopolies no longer hold control, the suppliers will respond with:
1) Superior products (teachers, books, supplies, and the successful implementation thereof)
2) Customer service (responsiveness, committedness, and a sense of obligation)
3) Cost containment—best dollar value.

And it will not always boil down to what something costs, but rather what something is worth.

Once the public education system realizes that it is no longer the only game in town it will either choose to respond by once again making itself an attractive entity, or it will become extinct. That will be its own choice.

For the first time in modern history the quality of education will improve while at the same time the cost will decrease due to competition.

As is so often the case good things lead to other good things. When parents see a direct relationship between the voucher they are given and the quality of education which can be provided if they shop around correctly, it will attune many of them to their proper involvement in the process. It will spur their personal interest in encouraging their children to take the best advantage of these educational opportunities.

This major change in the way we have allowed things to be run must be instituted. It is absolutely immoral to hold the taxpayer, our children, and the citizenry as a whole captive by a system that just no longer works, nor has any intention of improving itself.

Gun Control

The whole issue of gun control can be summed up in just a few brief words.

1) Have plenty,
2) Don't need any.

Who is calling for gun control, and to what purpose?

Could we ever hope to seize all the guns from those who would use them improperly, those of a criminal bent?

I'd like to introduce you to a statement made by Thomas Paine, one of the framers of the constitution, on just this subject:

> "THE supposed quietude of a good man allures the ruffian; while on the other hand, arms like laws discourage and keep the invader and the plunderer in awe, and preserve order in the world as well as property. The same balance would be preserved were all the world destitute of arms, for all would be alike; but since some will not, others dare not lay them aside...Horrid mischief would ensue were one-half the world deprived of the use of them..."

I hope that the logic of his statement does not escape you. It's just common sense.

Argue against that if you wish, but please keep things within the context of the statement.

Supposedly well-meaning people, like Mr. Brady, the man who was permanently brain damaged in the assassination attempt on President Reagan, answer all problems that concern guns with the call for more restrictive gun laws.

Let us examine, for the moment, the bill (now law) which bears his name.

The Brady bill calls for a five-day waiting period on the purchase of handguns, supposedly so that police can do a background check on the applicant. But is that its real purpose?

Proponents of the bill have already admitted that they intend to broaden its application to all guns now that it has been enacted. They are more hesitant to let you know that this legislation in no way *requires* background checks. It only provides for a period of time when they may or may not be done at the discretion of law enforcement agencies. Least of all do these people wish the public to be aware (gun owners in particular) that the five-day waiting period is a minimum. All that law enforcement personnel need to deny an honest individual a gun permit (and thus, ownership) is to neglect to act upon the application. They will be under no legal obligation to act upon any permit within five days, thirty days, six months, or indeed ever. This, even when there proves to be no reason to deny issuance of said permit.

I know many of you do not care to own guns and so are unconcerned about this. You shouldn't be. The same government which is capable of using a twist in the law to deny someone their rights in one area is but a small step away from extending that abuse into other areas as well. Perhaps next it will be in one that affects you.

If we do not pull together to fight this type of legislation, can you not imagine the day when drivers licenses are not renewed, building permits not granted, just because the government does not act upon them, and only because they have a hidden agenda?

The more you examine the Brady bill and what it was really intended to constrain, the more you are lead to conclude that its purpose wasn't to target the criminal at all (those who it should) but rather to make the lives of law abiding citizens more difficult.

A little gun control is like a little poison in your tea. When the brilliance of our founding fathers shone forth in crafting the constitution they knew full well that things did not tend to remain the same for long. To guard against government encroachment into that precious seed, upon the very intent of their new constitution, they stipulated within it that "these rights shall not be infringed." The concept here stated was not that they wished to avoid the day when the constitution might be destroyed, but rather they didn't even want those basic rights so much as tinkered with! The "not be infringed" clause basically and clearly says "hands off!"

The originators of the document were aware that allowing even small changes to occur will open the way for certain and steady change of an evolutionary nature, which brings about eventual metamorphosis whereby the end result looks nothing at all like the original intent.

Properly protected, they assure future generations that the strong foundation upon which the entire weight of this great nation sits would retain its integrity throughout time.

Only fools, and otherwise dangerous people could possibly think that you could dabble here, make small changes there etc., and not have to worry about jeopardizing the entire structure, given mere time coupled with a lack of understanding.

There currently stand on the books over twenty thousand gun laws. Why is it that with this incredible mountain of legislation that crime only seems to be moving upward? Is it just possible that gun laws have a neutral or even negative effect upon attempts to control crime?

Washington D.C. is ironically a most interesting example. The legislature had instituted a total ban on handguns in the city, many years ago. Despite this it has become the murder capital of the United States.

A number of years ago New York City spawned a cult hero named Bernard Goetz. Mr. Goetz had been mugged several times, and growing weary of being victimized he applied for a permit so that he could legally carry a handgun for purposes of self-protection. His application was denied despite the fact that any background check would have shown him to have been a model citizen, and one who had an obvious need.

When first instituted the pistol permit system was supposedly intended not to deny the honest individual the right to protect himself, but merely to keep tabs on who was so armed.

Liberalism has caused the system to evolve to the nth degree till it now results in a near total prohibition of legal possession, and of course it has no effect on criminal possession of any sort. This misuse of power and perversion of the law would appall our founding fathers.

Mr. Goetz, thus disarmed by a government which no longer trusts nor serves those who pay the taxes, was mugged still again.

Finally giving up any hope that the police would or could protect him, or even cared to for that matter, and giving up any idea that he would ever be legally allowed to protect himself, Bernard Goetz in violation of the law purchased a handgun without possessing the required permit.

He would not stand still for being attacked again without the ability to respond with proper recourse.

Goetz recognized that which millions of other Americans are becoming aware of: there is a natural law which man may institute: your God-given right to look after your own survival.

Not too many weeks after taking the protection of his life into his own hands by purchasing a handgun, the predictable happened. On a New York City subway car Bernard Goetz found himself surrounded by a group of four trouble making youths demanding money. The four miscreants gave him every reason to fear for his life, as they were wielding screwdrivers whose tips had been ground to sharpened points.

One can only imagine the images of past abuse which must have flashed through Goetz's mind as he responded in kind, pulling his revolver and shooting all four youths.

Bernard Goetz will forever be a controversial figure, now a permanent part of American folk lore. To many he is a modern hero, one man who did what most Americans wish they could do. He stood up against an unjust system and said, "Enough! This is my life, and I will protect it regardless of the consequences."

To others he is an example of the worst in our society. Someone who took the law into his own hands by possessing and using a gun without the required permit.

There are a couple of items which are difficult to ignore. Because of his actions Bernard Goetz is alive today, while otherwise it is most likely that he would not be. As an interesting side note, after his date with destiny overall subway crime went down over sixty percent and remained at that reduced level for more than six months. How many innocent lives were spared due to this lone action we will never know, but it certainly had a positive effect on crime control.

It is my contention that the last thing we need is more restrictions on a persons right to keep and bear arms.

Some one will always try to make the case for what happens when guns fall into the wrong hands. They will point to those instances where madmen have taken their frustrations out on harmless school children with predictable results.

While it would certainly behoove us as a society to produce fewer madmen, I must point out that much the same thing happens when the aforementioned lunatic uses a car as his weapon of choice rather than a gun. Yet why is no one calling for a ban on cars?

Firearms and automobiles are quite similar in that in and of themselves they are but harmless inanimate objects. It is only when used by people with bad intentions that such horrifying incidents result.

The average American citizen should neither be denied the right to drive a car, nor the right to own and carry firearms on the basis of what some madman may on rare occasion do. It is societies' responsibility however to identify and weed out those people and not expect the citizenry to suffer instead for their lack of ability or desire to do so.

Gun control laws by their very nature target exactly the wrong group of people. They have not and cannot have any impact upon crime except possibly to make things worse. No matter how many laws are enacted criminals will not adhere to them.

An instance where such laws actually make things worse is in fact the case of Bernard Goetz. There is little question that when those who operate in areas of criminal activity are aware that they face an unarmed public, that they pursue their illegal activities with impunity.

In New York City there is an average of over two thousand homicides reported each year. Think about it. That's about six murders each day. Those of ill intent are well aware that there is little chance that their intended victims will be in any position to defend themselves, and so crime flourishes.

There are those who say that "the right to keep and bear arms" as stated in our Constitution is being misinterpreted, and that it was only meant to be applied to a militia, or a standing army. But two important pieces of evidence shoot this theory down. The first is within the context of the second amendment itself. Clearly stated it says; "A well-regulated militia being necessary to the security of a free state, the right of the people to keep and bear arms, shall not be infringed."

You'll notice that the placement of the commas leaves no question that the authors of the constitution were referring to the peoples right to be armed and not the militia's.

The second evidence I would offer you is the other writings of the originators of the Constitution about what they meant with regards to the document itself. It only makes sense to examine this to find original intent and not later interpretation. Thomas Jefferson in 1823 wrote:

> "On every question of construction (of the constitution) let us carry ourselves back to the time when the Constitution was adopted, recollect the spirit manifested in the debates, and instead of trying what meaning may be squeezed out of the text, or invented against it, conform to the probable one in which it was passed."

That kind of makes sense now doesn't it? So let us take a look at a few of the things these fine gentlemen said back then:

> The Constitution shall never be construed...to prevent the people of the United States who are peaceable citizens from keeping their own arms."
> Samuel Adams
Debates & Proceedings in the Convention
of the Commonwealth of Massachusetts.

Notice again the reference to the people and to the citizens. Also notice it speaks of "their arms" not those of an Army, nation, or government.

James Madison, in the Federalist papers:

> "Americans have the right and advantage of being armed—unlike the citizens of other countries whose governments are afraid to trust the people with arms."

Again you see him referring to gun ownership in terms of being the right of the citizens. The only place he appears to be wrong is that today, our government IS afraid to trust its own people.

Those who started this country and did their best to look after its well being wanted the average person to be armed. This can be seen here as stated by Alexander Hamilton: "The best we can hope for concerning the people at large is that they be properly armed."

Some people honestly believe that the constitution is outdated, particularly in regards to the second amendment. These same people would of course balk at the idea that perhaps the first amendment, guaranteeing free speech, should be likewise considered obsolete.

Certain things stand the test of time and are never outdated. The fact that they are antiquated in no way makes them of lesser value today than upon inception. We have not yet bettered the wheel, a mother's love for her child, nor simple concepts such as common courtesy and civility. Our constitution is likened to these, wherein its basic goodness does in no way diminish with the passing of time.

Trying to avoid a day where a vocal minority or a foolish majority might undo our basic rights, Albert Gallatin pointed out in 1789:

"The whole of the Bill of Rights is a declaration of the right of the people at large or considered as individuals…It establishes some rights of the individual as unalienable and which consequently no majority has a right to deprive them of."

Albert Gallantin
New York Historical Society
October 7, 1789.

But if we were to go ahead and foolishly weaken the Constitution, and therefor our rights in this matter despite all I have mentioned herein, let us at least refrain from doing so at the federal level.

What seems right for one state, or one city, or one area of the country can hardly be expected to properly apply as well everywhere else. The wants, the needs, the desires (whether real or imagined) of New York City are vastly different from those in the hills of Montana. Just as you never would expect to take the 30 m.p.h. speed limit in Chicago and institute it on the open highways of Nevada, we should avoid the "one size fits all" mentality with regards to further firearms restrictions.

Lastly, at the risk of having you think that I am an alarmist, I must bring to your attention that the right to keep and bear arms as stated in our Constitution, is the only right which has the capacity to protect and preserve all the others. Fully aware of this, George Mason said: "To disarm the people (is) the best and most effectual way to enslave them"

In the event that this key right is abolished, whether wholesale or one small piece at a time, what is to stop our government from placing restrictions on our rights to free speech and others? It is a common misconception that the Second Amendment's main function was to allow the citizenry access to firearms so that they may hunt or so that they may protect themselves from other citizens. Again I point you to the Federalist papers. If you research these you must come to the conclusion that the prime purpose of the second amendment was that the people must be allowed to be armed against the possibility of oppression brought about by their own government!

History shows that of all the oppressive Fascist regimes which have sprung up within existing nations, the despots in question have found it expedient to first disarm the citizenry. Only when this is done is it possible to fully subjugate the people. This day may well come in America, but God help us if we assist in the effort.

This reason alone should be enough for any freedom loving American to say "no" to more gun control.

As I stated in the beginning:
    1) Have plenty
    2) Don't need any

To those who believe that no one should be allowed to own a gun I reply that EVERYONE should be allowed to own a gun. Everyone that is except criminals, the mentally deficient, children, and of course, themselves.

THE MILITARY AND NATIONAL SECURITY

Historically the United States of America has provided its people with a strong defense. Our Navy, Army, Air Force, etc., were unsurpassed both in strength and quality of personnel and weaponry. With the advent of the modern eras technological advance, we have continually upgraded our systems and remained on the forefront of quality and science, allowing us to respond to any offensive action in such a manner as to preclude the necessity of doing so under most circumstances. Simply put, this strong defense allowed us to say to the rest of the world "Leave us alone" with considerable authority.

During the failed administration of Jimmy Carter, it was felt by those in power that the U.S. could well afford a dramatic reduction in its military. This was due in part to a reduced perception of the need for self protection, coupled with a desire to save money in those highly inflationary times. The cuts instituted were so severe and so much damage was done to our military, that it took several years of effort on the part of the Reagan administration which followed, to return us to our former position of power so that we are now again a viable entity. As is quite often the case, a rebuilding effort of this sort cost us far more than was saved through the cut backs.

Never being of the sort that goes so far as to actually learn from our mistakes, it appears that we are in the middle of starting this ridiculous cycle all over again.

I do not contest the fact that we can afford to scale back our forces to some degree, due to the demise of the Soviet Union, but I do disagree about how much we can afford to do so and still maintain the ability to look after our own self-interests.

In his last year in office President Bush yielded to pressure and begrudgingly reduced military spending by five percent. The average interested taxpayer was quite naturally irate about the reduction being handled in such a token and meaningless fashion.

The proponents of drastic reductions believe we should aim at cutting back our military by as much as thirty five percent. The insanity of this move would of course leave us in an extremely weak and vulnerable position. Furthermore, they do not take into account two very important things. There are certain fixed costs, those of accounting, procedure, electronics, amortization of past bills, overhead, etc. Overall, cuts of thirty five percent will not affect these fixed costs at all. A cut this deep will reduce our effectiveness by up to fifty percent in areas such as personnel, and our ability to service and to support those personnel. As I hope you can see, a cutback of this magnitude will undoubtedly lead to a crippling of our national security.

The second thing to consider is what will happen when aggressive societies perceive that our defenses are weakening? Does this not set the stage for places like Iran, Iraq, and others to start testing us? At such times as these we may experience an increase in terrorist activities and attacks, as these aggressors dabble around our periphery to check and measure our response. We must not encourage this type of action.

Due to the circumstances of our present situation (and all that it implies) the appropriate amount to reduce our forces is around fifteen percent. This is three times the insignificant roll back offered by George Bush, but less than half the possible reduction which may be brought about by those who consider national security unimportant. This figure strikes a good balance, saving us substantial expense desirable with Russia gone from the scene, but still allows us to remain strong in defense.

A good solid defense position is what is needed with the increase of military action now seen in nontraditional areas of the world, (Bosnia, Kuwait, etc.) and the new rise in international terrorism.

As I write this, we are in the midst of deciding which military bases to close down entirely.

This is an error of the highest magnitude, but one we should become used to given the mentality of the present administration. It costs millions of dollars just to close each of these facilities. As you can understand, it will cost many millions more to reopen each one should they be found to be needed again in the future, as they undoubtedly will.

None of this takes into account the devastating impact that total base closures will have upon the support towns that have sprung up around each military installation. I am certainly aware that said bases do not exist for the purpose of perpetuating the economic viability of these neighboring towns. But if we do not wish to repeat the performance exhibited when an auto producing town dies, as what often happened in the Midwest we must, as I usually insist, do things my way.

Rather than closing these bases down entirely we should instead be scaling them back, and depending on our needs, each to differing degrees.

In some cases no loss of manpower will be allowable if it is found that the work is of such nature, and the staffing of such a low level as to preclude reduction. In other cases significant staff reductions will be feasible even to the extent of manning certain bases with skeleton crews.

By realizing our savings in this way as opposed to outright closures we can accomplish the necessary downsizing while giving ourselves the latitude to allow for the need of possible reexpansion in the future. This with the least cost, inconvenience time delay, and weakness in our defenses.

In keeping with our desire to retain a strong defense, I must question the wisdom of selling our arms to most of the rest of the world. Unless another nation is a friend and a proven ally (over time), we should refrain from supplying them with weaponry which we may soon find turned against us. Today's world is far too unstable and volatile to indiscriminately pass around guns to.

A perfect example is found in Iraq. Just prior to our latest problems in this area of the Middle East, we had been helping them with their war efforts against Iran. Little did we realize just how fast the tables could be turned against us, as indeed they were.

Nearly every time you turn on the news and see fighting, the side which opposes our interests can be seen wielding American produced M-16s, weaponry which we supplied them. This is only one example. Our stinger missiles and nearly anything else you can think of are constantly turning up where they don't belong. Why? We sold them to almost any interested party. Let us stop this madness. If our weaponry is superior to that of other producers, why should we wish to share this with anyone other than our staunchest allies?

England, Israel, Canada, and a few others have proven their allegiance to us over a number of decades. With the rest of the world however, I think it is time we recognized the need for a policy adjustment.

Moving on to a different subject, there is no reason for our country to start encouraging homosexuals to join the military.

The recent efforts by President Clinton to lift the ban on them is an enormous mistake made by someone who either misunderstands a great deal, or perhaps just doesn't care.

While his own service record is such that it is quite possible that he actively wishes to destroy our military and thus weaken our country's defense capability, it is more likely that he is merely acting out of ignorance, never having shown himself capable of normal thought to any reasonable level of depth.

Allowing, or perhaps even recruiting gays into our armed forces will have a sizable negative effect. You'll notice that the average person already in the service was not asked his or her opinion on the subject. This was of course by design, not accident. The Clinton administration does not wish the public at large to know the full extent to which the rank and file soldier is repulsed by concerns such as having to bunk in and share showers with known and professed sodomizers.

These are the individuals on whom the lifting of the ban will have the most impact, and it is they to whom we owe a debt of gratitude for their past service. Surly they are deserving of some consideration in this matter. Why is it that we entirely discount the demoralizing effect that this move will have on them?

I have no proof, but only my suspicions that it is the same administration which pressured the press not to report the rapes which were perpetrated on sailors by homosexual sailors in early 1993. It does not aid their cause to allow it to be known that these incidents do occur and are destined to occur much more frequently once the ban on gays is lifted.

All of this also ignores the fact that the sole purpose for the existence of our military is for the protection of our country, hence the term "National Security." It does not exist so that it may serve the individual soldier, but quite the reverse. It was never meant, nor should it ever be meant to serve as the proving grounds for some perverse social experiment.

While it may be true that there are any number of gays who might prove to be good soldiers, that is not what is at question here. Whether or not taking them on board will actually improve the military is. To view this as some sort of civil rights issue is to look at things from entirely the wrong direction. The only concerns here should be for the betterment of, the survival of, and the quality of the military itself for the armed forces exist for too important a reason to allow the clouding of the issue. As it is clear that a lifting of the ban on admitted homosexuals is in no manner necessary for improvement of the military itself, there can be no further meaningful discussion on the subject.

But if it is necessary to raise additional questions, what about the promotion of this lifestyle choice, and the spread of AIDS? Even were we to be so foolish as to pretend that this simply isn't going to happen, what about those homosexuals already infected who will themselves be dying from the virus? And the certain spread of Hepatitis? Must we always turn to the beleaguered taxpayer to take on yet another burden? Should there not be a moral imperative to act in a responsible manner toward those who will be footing the bill? With the lifting of the ban on homosexuals, due to the confusing of our priorities, we will not only be providing the citizens of the U.S. with inferior protection, but we would also impose on them the added cost as well.

Along a distantly related line I adjure you that there is no reason to break with our long standing tradition and start sending women into combat. Not only would this unnecessarily subject another faction of our society to the horrors of war, but it would have a dramatic negative impact on how others view us, and indeed how we view ourselves as a nation.

What kind of society sends its own women and prospective mothers off to die or become maimed in battles that are horrifying enough when they only involve men? What is the next level we will sink to, sending the children?

Our supposed gentler sex, our children, our homes, these are the very items and ideals we send our young men into battle to protect, and hopefully to return to. Where is the impetus to fight if the safety of those precious things is by design allowed to be jeopardized?

And even among the survivors it must be noted that whereas a scar on a man may add character, on a women it is a disfigurement. This is magnified if the place in question is on the face.

The loss of all or part of a limb is devastating enough for a man, how much more so for a woman? Or are we supposed to grow so cold in our cynicism that we never look at these things in this light?

Some would argue that only those women who wish to go into battle should be sent, that the choice should be left up to them. But what sense does this make? Men are not offered the same privilege of choice. Only in the case where both sexes are forced to respond to the draft, both sexes forced off to war without regard to their personal desires, could things truly be considered fair.

With all due respect to the women's movement, there are more stupid and ridiculous things done in the name of supposed "fairness" than can be contained in this book.

For a great number of reasons putting women in combat roles would be a mistake. We can either come to that conclusion on our own, or we will have it proven to us in time. The only difference is that if we wait for the later to happen, it will be too late to avoid learning the hard way, as we have too often done in the past.

The next question I would like to raise is how did we become the worlds policeman? For some inexplicable reason our nation has grown an enormous heart of compassion for everyone around the globe with the exception of our own people.

I too am distressed when I see the terrible things going on in Bosnia. I do feel for these people. However I do not wish to inflict upon the soldiers of my own country the same sordid treatment as some twisted idea of a solution. A solution by the way to a problem which does not, and should not, concern us.

My first moral obligation is my own countrymen, and unless we have a definite, and compelling interest in any foreign action, it is their welfare which must weigh heaviest in the balance.

An example of where we perhaps were justified in sending our troops was in the Persian Gulf war. Not only were we there to return stability to the region, but to keep our life's blood supply of oil flowing as well. Yet, even there I had and still have some reservations.

Even in this case our goals weren't clear enough. Too many people raise the point that targeting a leader like Sadam Hussein would make us amount to being nothing more than hired assassins. I disagree.

What would have been so wrong about specifically going after one particular leader (cutting off the snakes head as it were), and how is it then right that we should kill thousands of his soldiers? Is it their very anonymity which makes their demise at our hands so acceptable? Would we have held back in targeting Adolph Hitler had the opportunity arisen, due to the same ethical concerns? I doubt it.

Nothing is worse than leaving this kind of job unfinished. We are destined to pay dearly for that mistake. It would behoove us to make far fewer enemies, but to deal with them more decisively.

As to our humanitarian involvement in Somalia, I have many problems here as well. Few Americans do not share a genuine concern for these innocent victims of both famine and war. But what part should our military play, and why?

Our brave and self-sacrificing military men and women are dedicated individuals who are used to going to wherever they are sent, and without debate on the question. Do we not have a duty to be careful not to abuse this arrangement? Because of this country's long standing tradition with regards to its armed forces, there is implied the concept that while the soldiers involved may be dispatched at any given time to a place of war, the same soldiers would not expect to be called upon to sweep up garbage, police up after farm animals, or distribute campaign literature.

I think it is wrong of us to send our soldiers off to risk their lives (and indeed, several have died) to guard in the distribution of food. And again I say if we lack the creativity to offer alternative solutions to paying for our ideals with their blood, then shame on us. This type of misuse of their stated duties is not what they signed on for, so let us neither demean them nor count the value of their lives as unimportant. Let us keep the use of our military in areas that it obviously does belong. The savings in both American lives and taxpayers dollars will be the dividends in this needed change of policy.

Another area in which we waste much money has created within us a living paradox. For some unfathomable reason we will bomb the living daylights out of another country, and then in a few short months will pay to rebuild them! To add icing to this perverse layer cake, we will then send the taxpayers the bill for both.

Am I mistaken or can you name for me another nation on the face of the earth that pursues this insane policy?

If people like myself were to know beforehand that we were going to rebuild the enemy, then perhaps we might ask that on our bombing missions we do not do quite so good a job, and thereby save us a few bucks.

We also ask of both our soldiers and our citizenry that they allow us to turn their emotions on and off like a light switch. This is absolutely improper. In order to have soldiers willing to attack and kill any supposed enemy, we (as a country) find it expeditious to convince those being sent to war to come to hate the opposition. Likewise we do the same to the rest of our society in order to recruit their support. To a degree this is as it should be. How much more horrifying it would be to send a bunch of young men off to fight and kill others who they harbor no animosity for. That would have the effect of turning them into even bigger monsters, and cold blooded indeed.

Shortly after the last bomb is dropped, the last shot fired, we start reconstruction as we did in Vietnam. Then we push for a normalization of relations with a full compliment of diplomats all around, and damn the destruction we have wrought upon our own peoples emotions and psyche!

I was just now speaking on a spiritual and ethical level, but I must bring out that of the physical as well. Let us abandon this policy of destroy and rebuild, and as I said earlier, make far fewer enemies, but do our best to destroy them so as to no longer perpetuate this foolishness.

Perhaps you will finally agree with me if we begin rebuilding Bagdad?

The Military and National Security

Our new downsized military will not find it necessary to attract as many people as it has up until now. Therefore, it will not be necessary to offer quite the same package as is offered at this time to recruit enough personal to get the job done. It is then this area which presents itself as an opportunity to reduce spending. It is no secret that one of the largest expenditures in our national defense budget is the paying of retirement benefits.

In years past it was the rule to offer the individual a half-pay retirement after twenty years of service. In too many cases this means we are "retiring" someone at the age of thirty-eight, with half the paycheck that the individual receives while working, full medical, use of the P.X. etc. There is every good chance that same retiree will continue to draw retirement pay for thirty or forty or so years. Decades will have passed since he has ceased being productive for us, and in many cases on a ratio of more than two years of drawing benefits for each one year of having worked.

Another factor to consider is that while thus drawing a healthy retirement paycheck at such a young age it is most likely that the young retiree will seek a second career out in the private sector. This is additional competition that those who are chasing after but one career will not appreciate.

Not to belittle the efforts of these service men and women, but if we scale back our forces, and our desire and interest to use those forces as often, then we should likewise roll back benefits on our reduced military. Please note, this is for new recruits only, no contracts would be broken on those already in the military.

What I propose is that the contract we offer new recruits would be for half pay after twenty-five years (and incrementally adjusted for additional years) and retirement paychecks not collectible until a minimum of age fifty-five. This is to reduce the total number of retirement paychecks due. With the P.X. privileges, excellent health care packages, and other fringes, our military personnel would still enjoy an attractive package compared to most of the private sector.

With today's weakening of unionism, conversion of most double time to time and one half, and weakened job prospects in the outside world, these rollbacks for the military are not out of line.

If we adopt the plan I offer:
- no longer supplying arms to potential enemies;
- a fifteen percent reduction in our military;
- proper application of those remaining;
- maintaining those principles which have served us long and well with regards to gays and women; and
- a somewhat reduced retirement benefit in light of today's business climate.

With this we can save a significant amount of revenue while still producing the first class defense which this country desperately needs.

CRIME

I'd like to start by banishing from your mind one widely held, but ridiculous concept about crime before delving any farther into the subject.

There is a faction within our society that, quite unable to think clearly for itself, is doing its damnedest to see to it that your thinking is clouded as well. This faction would have you believe that much of today's crime statistics are the result of our high unemployment level. On the surface, this idea might have some appeal, and you might be tempted to buy into it provided you refrain from the practice of proper reflection.

The time our country suffered the highest rate of unemployment was during the great depression. Up to twenty-five percent of the people were out of work at any given time. Those who remained in the workplace generally received substantial pay reductions. Just how did this translate out to crime statistics? In actuality, crime rates across the board were quite low in comparison with today. But why is this?

Surely, we had teeming multitudes of people out of work? I believe the answer for this is rooted in two very basic reasons. We had a much better class of people back then whose natural inclinations were to always pull together and make the best of any situation, not to use hard times as a convenient excuse to sink to a lower level and become common thieves.

The second is that at that time, we did not have a large contingent of leftist leaning apologist and sociologists who, as they do today, would have been quick to excuse criminal and antisocial behavior on lack of employment.

"Blame society" is the hue and cry of today anytime things go wrong. The kind of things, mind you, that could easily be traced *exactly* to the chosen behavior of the particular individual involved in criminal activities.

What reason does the criminal have to turn from his evil ways? The poor unfortunate will always get plenty of support from others, so much so in fact that he will no longer need to come up with the excuses for his actions, even that will be provided for him. Notice that this outpouring of concern leaves a deficit when it comes to caring about the needs of the victim. After all, there is a limited quantity of compassion, so you can well understand that the actual victims of crime will simply have to fend for themselves. And if the injured cannot grasp this concept, what can one say? It's a rough world out there.

No, crime is not a function of unemployment, it's really no more complicated than this: when good people find themselves out of work, they suffer. They do not take their misfortune out on society. In the rare instance where a good individual is pushed past the breaking point, he may steal food, but that is about the extent of it. Bad people, on the other hand, pursue criminal activities whether there are sufficient employment opportunities or not. They live a life of crime not because they have no work, but rather *instead* of working.

Please do not allow yourselves to be distracted by all of the nonsense you will hear on the subject. I am about to give you the bottom line.

The largest single component responsible for the level of criminal activity we see today is our willingness to tolerate it. Next to this one factor, all others combined do not even come close.

We have judges who refuse to prosecute. We must fire them. We have police who refuse to arrest. Again, fire them.

Legislators who refuse to pass meaningful laws with teeth in them—impeach them.

Governors who side against proper punishment—give them the one-way ticket out.

And liberals who either say "we've got to understand things from their point of view" or "we must take into account their background"—silence them.

Many decry the "us or them" mentality which is widespread today. But they are the very ones who gave rise to the need for this approach. It *has* become a question of us or them due to their efforts.

If you have a cancer in your body, you do not operate yet leave a small bit of it behind in order to demonstrate some form of "understanding." No, not at all. Once you have made the decision to operate (and operate we should), you go in to remove all of it and in fact follow up with treatments of chemotherapy and radiation, many times just as a precaution.

It *is* us or them, and in reality, always has been. The "us" are those who choose to live our lives by a definite and by no means unbearable code of ethics. A moral protraction which has yielded a system of laws designed to protect the rights of our fellow man and our own in the bargain. We willingly bond ourselves to those laws for not only the furtherance of civilization, but because those laws are reflective of who we are. To a large degree, those laws define us and our worth as beings.

And the "them" are those who hold these principles, these codes of behavior, in contempt. They abandon moral guidance and anything that even suggests that someone or anyone should be allowed to intrude on their quest for not just freedom, but license. Many of these people are not only immoral, but truly amoral, having no code of ethics which they even hold themselves to.

Grouped also in the "them" category are those who willingly embrace the cause of situation ethics. Those who are not above offering even the most asinine excuse for that behavior which comprises illegal actions.

Some of these only lend lip service to this cause, while others are in fact to blame for the actualizing of it. Last year, when tennis player Monica Seles was stabbed in the back by a deranged fan of another player, who was the judge who after trial, imposed *no* jail time, but rather probation? He is one of the "them."

News Item: A German tourist is gunned down in cold blood during a visit to Florida. One of the accused is a thirteen-year-old boy with about (yes, count 'em folks) fifty previous arrests. Fifty arrests. My God, where did he find the time? Who are all of the judges responsible for seeing to it that he was returned to the streets to again terrorize society time after time? They are the "them."

The first step to crime control as I have alluded to in my chapter on the criminal justice system, is to get rid of up to half of the judges. If the ones who are currently making a very nice living from the bench find it a bit too much for their delicate stomachs to impose real sentences, let them be replaced.

A good line to draw in the sand is the question of homicide. In the United States the *average* time served for murdering another person is five and one-half years. Oddly enough, the corpse of the victim does not spring back to life after this period of time, only the murderer goes free.

By reviewing the records of all judges who have adjudicated criminal law for five years or more, we should fire or retire all those who have imposed sentences below the median figure (five and one-half years) in a majority of the sentences rendered.

This will cleanse the system of its most lenient judges, while sending a strong message to the rest that the party is over. No longer will the public tolerate judges on the payroll who are soft on crime.

A judgeship is a prestigious job. It is usually the crowning achievement, that last feather in the cap that most lawyers aspire to before the end of their career. With the position goes an excellent salary, much power and respect. Let only those who are willing to do that job properly remain in place. As to the rest, we must rid ourselves of them.

Most police officers do their job, but too large a portion of them do not. Often used is the excuse that the system will only release the criminal anyway, so why bother? To those officers, I say—Hand in your gun, hang up your badge and seek employment elsewhere.

The failure of one part of a system (which we must work to change) is no legitimate reason to stop holding up *your* end of it. To those who remain, I say—Do not be discouraged. Do *your* job to the best of your ability without respect to the inadequacies you see all around you. Be your own best critic so that you can at least be able to justly say, "I did my part and I did it well."

If judges continue to release your captures, go on the offensive. Work even harder to bring about more arrests. Flood the courts with captured criminals until those on the bench less responsible than yourselves get sick of seeing your faces.

Then join with the rest of us in demanding reform of the criminal justice system.

While I'm on the subject of the police, let me just bring up one further point.

Although crime is rampant, we do not need any more police. We must learn to make better use of the ones we have.

Despite protestations from the P.B.A. and police unions, subsequent contracts must force able-bodied officers out from behind desks and into the streets. Shame on us for having allowed it to continue, that men trained in the use of badge and gun are chained to paperwork, while everything they were trained for is wasted.

Professional clerks should be brought in to man the typewriters, fill out the forms and so forth.

And now to touch upon a sore spot. Just as police officers go out in their patrol cars cruising an area in search of problems, a citizens committee should also cruise an area in search of police goofing off. The taxpayer is understandably rankled when he hears how we need more police, yet he knows of several places where officers go to hide out. Although this is not true of the majority of officers, it must be rooted out to the degree that it exists.

Legislators, governors, mayors and so forth have one important thing in common. We elect them. Therefore, we can also replace them. But our battle starts long before Election Day, it begins prior to the primaries. It is our responsibility as the voting public, as the citizenry, to see to it that *each* candidate has a strong law and order platform. Never again should we let things get away from us so that we are forced to choose the least damaging of two weak fish. Soft on crime, leftist-leaning liberal societal apologists have no place in the future running of our country, if our country is to have a future.

There is a saying which I believe is particular to America. It says "Everyone is entitled to their opinion." But we really do not believe that, do we? Is Adolph Hitler entitled to his opinion? Was Jeffrey Dahmer? Do we listen to the rantings of madmen?

Someone decides that life is not worth living and so takes a one-way trip off a very tall bridge (without even having the decency to pay the toll). How many of us go along with him just to see if he is right? Not many I surmise.

The fact is that everyone *has* an opinion. But that in no way means that all opinions are of equal validity.

We know as a people who are fed up with being victimized, in what direction we wish to go.

When the naysayers object that we must be more understanding and more caring when it comes to dealing with the issue of crime, when these people tell us to take the background of the criminal into account, let us stop being afraid to stand and loudly say, "Shut up!"

We must make it known that we are not interested in their opinion on the matter. There is no time left for debate. We must meet the problem of crime in our society head on. The cancer must be removed or the patient will die. No alternatives. So you see, it all boils down to you. Unless you are willing to take a pro-active position on the politics and policies that shape the future of how our nation is to be run, things will continue pretty much as they have up until now. A continued slide, slower at times, faster at others, but always in the same downward direction.

One final note. Our personal blame in all of this. We must all, all of us who call ourselves good people, stop buying things which we know to be stolen.

You've seen the deals before. Some individual hawking items which have "fallen off the back of a truck." Let us not pretend that in buying questionable items, we are not somehow providing a market. Do not use the logic that if you do not buy it, someone else will. Let them. Accept your personal responsibility in this matter and no longer be even a small part of the problem yourself.

I've said this before, but it bears much repeating. The biggest single component in the existence of crime is our willingness to tolerate it.

Let's stop.

Prisons

Only a couple of generations ago there wasn't nearly so much confusion on this issue as we see about us today.

The Americans of our past knew full well what the purpose of prisons was meant to be, and unlike those of us in today's world, were not so easily sidetracked by foolishness masquerading in various forms.

The primary purpose of incarceration is twofold; to remove the individual in question from the opportunity to do damage to a society he has already threatened, and to punish him for having done so already.

Clemency, pardons, paroles, plea bargains, reduced sentences, leave, work release programs, what do all of these have in common? First off they are legal maneuvers designed to soften the effects of a just penalty or remove it entirely, and second their existence today is in stark contrast to the concept of incarceration of but a few years ago.

Today's expansion of criminal coddling has led to a predictable growth in crime for many reasons. Unlike in the past we might say, yes, crime does pay. The dissuasive element in punishment is reduced to a token or "wrist slap" under today's guidelines and when balanced out against the profit potential of committing a crime along with the much reduced possibility of capture and conviction, can make a life of crime quite appealing indeed.

As an example of this I draw your attention once again to something I mentioned elsewhere in this book. The average time served for homicide today is five and one half years. Only as an aside do I point out that at the end of this term the victim will not be released. Oddly enough he is still dead, but the perpetrator will go free.

Imagine if you will, that you are some petty thief who is caught in the act by a homeowner whose belongings you are attempting to add to your own. Should you be arrested under these circumstances and depending upon your record, you may get two to seven years in prison. But should you simply opt to shoot this busybody who has the audacity to protect his own household, you will likely only get the same term as for the burglary. That is of course if you are caught (unlikely) and if you are convicted (also unlikely).

Is it any wonder so many burglaries end in murder?

The average American thinks that most people are basically good. Let us take that as a given. There is of course a small percentage of our population who are basically bad. It is important that we recognize that in addition to those basically bad people, there is a larger number of people who, while not bad at heart, are capable of falling under that heading, in the right circumstances or if presented with enough temptation. We must remove that temptation by taking the profit potential out of crime.

Most things in life are regulated by natural balance. The fact that most people are neither obese nor morbidly thin is due to the principle that we usually eat when we are hungry, and stop when we are full, a natural control leading to balance.

If in the case of crime, grand theft auto for instance, the activity is profitable, it will occur. Again, a natural balance.

When stolen cars are worth a great deal, the chances of getting caught are slim and the sentences light in the event of capture and conviction, we can rightly expect a great number of cars will get stolen. This is the way it is today. Market forces if you will.

If, however, our system were vigilant enough to insure that one in three car thefts returns a conviction, and that five to fifteen year sentences were the norm, and finally if you will indulge me, that prisons were a wholly miserable place rather than a "sleep away camp," I assure you that few if any cars would be stolen.

The other major way in which unnecessarily short prison terms punish society is through returning to freedom criminals who will understandably see the system as a joke, and behave accordingly. He who has been sentenced to twenty years in some miserable hell hole will view his few remaining days as something precious, something not to be gambled with. And statistics show that those who have served out such harsh sentences overwhelmingly only wish to remain free.

It is unfortunate but true that the sole motivating force for most of us is self-preservation. The man who has served twenty or thirty years for child molestation is, upon being released, likely to seek out whatever help is available to him, (psychiatric, medical, support groups) not for the protection of society but rather to insure that the state will not have a future reason to return him for another prison sentence.

The man who has instead served eighteen months for the same crime is more likely upon release, to seek out another child.

The only change he will probably make is being more careful not to get caught. Perhaps he will even start killing his victims in order to cover his tracks. What did the short prison stay accomplish? It only served to make him more dangerous.

I know that the above goes against everything you will hear from such leftist groups as "The fellowship of reconciliation" and others, but it should be clear to you by now that they are part of the problem, and not the solution. So that second group of criminals created by lax sentencing, besides those who seek out a life of crime because it is profitable, is the returning non-repentant criminal. Recycling at its worst.

And all this because we have lost sight of the purpose of prisons to begin with: the protection of society, and the punishment of the offender.

Too many people nowadays miss this point. They have been convinced by sociologists, liberals, and others that prisons should exist for the purpose of rehabilitating the inmates. Again I am going to tell you something that is unpopular to think about in these terms, but is true nonetheless: The concept of rehabilitation is for the most part a waste of time. Allow me to elaborate.

Prisons should be divided into two types and two types only. Those to which we send first time offenders if their crime is sufficiently minor, and if we can have a reasonable hope of someday returning them to society in a more or less repaired condition. The second type of prison is the one to which we send repeat offenders, axe murderers, etc. It is there that we dump them and basically give up hope of their reform. Its only purpose is to punish criminals, and to protect society.

When I said that attempts at rehabilitation were a waste of time I meant as follows. That person who has indeed seen the error of his ways and genuinely wishes to change, will. There will be no holding him back. It does not require a team of psychiatrists, job training, or a free college education to accomplish this.

Similarly he who by his own strong will refuses to be rehabilitated will undo all your best efforts to bring him around. He has made his choice.

It is for the reasons I have stated that the recidivist rate in many state prisons is eighty percent within five years. After five years those who have truly gone straight remain that way. It would appear that it is easier to turn your back on society than to turn it on prison.

So what should this second type of prison be like, the one in which we house our worst criminals? Well perhaps the easiest way to describe it is to mention what it would not have.

It would not have cable TV...Many of the people whose taxes go toward housing convicted criminals cannot afford this little nicety for themselves, so by what means did this become an entitlement for the incarcerated? Likewise this prison would not have available VCRs and an extensive video tape collection. While I'm on this subject allow me to point out that out here in free society we are constantly being warned about the negative effects of sex and violence in television. And we want this for our prisons?

This prison would not have a weight room. Many prison guards justifiably feel threatened by inmates who have all the time in the world to work on their physique. Any number of them are capable of crushing a guards head with their bare hands if given an opportunity. The purpose of prisons is not to turn out competitors for the next Mr. World contest.

Medical facilities would be sparse. Why is it that we think that when someone becomes a ward of the state he should be entitled to medical care far in advance of that which he received prior to incarceration? Let he who goes into prison with either money or medical coverage provide for his own expenses if need be, and those who have not should receive the minimum care just as they would had they not been locked up. Let not the burden of maintaining the health of criminals be now shifted to the backs of the honest taxpayer.

Incidentally, no conjugal visits. How ridiculous.

What should prisoners be provided with? Perhaps a sand-lot style baseball field for recreation. A decent library for the mind. A small chapel for the spirit, and decent but rather ordinary food for sustaining life. That's all.

I must mention an idea proposed to me by my good friend Terry Eckert, an idea which I wholeheartedly endorse. What I have said so far will most certainly raise the ire of most Liberals and civil liberties groups, the same groups so painfully absent when it comes to victims rights. If they are so concerned about the plight of the poor misunderstood criminal, let them foot the bill for the window dressing. Prisoner rights advocates should feel free to send in non tax deductible contributions to improve the environment of those who are jailed. If they wish to see that each prisoner gets access to cable TV complete with the Playboy channel or whatever, let them pay for it. Let it no longer be a taxpayer concern. Soon we'll see how compassionate they can be when it is their money alone being spent and not yours and mine. If they feel like being that generous, so be it.

Why do I promote a "throw away the key" mentality? Had the criminal justice system done its job in instituting harsh sentences, had the prison system been of the sort which actually punishes criminals instead of rewarding them, the late James Jordan, father of basketball star Michael Jordan, would doubtless be with us this day. Just one example, there are thousands.

Rather than simply being allowed to languish, prisoners should also be put to good use. There are many lessons which can be learned from the South in this regard. In many parts of the South prisoners are routinely leased out to do road repair, forestry, et al. This idea could quite naturally be expanded to include refuse sorting for recycling as well as farming whereby prisoners could grow a substantial amount of their own food. A touch of enterprise here. The harder they are willing to work, the better the food they will enjoy.

Another lesson to be learned from the South is how prisons should be built and run. A number of years ago *Forbes* magazine had an article on the privatization of the prison system as it has been implemented in parts of the Southeast. The prisons are still built to the same rigid specifications that they had been, but with the whole project open to competitive bidding. Entire construction companies have formed around just such a program and have passed a substantial savings on to the state. These prisons are now staffed by a contracting firm which has done the job both better and more cost effective than going the old civil service route. The savings on both building and running the prisons comes to a whopping thirty percent. This idea is one which has been proven to work and should be instituted in every state of the nation.

So what do we do with youthful offenders, first time delinquents, and those who have committed minor crimes? Well nothing quite so harsh, but no country clubs either.

There are programs already under way that resemble military boot camps more than they do prisons. Their purpose is to straighten out young people who have just started their wayward journey in conflict with the law. The goal is to turn them back in the right direction while there is still time to remold their impressionable minds. Early studies show strong evidence to suggest a high success rate for the program. If time bears out the same results the program must be expanded.

If it becomes understood by its inmates that this represents one last opportunity to make personal changes and avoid moving on to "real" prison, this system will act to shortstop further criminal activity.

Clear-cut choices to behave or be jailed will lead to serious decisions on which direction to take ones life in, this second chance also being the last. No longer will we see cases like the recent one in Florida, where a thirteen-year-old suspect in a murder has fifty previous arrests.

By returning our prison system to the concepts under which they were originally created, in conjunction with an overhaul of the criminal justice system we can look forward to a substantially reduced crime rate, lower taxes, reduced need for police and insurance, and fewer horror stories about repeat offenders like the ones we now see daily in the news.

Capital Punishment

We must touch for a moment on certain religious teachings on this particular subject, for it is a moral dilemma which we attempt to settle when addressing the question of state-sanctioned execution.

In biblical history (both Jewish and Christian), we see not only an allowance for capital punishment, but an admonishment that justice shall be dispensed in accordance with "an eye for an eye, a tooth for a tooth," etc. Biblical scholars are divided on the reason that this pronouncement was given. Some say to make certain that punishment was enforced both sternly and equitably. Others equally astute in scriptural studies and history counter that civilized man at that point in time was really quite vicious, and capable of utter retribution. They contend that these were guidelines which implied "*only* an eye for an eye, *no more than* a tooth for a tooth" holding people back from exacting a far more severe punishment than was deserved. Which do I side with? It isn't important so long as we recognize the guidelines.

While we are at it we may dig a little deeper and notice that Scripture not only permits capital punishment for certain crimes, but indeed *insists* upon it. Now the reason I chose to break with the general philosophy of this book, and bring religion and morals into the subject matter, is that this is intrinsically an issue which can only be approached from a moral basis. Were we to devoid the question of any reference to religion or moral ramifications, and only view things from an antiseptic clinical platform, we could as easily reach our conclusion by flipping a coin.

Whenever anyone raises an objection to capital punishment, it is done so on a question of morality, and so I must defend it on that same question of morals basis.

This country has always recognized the ethical and constitutional appropriateness of invoking the death penalty as just payment of debt for the performance of certain crimes. Generally accepted as worthy of this punishment are murder, kidnaping, espionage and desertion during war time.

The only glitch in our record of accepting capital punishment as proper was when, for a short period of time, the Supreme Court was of the opinion that capital punishment was unconstitutional. This came about in 1972 on the grounds that it constituted "cruel and unusual punishment," a prohibition on what may constitute excessive recompense for crimes committed. The questions are therefore whether this *does* indeed constitute such cruel and unusual punishment, and historically how far that concept has been applied.

For the sake of this discourse, I would prefer to restrict dealing with this question only in terms of how it applies to the subject of murder. Even if you agree with the principle of capital punishment, it could forever be debated which crimes should be included for that punishment, whereas murder is the widely recognized common denominator.

In our society, or in any other society for that matter, there have been set up certain parameters of acceptable behavior. These are generally neither arbitrary nor illogical. Laws are passed in order to define the boundaries of behavior so that there will be a hard cold line drawn, not subject to the whims of individual interpretation. Cross over one of these lines and you are in violation of the law and subject to punishment including a suspension of your constitutional rights, provided there is due process.

Those who have destroyed the purpose of the law and shattered its understandable boundaries by going so far as to commit murder, have in essence made a statement. They have told society through their actions that they couldn't give a fig for our notion of responsible behavior, and as such they have forfeited their rights to be treated as human beings. At the point where they willingly take another's life with malice and intent, they have more in common with a rampaging animal than with a civilized man. I of course am not speaking here in the event where there are extenuating circumstances as in the case of self-defense or the like.

The issue of capital punishment has unfortunately been confused when certain well-meaning individuals raise the erroneous question as to whether or not its presence results in the deterrence of crime. It was never intended to act as a deterrent (although it well may) only as a punishment, which it accomplishes quite nicely. Beyond being punitive, it also serves another very important purpose. It removes the person in questions from the position of ever being able to inflict himself on others, to repeat the offense for which he is being punished.

Also fallacious are arguments on how the institution of capital punishment lowers all of society to the same level as the criminal. Only fools and evil individuals would even try to compare the metering out of retributive punishment to the willful and violent taking of an *innocent victim's* life.

There is, of course, much talk about prisoner/criminal rights, but there is far too little attention being paid to the rights of the victim and society as a whole. We all would agree that it is a crying shame whenever some innocent person is murdered. But how much more so when a *second* victim falls prey to the same person of evil intent after he has been released from a brief incarceration?

The first occurrence we can have little control over. We live in a dangerous world and in violent times where anyone might strike out at any given time without prior warning. But shame on us, if in our attempt to be "lenient" or "understanding," we have set the stage for a repeat performance.

Now as far as cruel and unusual punishment is concerned, are not all punishments what we would term as cruel? After all, what nation ever instituted what might be considered pleasant or comfortable punishments?

Likewise, what constitutes unusual? Anyone might agree that it would be both unusual and cruel if we were to extend the application of the death penalty to cases of failing to rotate one's tires correctly, or even to petty theft. But on the subject of minor crimes, have you never seen those signs which say "LITTERING—$250 FINE"? Remember, it isn't important what length of time is required for you to earn two hundred and fifty dollars, what matters is how long it takes you to *save* that amount. Let us assume that it takes a month. Is it proper then, that the state should deny you an entire month's savings for having improperly discarded an empty coffee container or cigarette pack?

Now as for proper recompense in relation to the severity of the crime, coupled with (in the case of murder) the inability of the violator to ever set things right again, capital punishment is neither cruel nor unusual at all but precisely what one might expect to be just punishment for certain crimes committed.

It is in fact the mark of a *civilized* country which insists that the punishment be commensurate with the crime, while those who pretentiously put on only the veil of civilization try to impress us with how "understanding" they can be. Far from being progressive as they envision themselves, they

Capital Punishment

instead project an attitude of "anything goes." In 1977, the Supreme Court reversed its decision, again permitting capital punishment, and there it has stood ever since. It has from that time become the responsibility of the individual states to make their own determination as to proceeding with execution as a reasonable reward for ill deeds.

The less responsible states have allowed their governor to make the decision, pretty much doing away with the one-man/one-vote concept, and the principle of self-determination. And in those cases where the governor has used his veto power to override majority rule, it becomes readily apparent what happens when those in charge care not at all about the wants, needs, desires, and even opinions of the people government was supposed to serve.

Since it has been determined by the Supreme Court (after much debate and one false start) that the death penalty is in no way unconstitutional, and that the decision as to whether or not to implement it has been handed to the states, let it continue to be determined in that manner. Let us make one small change however. We must see to it that the decision at the state level is always placed in the hands of the citizenry, those who will be most affected by the outcome.

Properly, it is the citizenry who should decide if they wish to see that justice is done or whether they would prefer that criminals are treated better than their victims. That determination would also include the question as to which crimes should be judged severe enough to warrant the ultimate payment and the decision will naturally vary from state to state. Some will decide that only murder in the first degree justifies execution, while others might take things as far as high level drug trafficking or car jacking. Let the public decide.

As a final note, I must mention something which happened here in New York, that mecca of liberal theology.

Here, thanks to the hardheadedness of one man, Mario Cuomo, we had no proper payment for crimes such as murder.

A radical group bombed the World Trade Center, killing six and injuring nearly a thousand more. This was not what they had intended. What they had really hoped for was to bring the entire tower (or both of them) down in a pile of rubble, killing tens of thousands and striking fear into the hearts of all Americans.

The signal we send, when even perpetrators of such crimes as these will not be made to pay appropriately, can only ensure their repetition in the future.

ENERGY

Several years ago the reigns which controlled most of the world's oil supply were held tightly in the hands of the Arab countries. As the price shot through the roof they enjoyed seemingly unlimited prosperity. They made, in my view, only one mistake. They did not press their advantage, and with those new found petrodollars capitalize on their opportunity to branch out. It was those extra dollars per barrel of oil which should have funded their efforts to develop alternate energy sources. Think of it. Had these Mideast countries had on their thinking caps they might now control the technology and patents for windmills, solar cells, solar panels, and geothermal energy. Perhaps they might have even delved into further research on nuclear fusion. Had they done it right, the world might have no choice but to turn to them for all energy needs, regardless of which types were chosen.

Fortunately for us, they did not pursue those avenues. Sad to say, neither did we.

There is still a long way to go in the development of the solar cell, and we have not expended nearly as much effort toward its development as we should have. Yes, I know that we have solar cells and that they do work, but the problem is one of cost versus life span. Unless a way is found to make them half as expensive, or last twice as long, they will continue to cost more per unit of energy produced than other sources do.

Wind energy production, once scoffed at, has taken parts of the nation by storm, if you'll excuse the pun. Portions of California have spawned great wind farms with vast tracts of land covered by hundreds of large modern windmills. Small farms all around the United States have returned to wind power at least as a supplement to existing utilities. We still have many areas which remain unexplored in this effort toward practical wind energy, and I will go into more detail later in this chapter. It is a shame that the very area of our country which would benefit most from wind generated power lacks the most basic ingredient in the recipe. The southeast, to which I am referring, simply does not have enough wind to make this form of energy practical, at least for where we are in our progress with wind machines.

There may or may not be great promise for the future of geothermal power. Shafts reaching many miles below the earth's surface to where the temperature is higher can allow us to power steam driven generators to provide much low cost electricity. Certainly the logistics of such undertakings are a long way from being worked out satisfactorily, but that day appears to be coming. If all were to go as planned, this system would be a bit like having your own pet volcano, only safer and more predictable.

The solutions to our energy problem like the solutions to most of all our problems are simple. All we need is the foresight and the fortitude to properly tackle these challenges. I propose the following: the federal government should fund efforts to move forward with the development of the most promising means of alternate energy sources.

Yes, I am aware that some people think that any concept of alternate energy is just so much hullabaloo. I'll thank them to remember, if they are capable, that the petroleum products we rely on so heavily today, were in themselves alternate energy sources not so long ago.

Energy

Prior to this century, hay was the fuel and the horse was either the vehicle or else the power that pulled the vehicle. Lamps were fired by tallow or perhaps coal oil before the rather recent applications of gas and electricity. You don't have to reach back too much farther to see Europeans heating their homes with wood, peat, or dung prior to a Mister Marco Polo returning home from a venture with tales about rocks that burned. Stories of the existence of coal were met with skepticism by the majority of people who he shared his experiences with, and he was undoubtedly branded either a madman or a liar by most.

With these things in mind, I hope you will take a bit more seriously what I have to say with regards to the search for alternate energy.

As things stand now, the possibilities I see as most promising include wind power, solar power, and geothermal energy as I've noted. A possible fourth area might be tidal flow power, taking advantage of low velocity but high quantity water flow which may be captured at yet to be created sea walls.

Firms in the private sector which have enjoyed a measure of success in any of these three or four subjects should be given seed money to help accelerate advancement of the developing technology. A financial reward should be offered to companies which do make breakthroughs. The inexpensive production of long lasting components is all that holds up the practicality of solar cells.

Much stands in the way of the wide use of geothermal energy, but its day will come. As with solar energy, it wouldn't hurt to give it a little nudge.

Wind power science still lacks the ability to extract energy at either high or low velocity levels. At low wind speeds, the answer may be the new breed of helical blade wind machines, possibly coupled with an electronically switched torque converter. An alternate might be wind turbines for this purpose. I believe I've stumbled onto the solution to the problem of excessive wind speeds. At the present time, windmill vanes spill off the extra wind when speeds get too high. This is usually accomplished by the blades rotating on their axis to present less surface area for the moving air to act upon, or by other similar methods. This is done for two basic reasons. Too high a wind may jeopardize the integrity of the tower which the windmill is mounted on. The other reason is that too high a wind overstresses the generator causing a number of small disasters. Motor burnout, winding explosions, bearing failure, and excessive output are the results. This is really a pity as at high speeds the best part of the wind is therefore wasted, gone is the best part of the wind energy curve. Air speed is indicative of the wind energy potential on a basis of geometric progression, i.e. a wind of twice the normal velocity possesses fourfold the energy. Think of the power we could get from a hurricane if we could only capture it!

Well, I believe we can.

If one were to make a windmill apparatus with a single drive shaft passing through two generators mounted in tandem, and having the second generator rigged with a centrifugal clutch so that it only engages, only comes onboard when wind speeds are high, each wind machine thus designed could capture twice the energy as a conventional unit. This would allow the device to operate at wind velocities approximately fifty percent higher than they do now. The only detail wanting is that of course the bearings and support towers would have to be appropriately beefed up to accommodate these magnum windmills. If successful in tests and practical usage, the concept might be extended to use several in line generators mounted similarly on a common drive shaft. The only difference would be the necessity of differing spring tension on each progressive clutch mechanism.

So how do we finance the development of these projects? How do we fund the attempt at development? Again, it's simple. Since it is fossil fuels which we are looking to replace (in the very long run), what better place to look at, than a one or two cent tax placed on each gallon of gasoline? You know that I am an antitax advocate, so please don't misunderstand me here. I am not at all proposing that we levy additional fines on the usage of gas, no, not at all. This penny or two per gallon should come out of the tax that the federal government is already collecting from us. It would remain the same amount of money, only now a portion of it would be going toward a more suitable purpose than whatever it is that Uncle Sam is wasting it on now.

My own figures, and being of course conservatively estimated, show that by this means alone, one billion dollars a year could be raised to fund alternative energy research, and all by simply earmarking a couple of pennies per gallon of gasoline for that purpose.

Next on the energy agenda is seeking out more of our traditional energy sources, oil and natural gas. We stand now poised at a unique time, a unique opportunity in history.

Everyone in the U.S. from right wing conservative to left wing Marxist seems to have their panties all in a bunch over the "necessity" of giving aid to Russia. Coincidentally, it has very recently been discovered that Russia is sitting on oil and gas reserves the likes of which, the magnitude of which are unequaled anywhere else in the world. According to reports, the Middle East is by comparison the proverbial drop in the bucket.

I propose that rather than simply gifting Russia multiple billions of dollars of our own taxpayers money (a response which we seem to have gotten far too used to) that we play instead a rather interesting game of "let's make a deal."

Properly set up and properly structured, we could find ourselves in the enviable position of never again having to beg our neighbors for a cup of oil. Never again could we be held hostage by Mideast power brokers holding all the good cards and all the oil to boot.

The best part is that we could largely avoid paying for the rights to these reserves with actual cash. Much more than our money, Russia is in dire need of our marketing expertise, as it makes the difficult attempt to secure itself a position among the developed countries with unregulated markets and free enterprise.

Technology is another priority item they sadly lack as well as tried and proven methods of business management. Our big corporation's C.E.O.s when unencumbered by government restriction are unparalleled in their expertise and their ability to engender in others the entrepreneurial spirit. We could both profit greatly with the exchange of this commodity for oil.

Our own coal and oil reserves deserve mention. At this time our oil, although of good quality, is expensive to produce. So much so that actually pays us to import that which we need. As strange as it might appear on the surface, it nonetheless really puts us in a good position. If we can keep the cost of imported oil at a reasonable level, it is to our advantage to keep our reserves as just that—reserves.

Kept in the ground, these reserves give us a strategic cushion, a safety net of sorts. Should we be cut off from foreign oil, these reserves will still be there, held available to bail us out. Their very presence in fact helps keep the Mideast oil prices down. Should the oil producing countries drive the price of their product too high, they are painfully aware that the move will stimulate us to provide more of our own.

Were the situation reversed, we would be in enormous trouble. Let's say we were to use all our own oil up first. That would put us at the mercy of foreign producers both as to supply and price. It is for this reason that I recommend that we hold on to our reserves against the day when we may need them (let's hope never), and do what we can to influence the world market price on oil so as to keep it reasonable.

Our coal reserves are, as they say, "a whole 'nother story."

The U.S. has vast, untapped coal reserves. Unfortunately, although they can be mined inexpensively, most of our coal has a high sulfur content, a major pollutant. Given time, our technology will catch up with our need, and we will find a way to use this type of coal in a more pollution-free manner. We might come up with a method of stripping away the sulfur during the mining process, but it is more likely that modified burning techniques, or a restructuring of the smokestack afterburners will be the answer.

In any event it is in our best interest to simply allow this technology to evolve naturally, and to continue to refrain from the use of this high sulfur coal until such a time as it does.

Again this puts us in a good position. By not having the use of this coal at the present time, it insures that it will be kept in reserve against the day when we have no other choice but to use it.

No discussion on modern energy would be complete without mentioning that greatest bugaboo of all, nuclear power. This nation has a poor track record on the proper use of nuclear power, second only to the Russians (Chernobyl, etc.). This source of power was supposed to be not only inexpensive, but highly safe. It has been proven to be neither. Despite glowing reports (pun intended) we have failed time and time again in our attempts to build nuclear power plants that do not contain a host of flaws, failures, and problems. And the cost has exceeded every other form of energy due to production cost overruns, litigation, "accidents," and disposal and shipping problems.

It is time we took a step back and carefully examined this energy source before plunging relentlessly on ahead. While there is much truth to the old bumper sticker "most nuclear power plants are built better than Jane Fonda," still nobody wants one in his back yard. While I am equally sure that few people want Jane Fonda in their back yard either, this is hardly the point.

Several other countries, notably France (yes, here I go with France again), have for decades been safely, successfully using nuclear energy, having experienced neither logistical nor financial problems in its use. Are we too stubborn, too proud to learn from someone else's success? I think perhaps we are.

We should postpone any new construction and implementation of atomic power facilities for a period of several years. Those plants which have been properly run we should not interfere with. Let us during this period study the success enjoyed by other countries to see what it is that they do differently, and place a moratorium on new construction here until such a time that we can guarantee top quality installations. At that time we should build one model plant. One. If it comes off without a hitch, and given enough time to prove itself, then we could build others. Only when we can demonstrate that we are at last on track with regard to cost and safety should we allow nuclear power to proliferate. My nearest guess is that at the rate we are going, that will take fifty years.

Cogeneration and reclamation are the last two things I wish to touch upon in my discourse on energy.

In many other chapters of this book I have mentioned cogeneration and the diverse ways in which we may take advantage of it, each time saving the equivalent in fossil fuel which is supposedly unrenewable. The heat from incinerators, both of solid waste and medical waste, as well as the heat produced in electrical plants are examples of what might be recaptured and recycled for their logical use. To varying degrees they could augment or replace existing heating or light at these facilities. In the past we were rather cavalier in the way we treated this resource. The time has come to take that which we have traditionally wasted, and put it to good use.

Reclamation is exactly what it sounds like. All over America are countless thousands of landfills. They range in age from relatively new to those which have long been closed. Most of them actively produce copious amounts of methane gas which is for the most part wasted. We have the ability today to reclaim, refine, and process this gas for use, and should not let this opportunity slip through our fingers.

Much of the waste from our sewage treatment plants could similarly be used to produce methane gas before disposal of the sludge. As I said, the technology is already with us, we have but to study the implementation.

So there you have a long term or perhaps permanent solution to America's energy needs. Let us now recap these in a more or less chronological order of how those different steps could best suit our needs.

First, let us bargain with Russia to secure the rights to those enormous pools of oil recently discovered there. This will take care of our immediate needs as well as providing a known future supply beyond the next century.

Concurrent with this move we must explore advancements in alternative energy. Allocations made from the federal gasoline tax will help here. It is important to seek to advance technology for alternate energy production not only because of its low pollution to output ratio, but because the day may come where we wish it to replace fossil fuels where possible, saving these for uses where there may be no other choice.

Cogeneration and reclamation projects should go forward to further reduce our dependence on petrochemicals as well as promoting the basic principles of frugality.

Atomic fission research must continue as I've outlined here, to be implemented only when proven safe, reliable, and cost effective.

Long term scientific study in the search for practical fusion reactors (especially along the lines of cold fusion) may someday provide us with the ultimate answer to most of our energy demands. The solution to the impediments to this are at least fifty years away if they are to be found at all, but because of the magnitude of what success in this quest may bring us, we must persevere.

Our own reserves of coal and oil should be kept aside, saved against the day when we have no other alternative but to use them.

The future holds much good news on the topic of energy, much promise indeed. As time passes, more ideas will crop up for alternative energy systems. Less polluting methods of energy production will be founds. Efficiency will increase as our technology evolves. Finally, it is inevitable that more oil, gas, and coal reserves will be discovered. If we make the concerted effort things will only improve, but we must get started now.

By use of the overall plan that I have presented here, our nation can easily provide for its energy needs not just for the foreseeable future, but forever.

SOCIAL SECURITY

It would almost be funny if it weren't so tragic. It seems that every time you turn on the television news, a congressman or our president is talking about making "needed" cuts in social security so as to reduce the deficit, balance the budget, etc.

Now it's not that I believe that there should be any sacred cows, but there is a certain perversion evident when officials whose salaries are between one hundred and thirty, and two hundred thousand dollars a year, decry allowing our aged a pension of a very minimal six to ten thousand dollars annually. This miserly pension was for the most part paid for by the retiree. So the reality is that they would be denied their own money.

Even the perks which our elected officials receive, far exceed the pension provided by social security. But somehow the recipient of a small social security check has become the bad guy. Perhaps these congressional perks might be an interesting place to look when considering needed cuts.

A person works all through life, from mid or late teens 'til that person is in his or her mid sixties. In addition to all of the other taxes, a special social security tax of fifteen percent is paid on most earnings (half provided by the employer). The government collects from this individual federal tax, state tax, property tax, sales tax, user fees, bridge, tunnel and road tolls, fines for parking in the wrong spot, or in the right spot for a bit too long, and on, and on, and on. Despite all these other taxes going in to feed the general treasury we are supposed to buy the premise that there just isn't enough, and that this is why our federal government has found it necessary to keep "dipping" into the social security account. Dipping? Yes, with both hands! It is for this reason and this reason alone that the fund is in trouble.

After decades of labor, with perhaps half of his income going to various taxes, the above mentioned individual looks forward to collecting a small monthly check for those few remaining years of life.

In this day and age the recipient of this check had better have made additional arrangements for his declining years, for there are few places where he could retire on this check alone. Quite naturally this is where those in Washington cast an eye with the idea of saving money.

Why? Does the pentagon need a few more seven hundred dollar hammers? Does our Vice President require another forty-two thousand dollars per year raise like the one granted to Dan Quayle?

Sure, let's put another burden on our aged. Why not? They've shouldered the burden most of their lives anyway, they must be used to it by now.

I'm sure there are many in government who would be delighted to eliminate social security entirely. Oh, not the tax mind you, we'd still have to pay that!

My way? As I've said I have no sacred cows, so by all means let us look at the possibility of cuts in this area. But not until we've done certain other things first. Let us begin by rolling back the salaries of congress to a more realistic level. (For this statement alone I'm sure I've earned their undying hatred and criticism. I'm sure they think I'm a very dangerous person indeed!) Let us reduce congressional staffs. In fact before I go on, please refer to my entire chapter on the congress. Likewise prior to cutting social security, let us address the possibilities as I've outlined in the chapters on Welfare, the military, AIDS, foreign aid, energy, and immigration. Why, the elimination of the electoral college alone would save us a small fortune.

Some people raise what appears to be a reasonable objection. "What about all the wealthy retired people who are also collecting a social security check?" Well what about them? It is never my purpose to excite class envy, that is the job of the liberals. And they do such a good job of it. I couldn't care less that a few millionaires who have also paid for decades into this program, should draw off of it as they are entitled. Pointing to any supposed inequality in this area is an old trick designed to draw your attention from the fact that our own government is stealing our future, and has been for quite some time.

The solution to our social security problem is simple. The government must stop raiding this fund to help out any more of its failed programs in the general budget. We must exercise belt tightening in all areas of government so as to not endanger this fund, which is when left alone, quite healthy.

Only when we have managed to put our many other houses in order, if there still exists a need should we look toward tinkering with social security.

It is my guess that if we clean up our act elsewhere, where real waste and excess exist, we will have no need to place a choke hold upon our aged, a group that we daily approach becoming ourselves.

Congressional Reform

Congress. The word alone stirs up images of inefficiency, ineptitude and corruption. I guess it was Will Rogers who said it first: "If pro—means for, and con—means against, then if progress means to go forward, what does Congress mean?"

Not much good can be said about this organization, and not much has changed since Will Rogers day other than the money which Congress costs us at every level. Their base purpose is to take large sums of your money, shuffle it several times, remove a big chunk of it for themselves and their ever expanding staff, and return to you what little is left in the form of overinflated services and idiotic projects which you have absolutely no interest in.

The whole kit and kaboodle could easily be replaced with an old calculator, a few cases of domestic beer, and a couple of monkeys, provided they possess the necessary predisposition toward evil.

With "pork" as their middle name they press onward in their goal to spend, spend, spend, secure in the knowledge that the money they waste is of course not their own. It is, or rather was, yours.

When good people, people who are citizens and taxpayers, are understandably upset about high taxation coupled with a poor economy (natural bedfellows it seems) they quite commonly appeal to their congressman to look for places where spending might be trimmed.

Since all evidence points to the probability that congresses desire is quite the opposite of actually saving money, you shouldn't be surprised when they respond that they haven't a clue how.

There is much that I could say on the topic of congressional reform, too much really. What needs to be said on this subject and related subjects could fill a book. Fortunately someone has already managed to do just that, and he has done an excellent job.

I can heartily recommend that you pick up a copy of *The Government Racket, Washington Waste from A to Z* published by Bantam Press.

It's author, Martin Gross, has really done his homework. The book is excellently researched and brilliantly written. His ideas for congressional and other governmental reform I couldn't agree with more.

If you do buy a copy of this book and agree with what it has to say, I make only one request of you. When you have finished reading it please forward the book to either the White House or your favorite congressman asking them to specifically implement his plans, and if not, to let you know why.

I have added up all of the major savings that his book proposes. While being a bit more lenient in certain areas than Mr. Gross, I was still able to come up with a yearly minimum savings of four hundred and fourteen billion dollars. Coincidently this figure approximates the current average yearly deficit, and wiping out current deficits will go a long way toward being able to position ourselves for battle with that even larger dragon, the national debt.

Mr. Gross also takes on that very question, and while his approach to the national debt is somewhat different than my own, I see considerable merit in his ideas.

To take things just one small step farther I must say that had our government applied that authors simple principles of common sense frugality but a handful of years ago, there would be no national debt.

To the solutions which Martin Gross has offered I only add a couple of my own which bear mentioning.

We should reduce congressional salaries to an even one hundred thousand dollars, while at the same time taking away their ability to vote themselves future raises.

But of far greater importance is our need as the people, the very people which this government was set up to serve, to take our power back. As I've mentioned elsewhere in this book, one of the best ways to accomplish this is to by any means necessary, and with any mechanism we can find, strip congress and others in government of as much power and as many perks as possible.

The money we would save would be considerable, but it is far exceeded by the importance of having returned the seat of power to where it belongs, to the hands of those who pay the taxes.

Congressional Term Limits

Every once in a while you run across a situation when the proper thing to do is to do that which looks better as second choice. There is only one major argument against term limitations and I am here to tell you that upon closer examination it doesn't hold any water.

Noted radio talk host Bob Grant is one of those who speaks out against term limitations. While in most instances I hold what Mr. Grant has to say with considerable respect, on this topic he is off target.

Yes, it would be far more preferable that we should "vote the bums out" when there terms are up. That would of course be closest to the Democratic process which most of us are in agreement with.

There stands only one problem. We are not doing it.

The majority of us are well aware of the shortcomings of Congress as a whole and would love to see them replaced *en mass*. The problem comes in when it comes time to vote on our own individual Congressmen. Somehow most people feel that their own Congressman is doing a quite serviceable job, and that it is only the ones from other states who should all be replaced.

But why is this?

Most of us are quite short sighted at times and tend to view things only on one plane or in one manner.

There are two components to what these elected officials do. That which concerns their state, and that which concerns the whole country. Unfortunately it is our inclination to pay closer attention to what our politicians do for us locally and we miss the big picture.

Only a small portion of time and money which our respective congressmen deal in, is directly related to their home districts. The majority of their time and our money is spent on those areas of national impact, but our tunnel vision causes us to more heavily consider the "what have they done for us" issues.

Should a congressman or senator be successful in bringing home a number of pork barrel projects, (as most are) their constituents feel that they have done a good job of looking after their interests, and usually reelect them.

It is to our detriment that seldom do we study the record of how they have been looking after the farm at the federal level.

Annually we have a federal budget of some 1.5 trillion dollars. For those of you who just don't know, it takes a thousand million to make a billion and it likewise takes a thousand billion to make a trillion, which we spend one and one half of each year. So that's one and one half thousand, thousand, million dollars or in other terms one-and-one-half times one million times one million. And that's only at the federal level!

This is all well and good except for one thing. The same Congress that approves this spending plan each year, is aware that we cannot generate more than 1.2 trillion dollars in revenues each year. Yet they keep spending more.

This budget gap, or deficit, is 0.3 trillion dollars or otherwise stated, three hundred billion dollars.

Each year we spend twenty-five percent more money than we take in, this despite the staggering burden of the taxes we pay. How is this done? Congress votes it so, that's how.

These yearly deficits, accumulated over time have given us our enormous 4.2 trillion dollar national debt. It now stands at three and one-half years total revenues.

Assume for a moment that your household income is thirty thousand dollars annually. Can you see what kind of financial trouble you would be in if you were one hundred and five thousand dollars in debt, three and one-half times your total income? And by this debt I do not mean for anything which has a down the line pay off such as a mortgage, whereby you eventually pay off a house. What we are talking about here is just day to day operating costs.

This is the kind of trouble we are in at a national level. Yet year after year our congressmen willingly vote to spend us deeper into debt.

And we reelect them?

This is but one small example of what a poor job they have been doing on our behalf while continuing to rake in over one hundred thirty thousand dollars in annual pay, plus many perks and benefits.

We should recognize our lack of discipline as voters, and do the next best thing to voting them out. Since we are apparently incapable of exercising good judgement in the voting booth, we should institute term limitations.

I once knew a man who was a recovering alcoholic. He joined A.A., and soon managed to behave himself all day long. But on his drive home from work he always passed his favorite neighborhood tavern on the way, for it was right along his daily route. More often than not he found himself yielding to temptation, and stopping in for "only one or two." He just did not possess the fortitude to drive on by.

He has been free from alcohol for a number of years now. The only way he was able to break the destructive chain was to begin driving a different route to work. He no longer passed by his favorite watering hole. This entailed an additional two miles to and from work, but even my friend who was of limited brain power, was able to see that it was the only solution.

We voters are much like my alcoholic friend. We know what we should do, but find ourselves too weak to follow through. Let us take a lesson from my friend. Recognize our failures, push through term limitations and remove the temptation out of our way.

There is one added benefit to be derived through term limitations. If these rascals are no longer able to become thoroughly entrenched in Washington, and in our lives, perhaps they will start doing their jobs for the jobs sake, instead of as an unending reelection effort.

No longer would they have the time to create monsters like the House bank, or the House Post Office either. Major embarrassments to us in the eyes of the rest of the world.

Some of you might be disposed to object to term limitations for the possibility that we may lose a few good representatives who we would prefer to hang on to. Of you I can only ask this: Is it worth it? Has it ever been?

A good house cleaning is in order.

The Non-Politician

"With all due respect, my opponent has no political experience." The incumbent will always be heard saying this whenever a challenger comes from outside the system to threaten his private little kingdom.

When we buy this line (as is usually the case) we have bought into two false premises. First is that the man holding office has any respect at all for his opponent or for the voters, and second that political experience is necessary to perform well in public office.

Since it is certainly not true that experience in office will guarantee quality representation, why do we take it as a given that the lack of past political experience negates any person's value as a worthwhile candidate?

The fine individuals who formed this country were not themselves professional politicians, nor did they envision that our government should be run by people who were permanently ensconced in positions of power.

It was their belief that governmental offices should be held for a period of but a few years, after which the ex-officials would return to the private sector from where they had come. Only in this way was the term of office in government truly served as a contribution to society rather than a career. "Helping steer the ship" was the more realistic approach as instituted back then, in comparison to today's concept of "being in charge."

Think of it. Our nation was set up by a collection of businessmen, smiths, inventors, and other representatives of the community rather than those who, from cradle to tomb, aspire only to government and the power and perks that go with it. Those who come up from the private sector can be truly representative of the people, while professional politicians almost cannot help but be out of touch.

Do not too quickly discount the type of contribution that can only be provided by those who have come from outside the system.

I cannot always tell you what will work, but I can show you what doesn't work. For approximately the last three decades what hasn't worked for our country is the standard political process, and our blindly following those pathetic excuses we have for leaders. In most races for office we, the American people, have been forced time and time again to pick between two ineffectual candidates, choosing the lesser of two evils. Where are the people of quality? Our country has about two hundred and sixty-five million people, approximately half of them adults. Surely somewhere among them can be found better alternatives to those now being offered?

We as a people need to open our minds and listen more carefully so as not to miss the sound of opportunity knocking.

Very occasionally one comes on the scene who has little or no political background, but wishes to run for public office. He is immediately rebuffed by the incumbent and others campaigning against him as "having no experience in politics."

But we must also exercise caution. As I hope this nation has learned by now, change for the sake of change is not in and of itself a good thing. We must make certain our goal is change for the better.

In 1992 our country made the mistake of voting for Bill Clinton because he pounded home his doctrine of "change." Soon that is all we will see for our paychecks. Loose change. We traded in the ineffectual George Bush for the Clinton Disaster Team, and we'll be paying for that error for many years to come.

Ross Perot siphoned off a considerable quantity of Bush votes. This was a non-politician and yet not of the sort I would ask you to support. As with many things in life he looked far better at a distance than he did up close, for only on closer examination did his many flaws become apparent. This is an example of where we must exercise caution.

Let us also remember an important point I make in another chapter, the need for runoff elections. We must restructure our political process so that the final election for any office always boils down to a choice between two candidates. This will make our choices clearer and remove the danger that a third party candidate will tip the scales toward the worst choice.

This being duly noted I say yes, embrace the non-politician under the right circumstances. Scrutinize his other qualifications, listen carefully to his platform, demand specifics and become a more educated voter. If he does not meet with your requirements then by all means give him no support, but do not dismiss him on the basis that he has no political experience. That is the incumbents oldest ploy for holding on to his job, his power.

The salvation of this country may well rest in the hands of the non-politician. We have seen what the "experts" can do.

Citizen Empowerment

Power and money. The two dynamics are as inextricably interwoven as it is possible to be. If it were our own power and money we're dealing with, all might be well. But when both power and money are being used against us as weapons for further subjugation, this is another story altogether.

In a better world (not a perfect one, just better) it would be easy to imagine government having no problem with allowing the power to revert to those in whom it properly belongs, you the taxpayer. This is precisely what the idea of initiative and referendum was meant to do. The fear of losing power over you is likewise precisely why the Legislatures at the State and Federal level are so reluctant to pass such measures. By this mechanism, we the citizenry, would be able to place on the ballot such bills and questions as we see important and the voting public would then determine their fate. A referendum is the voting process whereby popular vote would determine the outcome of any particular bill. As an example let us look at how things are done today, opposed to how they could be done under this system.

As things stand today an elected official, perhaps a member of the state legislature, gets an idea. Or perhaps he is leaned on by a special interest group to whom he owes a favor. This idea he then puts forth in the form of a bill. Let us say in this instance the idea is to build a new bypass along a certain section of highway. The bill goes to committee and is eventually voted on by the full legislature. Members of the body may vote in the affirmative for very good reasons, or perhaps rather because they owe this particular legislator a favor as well, which is often the case. Do you see how this can work? The measure (whether or not to build a bypass) is created, voted on and passed not because it is a good idea, but because a great deal of people owe a great deal of favors to others, most probably in reciprocation for having supported some equally questionable bill of theirs in the past! And so the bypass is built, going rate several million dollars. But was it needed? And by who? Did the citizenry want it? Were they ever asked? No? Will they be forced however to pay for it? Of course!

With initiative and referendum it is instead members of the citizenry which formulate proposals and they are then laid out before the voters as a whole, to decide on. A properly self educated voter will learn of the issues and make decisions based upon what he knows to be in his best self-interest. Additionally, proper market forces will come into play here as will the natural fluctuations of an economy. The voting public can decide how best to spend their money. True democracy can prevail as the public will learn to make their own decisions, perhaps at times their own mistakes, and of course hopefully learn from them as well.

Since this concept requires an enormous power transference from our present day politicians to the average taxpayer, as you can imagine there will be stiff resistance from those currently holding this power who do not wish to give it up. Oh they pretend to represent us all right, pretend to be servants of the people, but as I am certain you are aware, most of them hold us in contempt, and will do whatever they can to retain their power over us.

The solution in this case can be as easily done as said.

The voters must make the question of support for I+R a litmus test for all future elections, with impeachment as an understood for those who betray their commitment.

Power hungry politicians will yield to only one thing: The ultimate loss of their positions. Make no mistake, they would prefer to rule over us as does a King or any other sovereign, and will do their best to hold on to every advantage. But obscurity and forced early retirement is the abolition of all their existing power and an intolerable circumstance from their point of view.

When given the choice between willingly reducing some of their power into our hands, or loss of all power and privilege, the clear choice will be made to yield that power to us for a time, and try to figure a way to steal it back from us at some future date.

But I warn you: this is the only way that this can be done. Supporting I+R will only be done when our politicians are held over a barrel with the support thereof being a prerequisite for election.

The power for line item veto is something Republican presidents have been calling for time after time. Congress has always denied them this for the typical reasons. The overwhelmingly Democratic controlled Congress has a habit of spending money. Lots of money. Your money. This is where they get their power.

Generations ago, both Republicans and Democrats aspiring to the presidential office and to those of Congress made their appeal to a broad spectrum of the American voting public. Each party enjoyed success in their attempts at election and both parties served the public well. Truly great presidents and Congressmen were produced by both of the major parties.

In recent years however, and for whatever reasons, things have changed considerably. The Republican party continues to attempt to get its support from Americans as a whole, but for some reason the Democrat party has chosen to get its support by drawing together a coalition of minority interests. By minority interests I do not necessarily mean along racial or ethnic lines, although this is also done. They have become the party of the downtrodden, appealing to those who are perceived to hold no power, that they and they alone can represent their interests. Unfortunately once you go in that direction things tend to snowball.

If you gain your power from those who are viewed as being the downtrodden, the disenfranchised, it quickly becomes evident that it is to your advantage to see to it that as many fit into that category as you can!

If your entire power base consists of those who are unemployed, you find yourself looking at ways to see to it that as many people remain unemployed as possible. I admit that I am oversimplifying this for the purposes of demonstration, but it does work in a very similar manner.

Let's see how things work in party politics. If a congress puts forth a budget replete with fat, pork barrel projects designed only to pay certain factions back for their vote, they can ill afford to have those ideas struck from the budget. No payback, no vote next time around. Their whole house of cards is in danger of toppling down, because the structure was not built on the sound principle of what is best for the public as a whole, but rather on favors, trades, and coercion. This is one of the major reasons we end each budget squabble with an enormous deficit.

As I point out elsewhere, we currently assume that operating income at the federal level will be some 1.2 trillion dollars. But somehow that's just not enough. We spend 1.5

trillion dollars, or fully twenty-five percent more than we take in.

Being we are neither a poor nation nor one which is undertaxed, you are led to only one conclusion: Congress wastes an enormous amount of money.

One of the ways to stop this waste is to insist upon a line item veto. This gives the president the power to remove from the proposed budget any individual items he sees as wasteful spending, without having to reformulate the entire budget itself. The Congress is of course free to resubmit those provisions in a scaled down form, but will then be forced to be more honest in their approach. If they ask for half of the original figure they may get it, but if they insist on ninety-five percent they will probably get nothing. Again this will lead to a great diminishing of their powers (something we should all applaud), so they will resist.

And again I am calling upon you, the voting public, to make this a litmus test for all congressional candidates.

Those who support the line item veto are worth election, [all other things considered] those who are opposed should be sent packing. In this way we will not be able to change overnight, but within one generation we can have a Congress which supports these responsible fiscal principles. A Congress for a change, that works for us.

There are many ways of creating a budget, but only one sound one. In your home (if you operate on a budget) you probably tally up the expenses you must meet; food, shelter, clothes, taxes, transportation etc., and weigh those things against your projected income. The difference between those two sides of the ledger is your disposable income, or that which allows for discretionary spending (beer, movies, an upgrade on your auto, etc.).

In order to try to keep that margin of safety which is your surplus as large as possible, or in the case of those who live on a shoestring, in order to ensure that it exists at all, we try to keep the necessary spending as low as practicable by intelligent comparison shopping.

Each years budget for Mr. Average American is arrived at by taking last years budget and determining what might be pared away or gotten at a reduced price before formulating a new budget. Pretty good fiscal responsibility, and evidence of good stewardship, it is a laudable model of how things should be done.

Not so with Congress.

Their idea of coming up with a budget is to look at how much was spent last year, (never how much was actually taken in or how much was actually needed and spent well) and add to that a projected figure for expected inflation plus new programs. Is it any wonder each year produces a major deficit?

With zero base budgeting, each year every portion of the budget would have to be carefully scrutinized. All items, costs, reasons for expenditures, and cost comparisons would be shown in detail in order to justify inclusion in the current years formulation. In short, the fact that we may have overspent in any particular year will no longer be just cause for seeing that we perpetuate the error!

And since any given budget will no longer simply be built upon preceding ones, the impetus to spend (or waste) surplus funds before the fiscal year is over in order to ensure similar funding the following year, will be removed.

Who could be against such an idea?

Before I answer that, let me give you an example of why such waste exists.

Years ago I used to work in the motion picture industry. It was not in the least bit uncommon to see production budgets of thirty million dollars per picture with some going as high as sixty or eighty million dollars. At that time rarely would a major producer of films bother with low budget offerings. Why?

A small budget is by necessity run so tight that there is simply no way to hide an excess that you may then (through clever accounting) "steal." But with a forty million dollar budget, a little manipulation here, a little creative pencil work there and one wouldn't find it too difficult at all to skim off a nice chunk of that money for yourself. Even in cases where that type of dipping is not going on, a similar scam is. On big budget pictures the major players, producer, director, and sometimes cinematographer and the prime actors, virtually live off the picture. Forget their salaries for a moment. All hotels are paid for, all meals, flowers, entertainment, weekend air transport home, you name it, it is all taken care of in the budget. Oftimes, family member are put on the payroll in do-nothing jobs. But all this can only happen if a budget is sufficiently large.

With a budget of only a few million, all you will have money for will be the necessities. After paying for the raw stock of 35 millimeter film, developing, printing, editing, camera and equipment rental, actors and crew salary, location or studio costs, there will be nothing left for padding to allow certain bigwigs to live in the style they would like to. Perhaps now you can understand why there were so few low budget films made. This has recently changed, but this sordid bit of retrospective illustrates my point.

Well the same goes for government. Only when there is enormous spending is there room for waste. This waste may either be skimmed off by corrupt officials or simply be taken advantage of through excessive perks. At times this created excess is used to virtually guarantee reelection. A fat budget gives rise to many pork barrel projects, the recipients of which are indebted to the politicians, and round and round it goes.

Only when the people realize they we are not in this together, and that government thrives on excess rather than the avoidance thereof, will we have a chance of cleaning this mess up.

Zero base budgeting is the first step toward that all important task; a fiscally responsible balanced budget which is brought about solely through reduced spending. We are taxed entirely too much as it is. If we were to take the attitude that spending is right about where it should be, but that we are in fact taxed too little, picture the results. See what you would have left if you removed an additional twenty-five percent from your paycheck through higher taxes.

That's how much more Congress spends than it even hopes to take in, and that's how much more they think you should have to pay in taxes. It is irrelevant to them whether or not you will be able to live on what is left of your paycheck.

The way to get our taxes back down to a more responsible level and to eliminate the deficit at the same time is to insist on ZBB.

And the way to gain back Citizen Empowerment is to institute the principles of I+R, the line item veto, and ZBB.

This is the way things were supposed to be to begin with. You and I holding the power, not some "Government" official.

POSTSCRIPT

The Renaissance of America

Catch my vision. Picture a revitalized America, again a land of opportunity. A place where there are no whites nor blacks, just people. Where the citizens are more concerned with the strength and enhancement of their own country and way of life than they are with whatever ethnic background they may have come from. Pride is firmly rooted in accomplishment, not the happenstance of birth.

The citizenry enjoys a healthy living environment unencumbered by stiff governmental control, the government having been relegated to the small insignificant portion of our lives where it should have been all along.

Prosperity is out of control here, nearly overwhelming the people, charity abounds, for taxes are a minor nuisance not a destructive force. Thus, each individual's disposable income is enormous when compared to that of today. A plethora of investment opportunities greets each potential partaker of the American dream. Here the vision of a "kinder, gentler America," as only hinted at by George Bush, gives birth to the reality of the statement reaching into every economic level.

Neighborhoods are both safe and clean, for civic pride and a renewed interest in community standards precludes the toleration of those whose sloth and contempt for their fellow man tends to drag us all down.

Laws are set carefully and sparingly, having met with the approval of the people as a whole. Then these laws are strictly enforced in the court system which has once again begun to serve the people it has pledged to represent.

Any new diseases which may crop up are attacked vigorously without politically inspired distinction. The course and purpose is clear and the population is spared the ravages thereof due to problems of this nature being properly addressed by science rather than emotion or some perverse concept of "rights." The obvious rights of those not yet infected remaining of greater importance.

The world looks upon us once again with admiration and a bit of jealousy as we have reclaimed our position as the economic and ethical leader of the free world.

Health care is for everyone, not as a government mandate, but precisely because government has been removed from the picture. The cost has been placed within reach of the overwhelming majority of the people.

And yes, all of this is only the beginning.

Catch my vision.

What You Can Do

Stop listening to them. They who would continue to expand government's role in your life. Be aware that they who are responsible for the mess we find ourselves in today and who wish to further complicate it, get whatever power they hold over us from what you are willing to give them. Learn to turn things down on principle, not degree. Unless you learn this hard lesson, failure is only time away.

"No!" should be your most important and most commonly used word in regards to them. They will attempt to bait you into compromise. Do not fall for that old trap. Remember, their goal is to take it all. All your money. All your power. All your freedom. Offer them none.

We Americans have already lost too many of our constitutionally "guaranteed" freedoms to supposedly well meaning people. We have lost too large a portion of our economic freedom to taxes and always for "a good cause."

In the future, when you think or speak of taxes, do this only in terms of rollbacks. Holding the line is not good enough. When you think of government, consider it only in terms of how much you can shrink it.

You will recall that I began the preface of this book with the picture of a man dying from gunshot wounds and poison. That allegory was designed to show you the condition our nation is in. The America that I grew up in is not dead but it is most certainly dying. It got that way slowly but purposefully. Bad intentioned people who have given the store away, *your* store, are aided by those who through their inaction, do nothing to protect it. If this country is to live, it will be up to you. But there are many things you must do.

First, get angry and stay that way. Don't let them placate you with the crumbs remaining from the feast of liberties we once had. Demand answers. Refuse platitudes. Insist on accountability. Get used to saying "That's not good enough!" Learn to properly read statistics, seeing through the twists that have been added to fool you.

America is in desperate need of a lot of things, not the least of which is a heroic figure. We long for someone a cut above the rest, to come sweeping down on a white horse to do battle for us. But beware. While it is good that we should look for this type of leader, so that we do not overlook him should he appear on the scene, it would be just as easy for us to mistakenly follow the next Adolph Hitler. Exercise caution. Test everything. Be skeptical.

Be especially leery of he who is most charismatic. Examine and follow with your mind and not your heart.

Mold your children. Not through coercion or indoctrination but with the beauty and wisdom of irrefutable logic. Teach them lovingly how to use their minds. And spend on them your love, not your license. They are our future. Take it seriously. Become members of citizen groups, taxpayer groups and political parties. When you have become steeped in knowledge, take an active role in their evolution and set the course for a renewed conservative America. You have only one choice: you will either lead or be led.

You are always told "This is not the time for finger pointing." Well, Jirgal says "Most certainly yes, this is *precisely* the time!."

Remember, we have not the slightest hope of stopping the bleeding until we locate the wounds. Let us always nail down exactly who is responsible for the bad decisions we all detest, the decisions which drag us farther down the increasingly steep slope toward destruction.

While it may yet be true that "this is still the greatest nation on earth," we are fast approaching the day when that will no longer be the case. Much of our slide downward has to do with the lack of accountability. Don't let them get away with it. Stay angry. Demand. Point fingers.

Take copies of this book and figuratively ram them down the throats of your elected officials, insisting that they explain why our country is not being run by these simple concepts.

And pray. For unless the angels dance with us on this one, we will lose.

I do not apologize for the fact that I have no tolerance for optimists.

That type of fool not only insists that we see a glass as being half full, but smugly thinks that he is both morally and intellectually superior to the one who sees the same glass as half empty.

I am a realist, one who ignores both of these delusions and simply tries to make good use of whatever amount of water *is* in the glass. That is provided that the aforementioned glass is even mine.

No, the optimist generally becomes a stumbling block to progress. With a foolish "things will turn out fine" attitude, he sees no reason to get involved, roll up his sleeves, and make the effort to see that they do.

He is one who believes that our country, and the world for that matter, is just experiencing a temporary downturn, at the bottom of a natural cycle, which has always and will always repeat itself, moving in a circle between the extremes of prosperity and decline.

This person refuses to take into account that we are now witnessing a great number of things in the negative that have never existed before.

AIDS, a deficit that we are fast becoming unable to pay even the interest on, overly expanded markets with no room left for growth. Nuclear weapons proliferation, the cumulative buildup of toxins and pollutants, and the expansion and implementation of governmental economic philosophy based on perceived needs and not production ability.

He also neglects to mention the absence of many of the things that we had been able to count on to bail us out in the past.

The prospect of a return to economic growth, the energy of the American people, advancing education and a technological edge, a government willing and able to either steer the course well or get out of the way, and the willingness of the people to see things with a high degree of clarity and then act accordingly are just a few of those things missing.

Things are not going to get better by themselves. This *is* our last hurrah.

So again I ask, is there any hope at all? The answer is perhaps. Only to the degree that you, the reader, are willing to go on the offensive, to adopt the basic philosophies in this book, and to without restraint, without compromise, take back *your* government, wrenching it out of the hands of the spoilers, will you succeed.

As for me, I don't think you have it in you. Prove me wrong.

Suggested Reading

One of our greatest problems as Americans is our personal ignorance. As a people we are not particularly well read. As a result we lack the balance necessary in our backgrounds to permit us to make properly informed decisions. Learning is the beginning of knowledge and knowledge is the beginning seed for wisdom. Wisdom is what is desperately needed to make the correct choices in every area of our lives, as it is all too easy to make the wrong choices. As we have seen, the results of making those wrong choices can be disastrous.

Not everyone knows how to think. Most people are content in merely knowing what to think, and again this is often due to mental lethargy and the lack of well roundedness which may cause even the best of us to view things in a very narrow spectrum.

Some of the books I recommend are out of print and difficult to get. This is unfortunate as they are worth tracking down.

You will notice that the majority of the reading material I offer you in this segment is very conservative, just as you would expect from someone who is generally portrayed as being right wing. But there is another reason for this. Almost everywhere else in life you will be exposed to nothing but views from the left. So there is no reason for me to cover that ground again or give voice to it, as you will be bombarded with Liberalism everyday, and from every direction.

Consider this: Ninety percent of all network news reporters are Liberals by their own definition and admission. Eighty-five percent of all network news reporters voted the Democratic party line in the last five presidential elections. Our entire public education system has a heavy leftist slant, as does our federal government. The politically correct movement, or new fascism, is tragically alive and well. And in most public and school libraries you will readily find *Mien Kampf, Das Capital,* and the Communist manifesto while The Federalist Papers, The U.S. Constitution and The Bill of Rights are noticeably missing.

It is for these reasons that I offer you this list while maintaining that it is what will allow you to get a balanced view, and to be able to apply that most elusive of gems: LOGIC.

Some of the materials I suggest are not of a political nature at all but are only meant for the purpose of broadening your background information, while some are included for no other reason than being just good reading.

Finally, please be advised that except where noted, the books and magazines are not offered in any particular order of importance, this being highly subjective. Also, that this in no way represents a complete list, but rather a point from which to start, a foundation on which to build.

Books

The Bible
The Perke Aboth
Anything and everything by C. S. Lewis, with emphasis on *Mere Christianity, The Great Divorce, The Screwtape*

Letters, The Chronicles of Narnia, The Four Loves, and his space trilogy.

Something of Value
The Old Man and the Boy
The Honey Badger
    By Robert Ruark

Anything and Everything by Ayn Rand with particular attention paid to *Atlas Shrugged, The Fountainhead,* and *The Virtue of Selfishness*, in that order.

Biographical

Citizen Hughes by Michael Drosnin
Malcolm Forbes by Christopher Winans
The Sea Devil by Count Felix Von Luckner
Where the Trails run out by John Blashford Snell
The Cross and the Switchblade by David Wilkerson
Sage by Col. Jerry Sage
Born Again by Charles Colson

Novels, Studies, and Documentary

When the Sleeper Wakes by H. G. Wells
Animal Farm by George Orwell
Senatorial Privilege by Leo Damore
A Doctor Studies Crime by Perry M. Lichtenstein

Documents of Interest

The U.S. Constitution
The Declaration of Independence
The Federalist Papers

Papers and Periodicals

National Geographic (Perhaps the greatest single magazine ever.)
Safari (the official magazine of Safari Club International)
The Conservative Chronicles
American Spectator
National Review
Commentary
Forbes
Biblical Archaeology
The Wall Street Journal
The New York Post (should it still exist)
New Oxford Review
Imprimis
H. F. Langenberg's Fall Notes